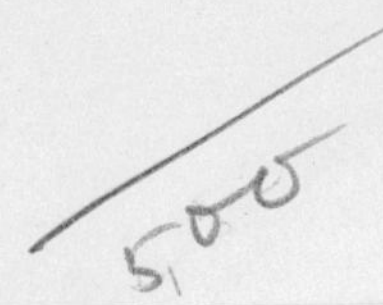

*The Irreverent*

**MR. MENCKEN**

*Photo by A. Aubrey Bodine*

Mencken at Sixty-Seven

EDGAR KEMLER

# *The Irreverent*
# MR. MENCKEN

*With Illustrations*

*AN ATLANTIC MONTHLY PRESS BOOK*

LITTLE, BROWN AND COMPANY · BOSTON · 1950

FIRST EDITION

*Published April 1950*

ATLANTIC–LITTLE, BROWN BOOKS
ARE PUBLISHED BY
LITTLE, BROWN AND COMPANY
IN ASSOCIATION WITH
THE ATLANTIC MONTHLY PRESS

*Published simultaneously*
*in Canada by McClelland and Stewart Limited*

PRINTED IN THE UNITED STATES OF AMERICA

# Foreword

As I SEE HIM, Mr. Mencken is a skeptic of the first rank—an American Rabelais, Swift or Shaw—who has somehow abused his gifts. As an artist, he might have written a *Gargantua* or a *Gulliver's Travels.* Instead he devoted himself almost wholly to the passing scene, and except for *The American Language,* the *Days* books, and a few selections from the others, has produced no works likely to endure. As a journalist, he had the power to reshape the minds of a whole generation of Americans. But here, too, his achievement has been qualified. For after having assaulted and demolished the delusions of one era, he became a spokesman of the delusions of another. As a result, I have been hard put to collect the odd pieces of his life and fit them into a plausible portrait.

Mr. Mencken has rarely, if ever, acknowledged these failings. Yet in the spring of 1946, after having written all that he cared to write about his own career, he consented to let me have a fling at it, and thereafter proved to be a model subject. He placed his papers at my disposal, entertained me at weekly luncheons in the Baltimore restaurants, wrote long autobiographical memoranda, and in numerous other ways put himself out to make my work easier. No points of information were ever denied me, nor were any suggestions made as to how I should handle them. There were times, of course, after the manuscript was submitted to him, when he could no longer suppress his feelings. Of the favorable passages, he exclaimed, "This is sweet stuff and far more accurate than Harvard"; of the unfavorable passages, he said nothing directly, but indirectly suggested that my judgment was open to question. Otherwise, he restricted himself to the correction of the most minute and uncontroversial details.

Many of Mr. Mencken's friends and associates have also been helpful, supplying data and even, in some cases, reading portions of the galleys, as follows: Joseph Hergesheimer, George Jean Nathan, Miss Thyra Samter Winslow, Gerald W. Johnson, Harry C. Black, Carl Van Vechten, Philip Wagner, Mrs. Edmund Duffy, James T. Farrell, the late William W. Woollcott, Henry M. Hyde, Mrs. Madeleine Boyd, Folger McKinzie, Mrs. Jim Tully, Professor Howard Mumford Jones, Professor Gilbert Chinard, Paul de Kruif, James M. Cain, James Branch Cabell, A. H. McDannald, Harrison Hale Schaff, John E. Cullen, Louis Cheslock, and Israel Dorman.

Others have contributed through their published works, notably: Charles Angoff, Carl Van Doren, Mrs. Emily Clark Balch, Burton Rascoe, Robert H. Elias, Ludwig Lewisohn, and again George Jean Nathan. None of these persons, however, is responsible for my errors of omission and commission. That burden I assume alone.

For assisting me with photographs and other details since Mr. Mencken's illness, I am indebted to his brother August; for helping me in the research, to Richard Hart of the Enoch Pratt Free Library (Baltimore), Julian Boyd of the Princeton University Library, John Alden of the University of Pennsylvania Library, and Joseph Katz, a private collector; for the use of personal correspondence and copyrighted material, to Alfred A. Knopf, Mrs. Theodore Dreiser and Sinclair Lewis; for patiently reading and typing the manuscript, to my secretary, Mrs. Eleanor Glushakow. Finally, for valuable and yet tactful criticism during an extended period of composition, I owe many thanks to Dudley H. Cloud of the Atlantic Monthly Press and Stanley Salmen of Little, Brown and Company.

EDGAR KEMLER

*Washington, D. C.*
*January 1950*

# Contents

# PART ONE

# *The Prodigy*

*C H A P T E R 1*

# Eruption in Baltimore

IN THE SPRING TWILIGHT the streetcar crawled along Fayette Street towards downtown Baltimore. Inside, a short, stout young man sat beside a housewife holding a basket of fish. There was nothing pretentious about him. He wore a plain blue suit, a striped blue tie and formal Belmont collar. He might have been a greengrocer or (with make-up) a German comic actor. His pug nose was stuck on his face like an organ stop. His features were so aligned from his short forehead to his firm chin that he might have made a cartoon of himself by pressing his face against the car window. As he stared at his fellow passengers, his eyes seemed to pop out of his head with an unaccountable astonishment. Now and again he twisted one of his ears through an arc of 180 degrees.

When the car halted at an intersection, the basket of fish slipped from the housewife's lap into the young man's. He returned it to its owner with a great show of politeness, lifting his hat straight up from his head. So far as the housewife was concerned the incident was closed. But in the mind of the young man it had many ramifications. Why, he asked himself, did the streetcar company permit this woman to stink up the car with her fish? And why, at the same time, was he forbidden to smoke his cigar? Which was more offensive to the average passenger—cigar smoke or the stench of fish? He had no doubt of the answer. Also, a week before, he had sat on an acid jar which had been left on a seat of one of the cars, and had burned a hole in his trousers. A small matter, to be sure. But he had wasted a half hour having the trousers patched; and the trousers themselves had declined in value from the purchase price of $5.98 to an estimated resale price of $2.50. This, too, he would bring to the attention of the authorities.

At thirty-two, Mencken was already a terror in the municipal life of Baltimore. The Baltimore *Evening Sun* had recently given him a column ("The Freelance" they called it) for the airing of his grievances. There were, perhaps, limits to what he could print, but he pressed very hard against them. Month by month he had expanded his range from domestic irritations like streetcars to great national movements like Prohibition, from profane targets such as the Baltimore Association of Commerce to sacred ones like the vice crusaders and the Methodist Church. His arrogance and his impiety were profoundly shocking to his fellow townsmen. In ten thousand letters they pleaded with him for more tolerance and more understanding. In church after church, ministers prayed for his salvation. But neither by the one means nor by the other could they exorcise the demon within him. "If a man is loved for the enemies he has made," it was said, "all Baltimore will attend Mencken's funeral."

This, however, was not an exact statement. According to Mencken's reckoning, there were two hundred people in the town civilized enough to appreciate what he was about. Who they were or where they lived he never revealed. But every Saturday night for eight years he had been playing music, drinking beer, and exchanging buffooneries with a handful of reporters, brewers, music teachers, physicians, and professors of medicine. This group had grown from a trio into a small orchestra, and from an informal gathering into an elaborate society, known as the Saturday Night Club. It held regular summer outings and had interlocking connections with a biweekly Sunday Dinner Club and a Friday Night Club. On this very night, while Mencken was nursing his grievances against the streetcar company, his fellow members were gathering in the back room of Hildebrandt's music shop for a meeting.

By 7:45 more than a score of them had turned up, and the little room was a bedlam of chairs flying across the floor, half-tuned violins, gurgling wind instruments, and loud voices. At one of the pianos, a bewhiskered musician had spread the sheets of his latest composition. While he picked out the theme, another musician stood listening behind him, convinced that it was drivel and determined that he would take no part in performing it. Behind them an impoverished street poet read one of his poems. Before the evening was out he would be hailed either as a great poet or as a great clown, it didn't matter which; but at the moment, nobody paid any attention to him. An eccentric financial editor held the floor with an exhibit of his latest invention, a collapsible tube for urinating in the upper berth of a Pullman car.

At 8 P.M. the din subsided somewhat, in anticipation of Mencken's arrival. He was always prompt. One minute before the hour, he pranced in, a cigar in his hand and his bowleggedness very much in evidence. Someone blew a fanfare for him on the piccolo; and he, on his part, greeted his admirers with some characteristic stage business. He raised his right arm to command silence. "We Dutch may be vulgar eaters," he boomed in a baritone voice, "but we still have some good men left."

As the members swarmed around him, Mencken took stock of the situation. Here, undoubtedly, was the most civilized club in the city. It had everything that a sensible man could ask for: "sweet noises," comic inventions, a solid corps of "amiable and decent" members. Yet even here, his mood of irritation persisted, and he was vaguely dissatisfied with it. Perhaps it lacked discipline. Perhaps it had grown too fast. Some of the members had been admitted under a misapprehension. They had proved to be "blank cartridges"; they played no instruments, nor did they contribute to the evening's entertainment. Confiding his doubts to Theodor Hemburger, the *Konzertmeister* and one of his closest friends, he said, "Soon or late, we shall have to get rid of them."

Mencken stripped off his jacket, exposing his paunch and his suspenders, and took his seat at the piano. Behind him Hemburger rapped a stand with his violin bow. Everybody fell silent except a couple of the "blank cartridges" beyond the circle of the orchestra. Mencken stared hard at them as if in warning, and then back at the music sheets spread in front of him. As the strings announced the first subject of a Mozart little symphony, Mencken accompanied them on the piano. He was a fluent reader. He could keep up with the professionals in all but the most difficult passages. Moreover, by the use of the loud pedal, he was often heard above them.

After the Mozart came Brahms's Second Symphony in

D Major. Again Mencken flashed a warning look behind him. Brahms was still a bone of contention both in the musical world at large and in the club. Mencken, converted by Hemburger into one of the most ardent Brahmsistas, was eager to do justice to him. For this he would need his full resources. Among other things, the melancholy themes of the second movement were developed by numerous fugal entrances; the piano part was extremely complicated.

Tonight (and everything was going wrong tonight) the work seemed more difficult than ever. The performance of the first movement was ragged; the fatal second movement, so far as it was heard at all, was hardly recognizable. As the little orchestra labored, the audience became restive. They began to talk and move about. Suddenly Mencken's hands dropped to his side. His wide plastic face froze solid into something not unlike Beethoven's death mask; his blue eyes turned to flint. With a voice that could be heard above the double bass, he shouted "*Maul halten!*" Not everybody in the room knew that "*Maul halten!*" was German for "Shut up!" but all of them got the point. Two of the standees were so frightened that without further prompting they picked up their hats and left. Others had to be assured by the serene Hemburger that Mencken had not meant to offend anyone in particular, and that it would be safe for them to continue in the room. At all events, when the music was resumed there was no question that a new note of discipline had been added. The final movements of the symphony and the final numbers of the program—some Slavonic dances by Dvořák and the Italian air "Funiculi, Funicula"—were executed without further incident.

At ten the members transferred en masse to the second floor of Miller's restaurant. There, as usual, the chef had ready for them a mess of raw beef and raw eggs to be mixed and ground into the notorious "cannibal plate." This appetizer did not sit well with the club's poet. Nor did Mencken make it more palatable by remarking: "That fellow at the chopper is a Hopkins surgeon. He has discovered that the rump and loin of unembalmed cadavers is both highly nutritious and palatable. Through his hospital connections, he has been able to obtain some choice cuts without expense to the club." Later, when the poet read his "Ode to the Spring," other members threw pennies at him and heckled him until Mencken threw his weight on the other side. "It is the best poem I have ever heard," he declared emphatically, and added, "I was a poet once myself. And not such a bad one either, by gar."

As Mencken recovered his *Gemütlichkeit,* the others responded in kind. Someone suggested a beer-drinking contest. Mencken took up the cry, defying anyone present to outdo him. For he could relax the muscles of his throat and pour the amber fluid into his stomach as through a funnel. The seidels were lined up in front of the contestants, emptied, and filled again by two waiters shuttling up and down the stairs. So it went, round by round. Mencken's eyes became watery, his conversation incoherent, his benevolence all-encompassing. But he was still as "thirsty as a bishop." By the sixth round, everyone had subsided except Mencken and Hemburger. A halt was called. The two men were proclaimed the champion beer-drinkers of the club and, by default, of all Christendom. Medals bearing the club's insignia, a seidel of beer on a cross, were pinned on them.

Outside the restaurant a spring shower was in progress. But the champion beer-drinkers ignored it. Mencken crossed the street and took his stand waiting for the westbound streetcar, while opposite him Hemburger waited for the eastbound. Pending the arrival of the cars, the two men elaborately bowed and doffed their hats to each other, exposing their hair as well as their clothes to the downpour. A half hour later, Mencken would be snoring in his Hollins Street bed, oblivious not only of streetcars and "blank cartridges," but of all the other irritations of his daily routine.

*C H A P T E R 2*

# Where He Came From

## [ 1 ]

ON FEBRUARY 9, 1713, the students and faculty in the great hall of the University of Leipzig fell silent when Johann Burchard Mencken arose to address them. He was dressed in the luxurious wig and the long black robes of Vice Chancellor of the University, and spoke in the name of "the Most Serene Prince and Lord, Mauritz Wilhelm, Duke of Saxony, Jülich, Westphalia . . ." A corpulent man, with hard blue eyes and bloated cheeks, he carried his many dignities with conviction. Only the other day he had reprimanded two guards of the garrison for having failed to salute him. Now, to everybody's surprise, he entirely forgot what was expected of him. Instead of congratulating the students for having become masters of art, he called them "quacks" and with great documentation proved that most of their professors were of the same stripe.

What could be more ridiculous, he asked, than their method of studying Greek and Latin texts? What was the point of trying to discover the number of oarsmen in Ulysses's boat, of blushing over the obscene passages (which were the most delightful), of accepting Plato as the last word in political thought? For himself, he placed his faith in modern science: he was skeptical about everything that could not be proved by scientific methods, including Newton's law of gravitation. Having said this, he looked up from his Latin manuscript to view the shocked expressions of his students and of the high dignitaries of church and state on either side of him. But he did not stop. He must insist upon the utmost freedom of speech, he declared, for the arts and sciences could never endure "in a republic of letters which knows fear and servitude." Two years later, when published under the title *The Charlatanry of the Learned,* this speech was banned at the request of a powerful Lutheran minister. But by that time it was too late: the shafts had already found their mark. Despite the Leipzig censorship, the book would be translated into German, Dutch, French, and Italian and be read throughout Europe for almost a century.

At the age of forty, when H. L. Mencken first read this work, he suspected that he owed much to his heredity, and when he surveyed the record of his other ancestors (Johann was of a collateral line), he became convinced of it. Otto Mencke, Johann's father, after a conventional beginning as a professor of theology, had declared himself "the biggest fool that the sun ever shone down upon." He renounced theology and founded the *Acta Eruditorum,* a magazine for the leading scientists and skeptics of Europe. Lüder Mencke, Johann's uncle, was so learned a man that he was called the "living lawbook": he ranked himself above Johann Sebastian Bach, whom he employed as choirmaster in his church, and only slightly below the nobility with whom his kinsmen were intermarried. About 1650, Eilhart Mencke, the Archpresbyter at Marienwerder, had established a perpetual family scholarship. For a century thereafter, there was hardly a single Mencke (or Mencken) who did not distinguish himself either as a professor at the University of Leipzig or elsewhere in the learned world.

Anastasius Mencken (1755? to 1806?) put an end to this tradition, but in a most significant way. He was a sprightly youth, a university graduate in jurisprudence, yet of a very sociable turn, with a fondness for composing ribald verse. After his family had almost been wiped out in the passage of Frederick the Great's army through Saxony, he deserted the academic life for the more glittering atmosphere of Frederick's court. There he rose rapidly. Frederick appointed him to an instructorship in the Prussian School of Diplomacy, and in his early thirties he was sent to Stockholm to negotiate a settlement with the King's sister, the Queen Mother of Sweden. Returning in triumph, he became officially Frederick's private secretary, and unofficially one of the most influential men in Prussia. His popularity lasted only until the King's death, four years later, after which he went into retirement. Meanwhile his extraordinarily beautiful daughter, Luise Wilhemine, was gaining favor in his stead. About 1808 she married a local cavalry officer, Karl William Ferdinand von Bismarck, and in 1815 gave birth to a son, Otto, later known as the Iron Chancellor.

Between the Leipzig era and the one which is the subject of this book, H. L. Mencken's forebears had neither the opportunity nor the inclination for such high adventure. His grandfather, Burchard Ludwig (b. 1828), found himself at the age of fourteen indentured to a tobacco merchant in the town of Oschatz, Saxony. The family scholarship was still available to him, but he did not apply for it; by this time, two generations had passed since his people had won a university degree, and three generations since they had held an academic chair. Yet as a tobacco merchant in Germany his prospects were not bright. Six years later, in 1848, with nothing in his pocket but a certificate of business proficiency and 500 taler, he joined the great exodus to America. He settled in the German section of Baltimore. Starting as a cigar maker, he became the proprietor of a general store, and finally a tobacco wholesaler. Mencken's father, August, was considerably more successful. At the age of twenty he founded a tobacco business of his own, and fifteen years later he owned a factory in Baltimore and warehouses in Maryland and Pennsylvania valued at $100,000.

With this growing fortune, August consolidated the Mencken position in the New World. He married the former Anna Abhau, a slim, attractive American girl of German peasant extraction, and soon afterwards bought a house, 1524 Hollins Street, facing the pleasant shrubbery of Union Square, a mile west of the tomb of Edgar Allan Poe. It had three stories, a shiny red brick finish, white steps and white marble trimmings, and except for its ornate cornice was indistinguishable from all the other houses in the block. Inside, it was furnished in the acceptable fashion of the time—with Brussels carpets, lace curtains, horsehair chairs, bird cages, and cuckoo clocks, all neatly arranged under the chandeliers. Outside, in the spacious back yard, it had an Oriental-style playhouse built by Mrs. Mencken's father, a cabinetmaker. For summer vacations, August Mencken acquired a large rambling house on what he called "Pig Hill" in the suburban community of Mount Washington. German girls were hired from time to time to help with the housework.

To this estate, Henry Louis Mencken was born on September 9, 1880. (Other children followed—Charles, two years later, Gertrude, six, and August, Jr., ten.) He was a healthy youngster, but otherwise unprepossessing. His head was too large and his limbs too scrawny; he was clumsy with his hands. At six or seven, when his father bought him a set of boxing gloves, he was floored at the end of twenty rounds by his younger brother Charlie. Later in baseball games at Mount Washington, he was demoted by degrees from pitcher to outfielder. Still later, when the neighborhood boys organized themselves into rival gangs, he hung around their several headquarters. But his legs were his only asset (he could run 100 yards in 13 seconds) and no gang would have him. Within the family circle, however, these defects were overlooked. He was the *Stammhalter,* the first born, and, as such, received special attention, not only from his father, but from his paternal grandfather as well.

The grandfather (who lived on till the boy's tenth year) was a crabbed, humorless, somewhat forbidding man, with a bald head and long parallel whiskers. No one had helped him get his foothold in America—least of all, his European relations. The shadow of the Mencken tradition hung over him, nonetheless, and obsessed him. On long buggy rides with Henry (or "Harry" as they called him), he declared that the Menckens were superior not only to all American families but also to all German ones. And to prove it, he pointed to his third cousin, Prince von Bismarck. His professorial ancestors did not interest him so much, but despite himself he was touched by something of their skepticism. Whenever he passed a certain Catholic seminary, he interrupted the outing to spend an hour or so inside, arguing with the Jesuit instructors about the existence of God. Then, thinking he had routed them, he told Harry that no clergyman would be permitted to attend his funeral, that he would die as he had lived, a freethinker.

Returning home, Harry would find his father storming about the menace of labor leaders or the villainy of the low-tariff Democrats. August Mencken, Sr., had no patience with the grandfather's sentimentalities. Only half German (his mother being Harriet McClelland, of Scotch-Irish extraction), he had the air of a successful American businessman, affecting a diamond stud pin and a Masonic watch charm hung upon a huge split-second Swiss watch. He was constantly preoccupied with large enterprises: if he was not off somewhere revolutionizing the cigar business, he was attending the national conventions of the Knights Templar; and if not there, he was running the Washington Big League baseball club, in which he had a considerable investment. He did not often play with his children. Occasionally he diverted them with stories about their fictitious Uncle Fred, a clergyman, or gave them cigar posters and the cast-off uniforms of celebrated ball players. But as Harry grew older, his father confided in him almost as he would in an adult, and gave him the cardinal articles of the capitalistic creed: that no man was worthy of respect who did not pay his bills, and that an employer must have paternal regard for his employees but must not allow them to dictate his policy.

[ 2 ]

Unfortunately, neither of the advisers had considered the possibility that the *Stammhalter* would be, not simply a reflection of themselves, but a throwback all the way to Leipzig. Harry, however, was such a docile and tactful youngster that he managed in his earliest years to oblige them both. At his grandfather's suggestion he was sent at the age of six to Knapp's Institute, a German private school, and given his first taste of Prussian discipline. Every morning he stood inspection for personal neatness and cleanliness, sang the German *Volkslieder*, and received lessons in penmanship. Four months later, Knapp sent back word that he was *recht fleissig und macht gute Fortschritte* ("very industrious and makes good progress").

The next year, he was sent to a Methodist Sunday School and remained under religious instruction of one kind or another until his confirmation seven years later in an English Lutheran Church. But neither his father nor his grandfather expected very much from him in the matter of religion, his father being interested chiefly in getting him out of the house during his napping hour on Sundays. So when Harry rebelled against the teachings of the Reverend Sylvanus Stall, his pastor, nobody realized just how deep-seated this rebellion would prove to be.

At the age of seven he had encountered and mastered "The Moose-hunters," a juvenile story that was printed by installments in the English magazine *Chatterbox*. Two years later he had consumed a fair sample of all the books in his father's library, which included sets of Dickens, Mark Twain, and Shakespeare, Bellamy's just published *Looking Backward,* Chambers' Encyclopedia, a history of Freemasonry, and *Life Among the Mormons.* This diet might well have choked a less sturdy scholar, but it tasted so good to him that he sought more of it in the local branch of the Enoch Pratt Library. His curiosity about the facts of human existence seemed inexhaustible. Yet in literature he had already acquired prejudices and enthusiasms. He was bored by Grimms' *Fairy Tales* and depressed by the contents and illustrations of Dante's *Inferno.* Reading *Huckleberry Finn,* he found that a story told with sufficient compassion and humor was the nearest thing to Paradise.

In his early teens Harry was so much at home in the world of the imagination that he commenced to fill it with objects of his own fashioning. He made sketches and water colors of the Patapsco River; but being slightly color-blind, he abandoned this art and turned to the composition of music. This time he was bogged down by his ignorance of harmony. Nevertheless, by trial and error on the piano keyboard, he wrote creditable waltzes after Johann Strauss and marches after John Philip Sousa, and he was moving on to the more difficult forms when he was suddenly overtaken by a passion for science.

Converting his workshop into a chemical laboratory, he made experiments and produced four or five explosions. By one such disaster, he breathed bromine into his bronchial tubes—enough, he later believed, to make him unusually susceptible to sore throats for the rest of his life. In the course of another experiment, he discovered a new and cheaper method of working a toning bath for silver. It was not an important discovery, as he was the first to admit. He had simply substituted platinic chloride for auric (gold) chloride, for "nearly everyone knows that gold and platinum are identical metals as far as their properties are concerned." But he prepared an article about it and would have submitted it to the magazine *Photography* had he not been so shy. All these endeavors (except, perhaps, his sketching) in some way left their marks upon his psyche.

It was not until his twelfth year that he tried his hand at literary composition, and not until his fifteenth that he had anything of interest to say. Then, while playing the piano at a teen-age function (he had never learned to dance), he fell in love with a German blonde. Borrowing heavily from the poet Robert Herrick and the French triolets and rondeaux then in vogue, he recorded the affair. In its early stages he spoke of love's arrow, which might have sailed over his stunted body, but which instead hit him squarely in the heart:

> I staggered, groaned and then—I smyled!
> Egad! It was a pleasant payne!

Love for him was something to be relished openheartedly. Rebuffed three years later, he accepted his defeat not with suicidal passion but with a chill expression of regret to be followed thereafter with an enduring prejudice against blondes:

> Still shines the moonlight; no more we walk together;—
> Yellow light and pale light,
> Glooming light and stale light;
> Shadows by the clouds cast, and signs of stormy weather—
> Cold falls the moonlight upon a desert land.

At fourteen, Harry was enrolled in the Baltimore Polytechnic Institute, a public high school, probably to bring him out of his ivory tower and back to solid ground. But the descent was not easy. Having graduated a year early from Knapp's school, he was younger than his classmates; moreover, being ordinary Americans, they were even less congenial than the German-Americans he had known. He was bored by the triple-expansion engines and other mechanical works that he was expected to master; his first-year performance in carpentry and blacksmithing was mediocre. On the other hand, he was so well versed in the classic subjects that at times he ventured to correct his teachers; and for his father's sake he made up his mind to master the other subjects with the same perfection. Three years later—that is, by the middle of his senior year—he had come abreast of the best student engineers, and by a tour de force of cramming, he managed in the final examinations to surpass them with a general average of 96. The principal, a retired Navy officer, was shocked. It was patently absurd that this impractical youth should have won the Polytechnic's Medal of Honor, and he withheld it from him. Harry made no complaint. Instead, with his tongue in his cheek, he delivered a class address in which he boasted that the boys of Poly had excelled even the Naval Academy in the rapid assembly of a triple-expansion engine. Also his spirits were lifted by a family prize of $100 bestowed upon him by his father.

After the congratulations came the hour of decision. What was Harry going to make of himself in the world? If he had doubts in the matter when he entered high school, he had none now. He had long wavered between a career as a chemist and a career as a man of letters, but incompetent pedagogy had by now dulled the edge of his scientific ardor. Furthermore, an English teacher, Edward S. Kines, who was not really a pedagogue at all, but an aspirant for the law, had taken an interest in him. Mencken quickly worked through the long list of classics that Kines gave him. Through Thackeray, whose complete works he read in one winter, Addison, Steele, Swift, Johnson, and Boswell, he became conscious of the enchantment of the English language as written by its masters. Somewhere in this garden of letters, he decided, he would find his life's work; and believing that there was no better way to get started, he told his father that he would apply for a job on the Baltimore *Herald.*

August Mencken should have known better than to tamper with something that was, apparently, in the blood. But since Harry would not accept either of the alternatives that his father dangled before him—namely, preparation at the Johns Hopkins University for engineering or for the law—and since August would not even consider journalism for his son, the young man found himself drafted into the cigar business. And here, for the first time, he floundered. As a salesman he was too timid with the customers; as an office worker he was even more of a failure. He could not keep his mind on the figures, his bills were occasionally garbled, his bank statements did not tally.

As to his literary ambition, the more it was frustrated, the stronger it grew. Quietly he enrolled in a correspondence school for writers. It was called Cosmopolitan University after the *Cosmopolitan* magazine which was the parent enterprise. His remote teachers advised him to avoid pompous verbiage, to write simply and directly.

And they gave him hope by telling him that his copybook short stories matched anything that passed through their hands.

After a year of captivity in business, he staged an open rebellion. The elder Mencken was as adamant as ever. Again Harry returned to the factory, his only comfort being that he had won over his mother as an ally. Six months later, August Mencken was unexpectedly stricken with a fatal illness. Four days after his funeral, on January 30, 1899, Harry entered the *Herald* office.

At eighteen the marks of his youth were still upon him; though an oversized cigar dangled from his mouth, he did not look at all like a prospective editor. After a month's wait he was given a beat—a vague area on Baltimore's northern city limits. Asking how far it extended, he was told contemptuously to "continue on out the road until you meet the Philadelphia reporters coming in." He was soon to turn the tables on his scornful associates. Most of the stories that he brought back, whether they concerned a United Brethren's church supper or a farmers' rally, found their way into print, and at the end of six months he was taken on as a regular staff member. He hoaxed one of his ribald fellows onto the water wagon by convincing him that liquor was endangering his health; he nominated another for Pope in succession to Leo XIII. At night he joined them in a bawdy house, where he played the piano for them long after the other hostelries were closed.

Ribaldry, it has been said, is the clever man's adjustment to a dull existence. Mencken already had had more than his share of dullness, and with suitable encouragement from his editors he now applied his wit to the hitherto dull city of Baltimore. Every Sunday he wrote reports of a wild man loose on the city line with dogs barking, children locked up, and half the police force baffled. Baltimore's Open Forum, which was as peaceful as London's Hyde Park, he re-created as a madhouse with the audience throwing beer bottles and the single-taxers chased through the windows by Socialists with butcher knives. If the town boosters found the weather fine in Old Home Week, according to Mencken's *Herald* it was even better: the air was composed of 99¼ per cent oxygen, "as invigorating as strychnine," and the rain was not made of water, but of "spheres of molasses incased in rose petals," "of chocolate soda water or old peach brandy, or smuggled Canary wine."

The details of his subsequent rise on the *Herald* need not detain us. In his school days he had already demonstrated a remarkable diligence and aptitude for learning, and with these plus his new-found ribaldry he swept all before him. He became in almost yearly progression drama critic, Sunday editor, city editor, managing editor, and finally, at twenty-five, editor in chief—the youngest "Old Man" in America. It was true, of course, that he had no serious competition to meet, for the *Herald* (the mouthpiece of an ice manufacturer who was trying to win the Republican nomination for the Senate) was a weak sister in Baltimore journalism, poorly equipped and, it seemed to Mencken, staffed mainly by chronic alcoholics. It was also true that his footing was insecure, that his rise was a direct reflection of the paper's descent. In any event, he made the most of his brief hour of glory. His opinions on the future of American journalism, that black headlines would remain and editorial "four-flushing" disappear, were given prominent space in the New York *Herald* (no relation to the Baltimore *Herald*). Moreover, in June 1906, when his paper folded under him, the other Maryland papers absolved him of all responsibility for the disaster, and nearly all of them (together with such out-of-town papers as the New York *Times*) offered him jobs.

Meanwhile, he had not forgotten that journalism was but a steppingstone to the higher arts; and having gained his first objective, he renounced all further ambitions in this direction. At $40 a week he joined the Baltimore *Sunpapers*, an institution which he had himself recently described as the "Uncle Joe Cannon" of American newspapers. He edited the Sunday paper and wrote drama criticisms (he stopped after twenty-three unfavorable notices in a row) and anonymous editorials. In 1910, when the *Evening Sun* was launched as an adjunct of the morning paper, he laid out its first dummies and subsequently was offered the rank of managing editor. He refused it, declaring that he was fed up telling other men how to write (on the *Herald*, in a similar capacity, he had often to take train rides to Washington to recover his composure), and demanded that he be allowed to serve without title as contributor and trouble shooter. His associates were amused at his perversity: they called him the "Honorable Prodigy "or the "Prime Minister without Portfolio." But had they known about the Mencken heritage, they would have been warned that something serious was afoot—that after two hundred years, another rebellious Mencken was at last coming into his majority.

*CHAPTER 3*

# How He Found Himself

## [ 1 ]

MANY PROPHETS of Christendom achieved their majority in the long silences of a desert retreat. Mencken during his critical years was never silent and never more than a few miles away from the turbulent headquarters of the Baltimore *Herald.* Yet his daily regimen provided him with all the conditions for self-contemplation. In his Hollins Street home he quietly cultivated his native agnosticism, his pride in his Germanic origins, his ribald and skeptical habit of mind. In the *Herald* office he soaked himself in all the disreputable facts of life as it was lived in an average American city. Inevitably, as the years rolled by, he felt the gap widen between himself and other mortals. But instead of lamenting his eccentricity as most other prophets had done, he reveled in it and gave it full voice, and so endeavored to lift himself out of the muck of journalism and into the world of letters.

From his eighteenth to his twenty-fourth year, he wrote a volume of poetry, forty short stories, and an advertising brochure for a Baltimore construction company. As a poet, under the stimulus of the Spanish-American War, he out-Kiplinged Kipling. Modern war was not lusty enough for him. He recalled nostalgically the day of hand-to-hand fighting when the "steel found rest in a brave man's breast and the axe in a brave man's brain." As a short-story writer he wrote robust but improbable tales about mutinous Negroes on Chesapeake Bay oyster boats, about crazy newspapermen dropping homemade bombs down office voice tubes. He was so facile in the arrangement of words that he could negotiate almost any form and produce a plausible product. Yet in none of them could he attain any real distinction. His stories, for example, were acceptable to the editors of the *Red Book* and other mass-circulation magazines, but not to their more discriminating colleagues on the *Atlantic Monthly*. Constantly rebuffed on this higher ground, unwilling to perform anywhere else, he abandoned fiction, as a few years before he had abandoned poetry.

By his twenty-fourth year he had come to the end of his rope. He was a misfit in the world of letters, and he knew it. Without the compassion and the warmth of feeling of the successful storyteller, he was also too egotistical, at once too cerebral and too frivolous, to be contained within the existing forms. It was a bitter year; yet throughout he maintained an unshakable hauteur. When Henry James remarked that newspapermen could not write proper English prose, he responded as though slapped in the face. In the *Herald's* editorial columns, he made his rejoinder: Newspapermen were so rushed that they could not be expected to write like Walter Pater. But what of literary men? Were they infallible? Did they have the right to condescend to their newspaper brothers? No, he replied, answering his own question. Even James wrote sentences that are not "sound in wind and limb" and his phrases do not "always keep to the track."

Meanwhile the thunder of other explosive egos was rumbling across the Atlantic. Combining philosophy with poetry, iconoclasm with drama, certain European writers were splitting the tight literary forms, brazenly exhibiting their superiorities, and condemning their countrymen as cows and idiots. The first blast of their heresy reached Mencken's ears in the most casual way. (He heard of Ibsen in 1900 from the skipper of a Norwegian tramp steamer; of Shaw a year or so later from the manager of a theater stock company.) But once having heard it, he could not get enough of it.

He read all the works of Ibsen and Shaw that he could lay his hands on, whether by purchase or by loan from the Enoch Pratt Library. He became acquainted with many of their contemporaries and antecedents—with Pinero, Sudermann, Hauptmann, and Maeterlinck. He explored the iconoclastic movement both in breadth and depth, until he had traced it to its ultimate source in the philosophy of the mad German, Friedrich Nietzsche. Only half of Nietzsche's works were as yet available in English, and the young Mencken's knowledge of German was shaky; but, in spite of these obstacles, he worked his way through the whole canon. No doubt, in the pursuit of so many new masters, he swallowed much of their doctrine without properly digesting it. At the same time, he worked so quickly that he became an authority on them before anyone else. In 1904 he published *George Bernard Shaw: His Plays*, an unpretentious handbook but the first full-length study of the Irish playwright. In 1907 he completed an undertaking ten times more ambitious, *The Philosophy of Friedrich Nietzsche*—the first popular exposition.

Whatever the merits of the latter book (and they are considerable), it is most interesting now for what it reveals of its author. Mencken, as we have seen, was already haughty enough. But under the influence of Nietzsche he had arrived at an intellectual perch halfway to the moon. From it he could contradict practically everybody. What difference did it make what the authorities said—the preachers, the professors, the statesmen, the pundits, the editorial writers? It was the natural infirmity of the human race to believe what was palpably untrue, and it was natural that the authorities should exploit and maintain such belief. The whole of Christian civilization was saturated with delusions. What would be more absurd than its basic proposition that all men are created in the image of God and endowed with immortal souls? Anyone versed in the Darwinian theory of evolution knew that man was descended from the higher apes. Yet the Christians not only preached their erroneous doctrine but founded a way of life upon it even more at variance with scientific facts.

In this welter of folly and hypocrisy, the facts could be observed by only a mere handful of "abnormal and (by the general standard) wicked men." Some thirty years before, Pasteur had discovered that disease was caused, not by evil spirits, as the majority of Christians had always believed, but by microorganisms. Even earlier, Schopenhauer had disentangled the truth about the war of the sexes from its Christian trappings. By these discoveries and others equally disillusioning, Pasteur and Schopenhauer had pushed the human race several pegs ahead on its upward course. Such men, whether scientists, engineers, or iconoclasts, constituted a separate caste. No nation or institution could claim their allegiance; they were entitled to freedom up to the limits of the endurable. Fifty thousand years hence, perhaps an even higher type of mankind would emerge, the superman, as remote from the ordinary man as the ordinary man from the higher apes. But his character was already foreshadowed by present truth seekers. He would be a super-scientist, a super-engineer, a super-iconoclast completely liberated from all superstitions.

The upshot of this revelation was that Mencken, by an extremely rare accident of birth, belonged to this superior caste. Henceforth, instead of wasting his time writing jingles and amusing stories, he would dedicate himself to "the most noble and sublime task possible to mere human beings: the overthrow of superstition and unreasoning faith." In Europe his eminent precursors (and Shaw most conspicuously) had made great progress in this direction. If they had not exactly overthrown the superstition of the Victorian era, they had done it much violence. In America, on the other hand, he had no precursors of any stature and few rivals. And here, inevitably, superstition flourished as nowhere else, under many names and in many shapes—progressives, vice crusaders, patriots, Methodists, osteopaths, Christian Scientists, Socialists, single-taxers.

For a moment, perhaps, Mencken was humbled by the magnitude of the challenge. It would not be easy to stand as one man against the sacred convictions of a whole people. For every blow that he struck home, he could expect a thousand in return. But at this point there was no turning back; humility did not become him, nor timidity. Besides, in a vague sort of way, he believed that history was on his side. "The masses on the surface," he said, "are still law-abiding and religious, but even amongst the lowest of the slave caste there is a mute, uncertain sort of willingness to follow any iconoclast whose crusade contains aught of romance."

For such an ambitious role as this, no affectation of dress or manners would have been excessive. Yet outside of his writings Mencken did not intend to flaunt his heresies. His war was with ideas, not with customs or decorums; and he was satisfied to follow a way of life almost indistinguishable from that of his "most pious and virtuous" fellow citizens. Only there would be no hypocrisy or cant or pretense about it, and, like Nietzsche before him, he was committed to a lifelong bachelorhood. "The ideal state for a philosopher [that is, an iconoclast]," he insisted, "is celibacy tempered by polygamy. He must study women, but he must be free, when he pleases, to close his note-book and go away and digest its contents with an open mind. . . . A man whose sole existence was colored by one woman would invariably acquire some trace of her feminine outlook, and so lose his sure vision."

[ 2 ]

Now and again, while propounding Nietzsche's philosophy, Mencken pushed the mad German aside and performed verbal gyrations of his own. To illustrate why Nietzsche had a distaste for the herd, he declared that the "majority of white men today still believe in ghosts, still fear the devil, still hold that the number 13 is unlucky, and still picture the deity as a patriarch in a white beard, surrounded by a choir of resplendent amateur musicians."

Discussing Nietzsche's sex theories, he predicted that someday woman will be the producer and man the parasite—"a condition of affairs," he quipped, "obviously identical, in all its essentials, with that which obtains today." Such passages had offended his publisher, who tried to excise as many of them as possible. Yet nothing could halt the emergence of the mature Mencken style. It was the natural vestment—at once the armor and the armament—of the apostle of the superman.

Where did the style come from? In his first efforts as the *Herald's* drama critic, Mencken had taken the pontifical William Winter as his master. Parading an ill-digested erudition, he had attempted to hand down exacting justice in his every review. Robert I. Carter, then managing editor, saw that the young man had started off on the wrong foot and gave him this advice: First, that it was more important to write an amusing story than to produce a sound judgment. Second, that his opinion was worth as much as anyone else's in the audience, and probably a good deal more. Third, that all actors and most playwrights are mountebanks and should be dealt with accordingly and without compromise. These points Mencken never forgot. They became the cardinal principles not only of his dramatic criticism but of his writing on all subjects.

He now looked with an appreciative eye to every literary showman who applied these principles and got away with it. There was in him a boyish diffidence which he had yet to exorcise. At first he received the greatest help from an editorial writer, Edward Kingsbury, who demolished politicians, particularly reformers, with a wry sarcasm in the columns of the New York *Sun*. For years

Mencken endeavored to do everything that Kingsbury did, and the controversial technique that he acquired in this way was to become far more famous in his hands than it had ever been in his master's. In essence, it consisted of the treatment of contemporary worthies with an affected scholarly precision, referring to them always by their titles, real or imaginary, such as Honorable, Doctor, or Professor, and crediting them with the virtues of some famous prototype: a Southern Baptist preacher became "a village Bossuet" and an obscure newspaper critic became the "Texas Paine."

At the same time, on the higher level of literature, he took lessons from the charm and electrical allusiveness of James Gibbons Huneker, the epigrammatic art of Ambrose Bierce, the ribald lyricism of Rabelais, the omniscient manner of Macaulay. When he encountered the writings of Nietzsche, he might conceivably have gone overboard for this greatest exhibitionist of them all. But while he was learning to mock and to gush, to crackle and to sparkle, he did not care, as yet, to explode. He was appalled at Nietzsche's more extravagant epigrams, by which Dante was made into "a hyena poetizing in a graveyard," George Sand into "a milch cow with a grand manner," Schopenhauer into "a king counterfeiter." "There is a wit upon some of these tags," Mencken wrote at the age of twenty-seven, "and a few have wisdom too, but it is obvious that such studied striving after mere verbal brilliance, while it may produce prettiness, scarcely serves the cause of critical art." Thus there was a final hurdle—a concern for the truth—that the young man would have to leap before he could emerge into the highest ranges of intellectual demagogy. Ten years later, after he had disposed even of this, he declared out of the other side of the mouth that it was "a million times more important" to make criticism charming than to make it true.

The experiment with various flamboyant styles and manners was not to conceal some inner squalor, but to release what was already a commanding personality. The world seen through his window was filled with colors, shapes, and textures never before encountered. To communicate them, he had, in the final analysis, to manufacture a new idiom. Thus he began to stockpile all the most highly spiced and dramatic words of the language; and when standard English fell short, he made up the lack by borrowings from slang, from Latin or German, from scientific and especially medical terminology, and by sheer invention. Whenever he encountered a rare but an illuminating word, he went to the *Sun* office dictionary for its origin and meaning and noted it down in his file cards for later use. He made his sentences dance by frequent use of archaic verbs and phrases—"to fetch," "the which," "to haul up," "to have at." His imagery became a carnival of "circus horses," "frying fish," "hoggishness," "wenching," "fornication," "unfaithful charwomen," and the like. His sentences became increasingly epigrammatic. He amassed a rich fund of billingsgate for the abuse of all unspeakable classes of men from college boys to Sunday School superintendents.

By 1909 he could write occasional paragraphs of Menckenian proportions. By 1912 he could conduct whole discourses with them. A few years later he could put his unmistakable stamp upon almost every sentence that he wrote. In the process, many virtues of his masters escaped him—the easy charm of Huneker, for example, and the intellectual dexterity of G. B. Shaw. Yet in the demagogic business of overstating and grossly distorting ideas he was surpassing them all. It was, as a later critic put it, almost impossible for him to tell the truth. And he might have added that no writer, except Rabelais, ever argued a case with so much animal spirit or visceral force. At his height, he would be like a ribald, scowling Teutonic god. The world of ideas would be his bowling alley, and he would topple the pins of men's faith as he pleased with his clattering verbiage.

[ 3 ]

In the assembly of this verbal armament, Mencken not only leaned heavily on the jargon of the American "boob" but became enamored of it. On all other grounds he despised the average American. But as one word-master to another, he admired him with an unblushing patriotism. The common American speech was the best possible vehicle "for the terse and dramatic presentation of ideas." It was succinct and clangorous; its deficiencies of sweetness, tone color, and delicacy of phrasing were more than offset by its sturdy rhythms and resonance. On the strength of this conviction, he predicted a development of major importance. The common American speech was uniquely the speech of the most illiterate elements. The gentry spoke and wrote "pure" English after the English of the mother country; and through their agents, the schoolmarms, they resisted all innovations. Yet, in the clash of dialects, vulgar American was bound to make inroads upon polite English. Eventually a compromise would be reached between the two, producing an American language as distinct from English as Bulgarian from Russian.

That the young Mencken was capable of making a generalization like this one was already clear. But that he would henceforth devote the best years of his life to proving it was not so clear. In the first place, it was not a project for a sham-smasher: there was, after all, nothing very original or very subversive about his thesis. In the second place, it could not be developed except by a scholar, trained or equipped for the most plodding, persistent, exacting, and painstaking kind of research. Yet, unbeknown to the public, Mencken was just such a man. It had always been his way painfully to learn the facts of a subject (as with the Nietzsche book) before doing violence to them. Moreover, he had mastered the arts of demagogy only by suppressing an underlying pedantry, which he regarded as his "worst internal enemy." The urge for demagogy he attributed to his mother's peasant blood; pedantry was his inheritance from the Mencken professors of Leipzig. Now, with his pedantry uppermost again, he asked himself what the precise differences between vulgar American and polite English were. American philologists had described some of them, perhaps; but there were many others, totally neglected—the peculiarities of American spelling, pronunciation, and grammar, for example. And since none of the professionals were investigating these things, he felt compelled to do so himself.

The cornerstone of this prodigious undertaking was laid circa 1908. He was then Sunday editor of the Baltimore *Sun*, and as an additional duty read the British press and wrote editorials on British politics. Observing for the first time the wide divergence of English and American usage, he noted down every instance of it on six-by-four file cards. In 1910 he printed in the *Evening Sun* an article called "The Two Englishes." From then on, language became a regular feature of his newspaper repertoire. He made copy, for example, out of sixty synonyms for "beard" and an apologia for such saloon rhetoric as "I went broke," "she's het up," "it's me," "swat the fly." In 1912 he devised a theory to explain the violations of schoolbook grammar. He drew up hundreds of case histories showing how the illiterate man reduces the orthodox tenses from six to three, breaks down the distinction between nominative and objective cases, merges singular and plural.

In 1915 Mencken commenced the first draft of a comprehensive "Inquiry into the Development of English in the United States." He went at it with more perseverance than he had ever before exhibited. He bought a complete file of *Dialect Notes* (which dated back to 1889), ripped out all the articles that concerned him, and threw away the husks. He took notes on some four hundred learned works—books and articles. His eye was now so constantly alerted to Americanisms that in everything he read, from the current crop of novels to the *Congressional Record*, he was always coming up with new discoveries.

From time to time, various academic philologists, attracted by his articles, offered to read his manuscript and to help extricate him from his pitfalls, for inevitably he was falling into them. But Mencken as yet spurned all such collaboration. He preferred to print his tentative conclusions and publicly to stand or fall upon them. Whatever his deficiencies in training, he felt that he had several advantages over the professionals: first, that he was his own man, not bound by any precepts or traditions; second, that he had a broader grasp of American cultural background; third, that he could write well enough to make a complex, technical inquiry seem not only interesting but exhilarating.

In the first edition of *The American Language,* Mencken claimed to have done no more than "a first sketch of the living speech" preparing the way for a "really first-rate philologist." Yet this first sketch was so successful that he became committed to a lifetime of corrections and expansion, and what was started apologetically as a book has become an institution, unique of its kind. To philologists, it is an exhibition hall in which Mencken presents the results of their collective scholarship. To writers generally, it is a constant stimulus to greater inventiveness, more robust Americanism. A cult of amateur word-addicts has grown up about it; in every state of the Union and in almost every English-speaking community around the world, thousands of shopgirls and ranch hands, schoolteachers and convicts, observe and report back the slightest swerve in the linguistic stream. In this way *The American Language* has grown both in depth and breadth. From the First Edition in 1919 to the Fourth Edition in 1936, its pages more than doubled. And from the Fourth to the Two Supplements in 1945 and 1948, they doubled again, for a total of 1629, including text and word lists.

It is important to recall that during the years of his self-discovery, Mencken conceived of himself primarily as an iconoclast, and it was this that determined the career related in the following pages. Language was simply a diversion, then and later. In moments of great stress he shuffled his thousands of index cards to find there the emotional relief that other men find in a stamp collection. And he made his greatest strides as a philologist when, for one reason or another, he could not get a hearing as an iconoclast. Yet, as things have turned out, *The American Language* is the most imposing of his monuments, and at this date the only palpable and enduring one. One can imagine what a range of marble mountains Mencken might have carved if all his energies had been harnessed to enterprises like this. But his mind had been permanently unsettled by Ibsen, Shaw, and Nietzsche. In his eyes, the slaughter of American sacred cows was an equally honorable enterprise—and far more exciting. Nor could any arguments or demonstrations ever persuade him otherwise.

# PART TWO

## *The Rebel*

*C H A P T E R 4*

# The Young "Literatus"

## [ 1 ]

After the success of *The Philosophy of Friedrich Nietzsche,* Mencken attempted in various ways to apply his strange doctrines to the American scene. As a prospective political commentator he crossed swords with R. R. LaMonte, the editor of the Socialist *Sunday Call,* in a long letter-debate; in the spring of 1911, as we have seen, the *Evening Sun* gave him a considerable license to "stir up the animals" of Baltimore; also, joining forces with Dr. Leonard K. Hirschberg, a local physician, he launched himself, for no apparent reason, as a pioneer of popular medicine. None of these enterprises was particularly successful. When the debate with LaMonte was published (it was called *Men vs. the Man*), the New York critics were obviously more shocked by Mencken's defense of capitalism than by his opponent's plea for Socialism. The book sold less than five hundred copies. And from his Baltimore experiences he found further evidence that he was living not in an iconoclastic age, as he had thought, but in an intensely righteous one.

Meanwhile, in a less exciting arena, an opportunity awaited him. In the eighties and nineties many American authors had openly defied the Puritan tradition and portrayed human nature in all its unlovely aspects. They included such men of genius as Stephen Crane, Frank Norris, Mark Twain, Theodore Dreiser, and, of a lower order, Hamlin Garland. But their revolt was ill-fated. At the turn of the century, William Dean Howells laid it down that such realists had no place in the American scheme of things—a dictum that was promptly reiterated by all the genteel magazines and incorporated into the platform of the newly formed National Institute of Arts and Letters. Since then, Norris and Crane had died; Garland changed sides; Mark Twain locked up his most interesting manuscripts for posthumous publication. Only a handful of rebel critics remained in the field.

In the pages of the *Bookman* and in the New York *Sun*, James Gibbons Huneker continued gushing ecstatically, as in Mencken's nonage, about European "immoralists," "egoists," "iconoclasts," and "melomaniacs." In *Town Topics*, a sister publication of the *Smart Set*, Percival Pollard, an American of Anglo-German education, had for many years attempted to carry the war against the Puritans into their inmost citadel, but he had done little more than hold his bridgehead: reputable publishers would not print his volumes, and his name was virtually unknown outside of a limited circle. Repeatedly, he had urged better men to take over from him. "Is there a Don Quixote to step into the breach?" he cried. "Let him not be abashed by what those fine swashbuckling Irishmen, Wilde and Shaw and Moore, have done; the American field is quite virgin for candor; let him take heart; he will have no competition on this side of the Atlantic! The wilderness of hypocrisy is so dense that the question is whether any ever so doughty egotist could ever blaze a trail through."

Mencken had no doubt that he himself was the Don Quixote in question, but it was only after the personal intervention of Theodore Dreiser that he finally became convinced that literary criticism was his proper profession. Their meeting was fortuitous. Dreiser, now editor of the fashionable *Delineator* and of the Butterick publications, was buying articles on medicine at the same time that Mencken was selling them. In March 1908 he summoned the latter to his office.

"With the *sangfroid* of a Caesar or Napoleon," Dreiser later wrote, "he [Mencken] made himself comfortable in a large and impressive chair which was designed primarily to reduce the overconfidence of the average beginner. And from that particular and unintended vantage point, he beamed on me with the confidence of a smirking fox about to devour a chicken."

"So you are Theodore Dreiser. I know all about you," Mencken began confidently, for he had obtained and read a copy of the suppressed *Sister Carrie* some years before.

Dreiser, for his part, had seen many aspiring authors, but never one with such an exterior as this—an exterior, he thought, appropriate to a small-town roisterer, a crude college sophomore, or perhaps even more to an overfinanced brewer's son.

"Well, well," he mocked, "if it isn't Anheuser's own brightest boy out to see the town."

"Why not?" replied Mencken. "See these yellow shoes and this gaudy tie? Every jack-dandy and rowdy-dow in Baltimore wears them. Do you expect any less from me?

My father is the richest brewer in town, and—God—he brews the best beer in the world."

Despite the "palaver and yoo-hooing" that followed, "an understanding based on mutual liking was established" and from then on Dreiser counted Mencken among those he most prized—"temperamentally as well as intellectually." At first, perhaps, he accepted Mencken at his face value—that is, as a medical popularizer. The latter's article, he later declared, was "the most refreshing and colorful bit of semi-scientific exposition that I had read in years, bristling with gay phraseology and a largely suppressed though peeping mirth." But after commissioning Mencken to produce further articles in this field, and a book, *What You Ought to Know about Your Baby*, he began to push him into deeper waters. He had him listed as one of the *Delineator's* literary advisers side by side with Charles Hanson Towne, Ludwig Lewisohn, and Gustavus Myers. In 1909 he bought control of the *Bohemian*, a pioneer magazine of sophistication, and there exhibited several characteristic Mencken essays—"The Psychology of Kissing," "Bachelors and Progress," "American Music"—and a one-act skit, "The Artist." (He was unable to pay for most of them, but Mencken assured him that this was a matter of no importance.) Meanwhile he was spreading the word among his fellow editors that Mencken was a young man of highest literary promise.

A few months after their meeting, Mencken's name was mentioned in the *Smart Set* office as a prospective book reviewer, and partly upon Dreiser's recommendation he was brought to New York for an interview. Mencken had never written for the *Smart Set* (though earlier he had tried unsuccessfully to sell it some poems), nor had he written any book reviews except occasional newspaper pieces. Hence he was utterly unprepared for what followed. "Boyer [the managing editor] introduced me to his chief Fred Splint," Mencken later recounted, "and Splint forthwith offered me the situation of book reviewer to the magazine, with the rank and pay of a sergeant of artillery. Splint engaged me with a strange and suspicious absence of parley, Boyer gave me an armful of books, and the two of us went to Murray's for lunch (I remember a detail: I there heard the waltz, 'Ach, Frühling, wie bist du so schön!' for the first time)." Indeed, it all happened so fast that Mencken had no time for second thoughts about it. Perhaps he was still not wholly reconciled to a career as a literary critic. But as a practical matter, he knew that such as job would not be offered very often, and he was determined to make the most of it.

In his first reviews he was afflicted somewhat by adolescent mannerisms—witness his titles, "Oyez! Oyez! All Ye Who Read Books," "The Novels That Bloom in the Spring Tra-la." Nor was his literary background particularly rich. (He had read most of the American realists, including Crane, Norris, and Mark Twain, but only a handful had stirred him.) Yet in the application of his Nietzschean prejudices to current letters he emerged full-blown. He dismissed Howells as a has-been; James as "no more an American than the Sultan of Sulu"; Edith Wharton, Gertrude Atherton, Robert Herrick, Robert W. Chambers, and others as "the heaven-kissing heroes of the $1.08 counter." "The purpose of novel writing, as that crime is practiced in the United States, is not to interpret life but to varnish, veil and perfume life—to make it a merry round of automobiling, country-clubbing, seduction, money-making and honey-mooning, with music by Victor Herbert." Until Dreiser's *Jennie Gerhardt,* few works evoked his critical enthusiasm, and these were written by the muckrakers whose political notions repelled him. He placed David Graham Phillips at the top, and gave high rank to Upton Sinclair.

If Mencken had expected to be recognized at once as the leader of the rebel movement, he was soon forced to change his mind. In the first place, most of the rebel critics, like most of the rebel magazines, were located in New York, and by keeping his headquarters in Baltimore he was in effect cut off from the main body of his potential forces. (As it was, it was not until his fourth year that he established contact with Huneker, and even then Huneker talked steadily for four hours and he could not get in a word edgewise.) In the second place, he was too critical. The bulk of his fellow critics he regarded as "specious, momentary successes—pleasant playboys for a day or two, but depressing fellows in the long run"; hence he preferred to keep his distance from them. Yet Mencken could see no reason at this time to compromise his standards. If Mohammed would not go to the mountain, someday, he thought, the mountain would come to him. Meanwhile he sat at his desk in Hollins Street, committed to a regimen of "slow, steady striving with a definite goal in mind."

[ 2 ]

In his second year, the *Smart Set* was rocked to its foundations by a scandal in the editorial office; and after several reorganizations Mencken was offered the editorship. On the face of it, this was just the opportunity he was looking for. Conceived in 1900 as a literary organ for New York debutantes, the *Smart Set* had surmounted its origins and gained a reputation as the proving ground for such rising authors as O. Henry, Damon Runyon, Jack London, Hugh Walpole. But Mencken could not agree with John Adams Thayer, its new owner, about a change of policy. In his former role as publisher of *Everybody's*, Thayer had made a fortune exposing the Wall Street financiers, and in his present one he intended to make his peace with them. The *Smart Set* should appeal, he declared, to "acute, nimble-minded, up-to-date people"—people who patronized Tiffany's and who liked stories that were arty but neither offensive nor "ultra in any sense." What Mencken wanted, on the other hand, was a Nietzschean review so shocking and so uncompromising that any collaboration between the two men was out of the question. But because Thayer could find no one of comparable stature to fill the job, throughout the fall and winter of 1911–1912 he kept dangling it in front of Mencken's face.

Meanwhile Percival Pollard, the rebel drama critic, was brought to Baltimore by his wife and admitted as a patient at a small homeopathic hospital. Mencken was deeply concerned. Four years before, he had met and befriended the critic at the Baltimore showing of one of his plays. (Indeed, Pollard had stayed on for several months, planning a joint Mencken-Pollard translation of some German poems.) At first, nobody could tell him precisely what was wrong with the critic, and after the latter's condition had deteriorated, the homeopaths called in Dr. Harvey Cushing, the Hopkins brain surgeon. It was, Cushing said, a brain abscess; he recommended an immediate operation, pending the consent of the next of kin. But Mrs. Pollard, prior to the crisis, had returned to her home at New Milford, Connecticut, to refurbish her wardrobe. She could not be reached; apart from Mencken and one other friend, none of Pollard's relations and friends were anywhere about. Well after midnight, there was a phone call for Mencken from the hospital. Would he authorize the operation? He did not hesitate. Pollard was promptly removed to the Johns Hopkins Hospital and his brain laid open. Six days later, he died without ever having regained consciousness.

The fact that Pollard had been his direct precursor was not wasted on the young Nietzschean. Mencken did not esteem him as he did Huneker. Still, Pollard had stood forth in American critical circles "like a truth-seeker in the Baptist college of cardinals." Hence, when Mrs. Pollard left the arrangements to Mencken, he ordered obsequies that would be appropriate to a kindred soul. He saw to it that the Episcopal formality was observed, but also that the service was conducted by a friend, an eccentric Episcopal minister who was an amateur cellist and a Johns Hopkins Ph.D. in philology, and clearly not a believer. Likewise, Mencken could count on the skepticism of the two chief mourners—Pollard's publisher, who had arrived from Washington with a copy of *Vagabond Journey*, Pollard's last book, in his pocket, and Pollard's friend Ambrose Bierce, the literary master of death clocks, walking cadavers, and all the shadowy world between life and death.

After the services, the funeral party proceeded to the crematory. Bierce and Mencken rode together in the same carriage. Bierce had never heard of Mencken (later he would be amazed that this young man wrote "so devilishly well"), but he knew he was in the presence of a fellow scoffer, and he treated him to an outpouring of macabre and profane speculations. He predicted that the foundry would catch fire and singe the mourners. He laid a wager that Mrs. Pollard would throw herself into the flames after her husband's body, and he advised Mencken to observe carefully every detail of the cremation. At the crematory, Mencken hesitated for a moment, believing that it was his duty to remain with the widow in the anteroom. Then, venturing into the foundry, he stood by Bierce's side and heard his parting jest—that the ashes should be collected and molded into bullets and fired at hostile publishers.

The influence of Bierce's ghoulishness lingered long after the funeral. On a sleety Christmas Day a week later, Mencken and his brother August went over to Loudon Park to "see how Percy is getting along." The two young men found the crematory deserted except for an old Irish attendant who informed them that the job was only half completed. He showed them the large bone clinkers and the skull still bearing the marks of Dr. Cushing's drill; and he explained that these would have to be reduced to ash. Mencken was fascinated: he wanted to know just how it was done. And the attendant, in demonstration, began to grind up the remains in a large mill. Up to this point, Mencken's taste for the macabre had seemed inexhaustible, but at the sound of crackling bones he felt his own underpinning give way. He summoned his brother and beat a hasty retreat.

Some months later it fell to him to ship Pollard's ashes

to their final resting place in Washington, Iowa, and this time, with the ashes safely boxed up, he recovered his self-confidence. As he walked into the express office, he proudly exhibited to his friends a container that looked like a cigar box; with great relish he told them, "Here's Percy Pollard. I'm shipping him home."

Following Pollard's death and in part as a consequence of it, Mencken was thrust into his first literary conspiracy. At his suggestion Willard Huntington Wright, the literary critic of the Los Angeles *Times* and one of his most ardent admirers, was brought East to fill Pollard's old post on *Town Topics;* and soon after his arrival Wright informed his benefactor that he was eager for further adventures in the magazine world. In particular, he wanted to launch an anti-Puritan journal of letters and opinion. Mencken might easily have dismissed such a fellow as an upstart. But, as we have seen, Mencken's ambitions ran in precisely the same direction; hence it occurred to him that by joining forces—with himself as the remote control and with Wright as the leg man in New York—each would have something to gain. Wright, for example, could be introduced to Thayer and to the *Smart Set* staff. He could be recommended for the editor's chair, which fortunately was still vacant, and once in office he could perhaps launch his weekly as a subsidiary enterprise for the benefit of Mencken and all other Nietzscheans.

For his part, Wright had no reason to doubt that he would live up to Mencken's expectations. Of Dutch and English extraction, educated in small California colleges, with a year of graduate study at Harvard, he had married and paid his way, more or less, on his earnings as a newspaper critic. Younger than Mencken (though he probably exaggerated his precocity), he was considerably more rounded and possibly more erudite. He knew about fiction, poetry, drama, food, women; he understood the unintelligible post-impressionist painting, his brother MacDonald being one of the earliest American practitioners of this school; and he could write music in the strange new harmonies of Strindberg and Stravinski. Whether he became addicted to the Nietzschean gospel before the appearance of Mencken's book or after is not clear; in any event, he not only believed in the superman but behaved like one—in which business, again, he went to far greater extremes than his master. Clever, arrogant, theatrical, slightly unscrupulous, he was at bottom a morose and callow young man with no great force or originality. And if Mencken did not perceive this at this time, it was because Wright had borrowed whole hog his style and manner. As yet unaccustomed to imitators, Mencken continually egged him on: "You have got into English the thing that Nietzsche got into German—a loud heart beat, an assertive clang. If anyone talks to you of your style, bidding you read Addison and Walter Pater—my curses on him!"

A third young critic was also involved in this scheme, George Jean Nathan, the *Smart Set* drama critic. Two years younger than Mencken, he had come to the magazine almost immediately upon Mencken's heels, had made the first friendly contacts with Thayer both for himself and for Mencken, and now joined wholeheartedly in the deliberations, contributing, among other things, the name of the proposed weekly, the *Blue Review* after a prototype in H. G. Wells's *The New Machiavelli.* Nathan was no rubber stamp like Wright; nor was he, strictly speaking, a Nietzschean. But in all other respects he was the perfect model of a sophisticate—so perfect, in fact, that though he was born in Fort Wayne, Indiana, he had managed to efface all traces of his provincial origin. His father, the proprietor of the Eugéne Perét vineyards in France, had provided him with private tutors to keep him out of the Indiana school system. Nathan himself had chosen Cornell for his higher education, because Cornell appeared to him more Continental than the other universities. Upon his graduation he had traveled in Europe after the fashion of the great Huneker: he had learned foreign languages and soaked himself in the advanced theater of Hauptmann, Sudermann, Ibsen, and Maeterlinck. When he settled at last in New York, the newspaper editors for whom he worked did not know what to do with him: he would not cover the police courts, and as a sports reporter, on one occasion, he described the Vanderbilt Cup race from the vantage point of a mid-town barroom. As drama critic for some half-dozen periodicals, however, Nathan had found himself, and though Mencken had lost his earlier enthusiasm for the theater, he was convinced (and rightly) that Nathan was the best critic in the field.

Thus joined together, the wily Mencken, the suave Nathan, and the brash Wright were too much for Thayer. In November 1912, after a six months' siege, he capitulated; he designated Wright editor in chief of the *Smart Set* and incorporated most of Wright's demands in a written contract. He did not make any clear commitment on the new weekly, the *Blue Review*, but this, Mencken said, would come in due course: "I believe it possible to lure him [Thayer] into the very sort of thing he fears and detests. . . . The next six months may see some fun."

On the eve of Wright's inauguration, on a Saturday in March, 1913, Wright and Nathan went to Baltimore for a final week-end conference. Mencken welcomed them and endeavored to make them, cosmopolitans though they were, comfortable and at home in his *gemütlich* provincial world. He had them registered at the best local hotel. He took them to Cator's secondhand bookstore and diverted them with one of his favorite devices—stealing books out of Cator's sidewalk display troughs and reselling them again to Cator in the rear of the store. Passing on to the Rennert basement café, he had them sample the specialty of the house and his own, turkey wings smothered in oyster sauce. Then, promptly at eight, he took them to the back room of Hildebrandt's music shop for a session of the Saturday Night Club—that is, for "a refined and intellectual struggle with the Rum Demon, with music by Haydn."

Now and again the proceeding was interrupted by a display of temperament from one of the cosmopolitans. At dinner, Wright snarled arrogantly at the waiter because the oysters were not cooked as he insisted they should have been cooked. Later, Nathan had a *mauvais quart d'heure* when certain members of the Saturday Night Club asked him some oafish questions about the morals of Broadway actresses and at midnight, when the local liquor curfew went into effect, it became clear from his remarks that Nathan would never become wholly at his ease anywhere within the city limits of Baltimore.

On Sunday afternoon, the three young men met in the living room of Mencken's middle-class home. Wright suggested, in passing, that Mencken adorn it with some modern canvases. But Mencken was not in the market:

"If I had a lot of money, my house would be filled with beautiful woods, metals and pottery, but there would be darn few pictures." As soon as Wright began unfolding his editorial plans, all such matters were forgotten. They talked of renovating the *Smart Set* with ribald and impious departments. They mentioned the salient authors they would bring to the fore—Huneker, Dreiser, Cabell and Untermeyer, and Europeans whose names were almost completely unknown. That they would create a sensation in the literary world, none of them doubted. Far behind were the "graceful charming days." Ahead was an era of "genuine remarks, poignant asservations." As the enormity of it all became evident, Wright's blond mustache became more pointed than ever, Nathan's flashing eyes belied his suavity, and Mencken could hardly contain his delight. "Eureka!" he exclaimed. "I feel like a new man. Once the weekly is launched, it will become a pleasure to manufacture prose."

*CHAPTER 5*

# The *Smart Set:* Two Men in a Tub

## [ 1 ]

MENCKEN deluged the new editor with manuscripts at the rate of two or three a month, including a half-dozen chapters of *The American.* This book was in effect a first draft of his postwar *Prejudices.* In the prevailing atmosphere, it struck such a discordant note that no other magazine editor, and certainly no book publisher, would print it. One chapter was too offensive even for Wright. On the other hand, when Mencken boiled down his observations into such neat little epigrams as "Sunday School: The first refuge of a scoundrel" and "Courtroom: A place where Jesus Christ and Judas Iscariot would be equals," and interlaced them with such glimpses into his private life as "The charm of a man is measured by the charm of the woman who thinks he is a scoundrel," Wright was highly enthusiastic. He had them printed along with Nathan's epigrams and his own in a special department called "Pertinent and Impertinent"; and whenever he found himself with empty spaces in a forthcoming issue, he would plead with Mencken to send him eight or ten scintillating lines. Mencken always protested that his files were empty, that he did not like to reprint the epigrams from his "Freelance" column, and that it was "suicide" to turn out such high-grade stuff at only five cents a word. Yet he always obliged.

After Wright's inauguration, Mencken expanded his sphere of operations to include Wright's apartment over a store front in upper Lexington Avenue and Nathan's suite in the Royalton Hotel, and they in turn expanded theirs to include the capitals of Europe. In London and Vienna, Wright spent his vacation "on the trail of a thousand girls"; while, in Paris, Nathan devoted himself to the lovely Paquerette "in whose lips new worlds were born to one." Mencken stayed home, having spent the previous summer in Munich "drenching his heart in the nut-brown flood" of Spätenbrau and filling his arteries with "its benign alkaloids and antitoxins." In 1914, however, they joined forces in Paris. They took a whimsical tour of the honky-tonks and refused to pay the guide because he had failed to provide them with the entertainment they had expected. Then they amused themselves by convincing one of Mencken's traveling Saturday Night Clubbers that there was a warrant out for his arrest.

Wright had secured Thayer's sponsorship for his first European expedition, and also Thayer's consent for a series of Mencken-Nathan-Wright travel sketches. At that time, Thayer had looked forward to a very congenial administration on the basis of Wright's declared policy "to entertain minds that are not primitive." But Thayer's ear was carefully attuned to sex in all its literary forms, and after Wright's return, he discovered that he and Wright were at opposite poles on what constituted a primitive mind. His attitude was reinforced by that of his friends and associates. Everywhere there was talk of the "unspoken assumption of ethical callousness," "the broad hinting at immoralities," and the "startling brilliancy of style" of the three young sophisticates. Thus, when Wright began to receive the European articles from his two associates, Thayer stood at his elbow, wringing his hands over every saucy passage.

In this crisis Wright turned to his Baltimore protector, and Mencken, who was now inclined to look at the dark side of events, advised his friend to "be very careful with the sexual stuff at least for the present." In the *Sun* office, he declared, he had long been faced with exactly the same kind of censorship, but by the exercise of literary tact had managed to evade it. Moreover, in criticizing the first draft of Wright's article "Night-Life in Vienna," he explained to his protégé just how this could be done. In the first place, he wrote, the title was badly chosen, being more appropriate to the *Police Gazette* than to the renovated *Smart Set:* "It has the air of lure held out to the Puritanical and the dirty-minded." He suggested "Wiener Blut" as an alternative. In the second place, he said, Wright had misunderstood the purpose of the series, which was not erotic, but satirical: "You are trying to picture the adventures of the true yap, the snouting American tourist. . . . Kid him more in the introduction." In any event, if further retrenchments became necessary, Mencken had no objection to Wright's eliminating the "Pertinent and Impertinent Department" and the other columns in which the three men collaborated.

Unfortunately, Wright had few of Mencken's strategic resources, and nothing of his pliability. A stubborn, truculent man, the greater the pressure against him, the more determined he was to carry out his original program. He not only printed the Mencken-Wright-Nathan series on

Europe (which he later collected as *Europe after 8:15*), but also bought stories by the most sex-conscious of contemporary Europeans, D. H. Lawrence and George Moore. And he encouraged such young American writers as Albert Payson Terhune, Floyd Dell, Barry Benefield, and the poet George Sylvester Viereck, to apply the same candor to the domestic scene. No subjects were now too sordid or too offensive for the *Smart Set*—neither decayed whores nor uninhibited circus girls, nor pimps nor Broadway Caligulas. Already by the fall of 1913 Wright had, as later critics put it, dispensed more realism in one magazine than any other editor on the North American continent. Yet he dreamed of the even more outspoken anti-Puritan *Blue Review*, and without consulting either Mencken, Nathan or Thayer, had a dummy issue of it printed at the latter's expense.

This proved his undoing. Thayer refused to pay for the dummies—or, for that matter, for any of Wright's incidental expenses; and noting that there was a difference of view between Mencken and Wright, he resolved to capitalize on it. One cold December morning he suddenly descended upon Baltimore, taxied into Hollins Street, routed Mencken out of bed, and for four hours presented him with a devastating indictment of the Wright administration. In conclusion, he declared that since Mencken was Wright's original sponsor, Mencken had no alternative now but to change sides and to support him in breaking Wright's contract.

It was a difficult position for the young critic. Many of the facts that Thayer recited, Mencken could not deny. Despite this, he reaffirmed his faith in Wright: "Between your policy and Wright's, I am for Wright's, as is everybody whose opinion is worth hearing. I have stuck by the *Smart Set* because it is the kind of magazine that gives me the leeway I want. Before Wright came, I didn't have that leeway. After all, I get very little money for my work. I take my reward in having printed the stuff I believe in." As a practical matter, however, Mencken agreed that the situation in the office was intolerable and that Wright had no recourse except to resign. But he cautioned Thayer that the resignation should be effected by a gentleman's agreement and not by a one-sided breach of contract.

"But what about you and Nathan?" Thayer asked. "Will you resign if Wright leaves?"

"I am not a breaker of contracts," Mencken replied acidly; and later Nathan made it clear that he was of the same mind.

On his return to New York, Thayer promptly forced Wright's resignation, leaving him with the impression that he had been sold out in his critical hour by his friend and mainstay. To clear the record, Mencken sent Wright a carbon copy of a letter to Thayer, reiterating his stand at the Baltimore conference. He advised Wright not to drag the case into court, but gracefully to retire. "I let you in for this past vain and disheartening year, and I offer my apologies. I was in hopes all the while that something could be swung." In reply, Wright said that he had never doubted Mencken's loyalty, and that he could always count on his friend's "decency whether or not you agreed with my policies." Subsequently, Mencken made amends to Wright by helping him get re-established as the literary critic of the New York *Evening Mail*. They remained close friends.

[ 2 ]

So far as Mencken was concerned, the lesson of this episode was that a magazine revolution could not be operated by remote control using Wright or any other protégé as his agent. Sooner or later he would have to emerge from his Baltimore stronghold and take over for himself. Yet during the six months following Wright's collapse, the requisite conditions did not exist. Without Wright the *Smart Set* slipped back into its former routine, becoming, Mencken said, as "righteous and decrepit as a converted madame." Though Thayer once more offered him the editorship, he refused it, and for a time even considered breaking off his connection as a literary critic. As to the ill-fated *Blue Review,* he did not mention it again until ten years later, when he considered it as one of the alternative names for the *American Mercury.*

Then came another of those benevolent sequences like the one which had brought him to the *Smart Set* in the first place. In July 1914, upon the outbreak of World War I, the stock market broke and Thayer, among others, was caught short. Hardly pausing to gather his effects, he left the *Smart Set* to his chief creditor, Eugene F. Crowe, the paper magnate, who appointed Eltinge F. Warner as his office manager. Warner had made a success as publisher of *Field & Stream;* he knew well many literate hunters and fishermen, but he was admittedly lost on a literary magazine. On principle, he fired everybody in the office and then, bit by bit, worked his way down the list of *Smart Set* contributors. At the name of George Jean

Nathan he paused. He recalled that he had met the drama critic a few months before on the S.S. *Imperator* en route from England to New York, and that Nathan was then wearing a modish gray coat exactly like his own, and made by the same Bond Street clothing firm. Observing that Nathan was also a contributor to some half dozen other magazines, he summoned him to take command.

This was not the first time that Nathan had been offered the editorship of the *Smart Set*. Time and again Thayer had tempted him with it. Yet on each occasion he had refused it, just as Mencken had in his turn, and the two men had long since agreed to do nothing about the magazine without consultation. So at the first news of Nathan's windfall, Mencken came posthaste to New York. "I am much too busy to edit the *Smart Set* by myself," Nathan told him. "Perhaps you would be willing to share the job with me." Nathan, the senior partner (his name would appear first on the flagstaff), could take charge of the home office in New York; Mencken could round up authors by correspondence from Baltimore. And by a system of checks and balances, both men could exercise control over the magazine's contents. Nathan would sift out the obviously unfit manuscripts on first reading; Mencken would then make his selections from the others and return them to Nathan for the final approval or veto. Every third week, Mencken would come to New York for conferences with his colleague.

Unfortunately, Mencken and Nathan had refused the editorship of the *Smart Set* so long that now, to an unperceptive observer, the magazine seemed hardly worth editing at all. Its circulation was "cut to pieces"; its advertisers had fled, its debt was $24,000 and growing at the rate of $2000 a month. Warner made no attempt to conceal these facts from his prospective co-editors. He fixed their salaries at $50 a month and advised them that even this modest sum would be withheld until the magazine was solvent. On his side, Mencken made but one demand: that he and Nathan be given gratis several shares in the new *Smart Set* corporation. In other respects, he was perfectly satisfied with the situation—so much so, in fact, that he began soliciting manuscripts before Warner could make his reply.

In the inaugural issue of October 1914 there was little indication that the *Smart Set* had come under new management. Significantly its motto—a definition of "smartness" out of Webster's Dictionary—was removed from the masthead and the epigram "One civilized reader is worth a thousand boneheads," attributed to Aristotle, installed in its place. In a house ad, the readers were promised (*a*) a revival of the "Pertinent and Impertinent" epigrams whose author, "Owen Hatteras," had suffered "a serious brain sickness"; (*b*) an exhibition of national absurdities to be called "The Purling of the Platitudinarians" (later changed to "Americana"); (*c*) "a brace of fiction stories by H. L. Mencken and George Jean Nathan respectively" (Mencken's had been written circa 1903–1904); (*d*) additional stories by Brieux, Alexis Tolstoi, Terhune and others—"the whole subject to change—*for the better.*"

Behind the scenes, however, Mencken and Nathan had mapped out a program for the real inauguration that was to follow. As Mencken explained it a few months later: "The experiment with whores and horrors [under Wright] has failed; the experiment with cheap melodrama [under Thayer] has failed; we had to try a new tack or go down.

We guessed that satire would save it [the *Smart Set*]."

He soon discovered that they had to deal with a condition, not with a theory. Most of Wright's school of writers they automatically black-listed. The "red-ink boys" (that is, Socialists) of Greenwich Village they tolerated, but not one in fifty could turn out an acceptable story. Nor could he and Nathan compete with the *Century* and the *Saturday Evening Post* for Ring Lardner or Montague Glass and the few other authors who met their requirements.

Necessarily, they specialized in literary misfits—in stories that were too long or too short, too subtle or too cynical, too thin or too plotless for a market that was still dominated by the slick O. Henry story. Subsequently they acquired Somerset Maugham's "Miss Thompson" (later called "Rain") when the more reputable magazines would not buy it. But such breaks did not come often, and after their first six months in office they had discovered or introduced only one important name, that of James Joyce.

At this point his friends could not conceal their disappointment. If Wright had moved too far and too fast, Dreiser wrote in April 1915, Mencken had erred on the opposite side. The *Smart Set* had all the "persiflage and badinage of a Broadway and 42nd Street curb actor." It was amusing now and again, but it was far less stimulating than the Socialist *International*. On the other hand, the rank and file of *Smart Set* readers (the "fat women trying to keep awake in Pullman cars after heavy greasy meals," Mencken called them) were equally disaffected. They responded well enough to the circulation-teasers, but whenever Mencken and Nathan tried "to lift the thing," they were bored and uncoöperative. "We have to give them, to some extent at least, what they seem to like," Mencken explained to Dreiser, "and more particularly, what we are able to get. I agree with you that 'When Fancy Leaves the Narrow Path' was an execrable novelette. But, believe me, it was the verv best that we could get."

How uncomfortably Mencken sat upon the horns of this dilemma we can well imagine. To fail in this, the one great opportunity of his life, was unthinkable for him. According to his harsh creed, no writer—and certainly no editor—had any right to live unless he could sell his wares in the open market. At an early age he had learned the arts of intellectual demagogy—that is, of selling his ideas—and in every enterprise thereafter except this one, he had successfully applied them. (His average total income at this time was about $75 a week.) In this case, circumstances were very much against him. Yet he did not complain, for even an unlucky man was outside the range of his sympathy.

It remained for Warner, apparently, to come up with a desperate expedient that had not been considered. Why not, suggested the publisher, launch one or more pulp magazines, fill them with circulation-teasers, or worse, and employ the resulting profits to liquidate the *Smart Set*'s debt?

The *Parisienne* was Nathan's idea, and an ingenious one. With the war raging in France, French propagandists were making much of the historic friendship between the two democracies; moreover, France was a perfect setting for high sexual adventure. Why not, asked Nathan in his turn, combine patriotism with sex? The *Parisienne* could portray the dalliance of counts and countesses in the sumptuous villas of the Riviera. Such trashy stories were available in carload lots. Even if the details were not quite right, Nathan could always paint in the French background and grade up the characters into the higher strata of European society. *Saucy Stories* was Warner's idea, but again Mencken and Nathan expanded on it. Colonel Mann, the *Smart Set*'s founder, had launched a pornographic pulp, *Snappy Stories,* adopting for its cover the same two sinuous S's that were on the *Smart Set*. Deliberately, it seemed, he was attempting to confuse the newsstand patrons and to destroy what was left of the *Smart Set*'s reputation. Perhaps the new *Saucy Stories* would prove to Colonel Mann that two men of letters could play the same game.

There was, of course, a cynicism to all this that was very much to Mencken's taste. Yet, after the preliminary discussions, the responsibilities were multiplied threefold; and though the "louse magazines," as he called them, made money almost immediately, he could not believe that the crisis was over. For a year, he spent two thirds of his time worrying about circulation and advertising business; for a year he "slept, ate and dreamed paper." When the New York Vice Society declared one issue of the *Parisienne* too indecent to be circulated, he and Nathan managed somehow to have the ban lifted, but the panic that then seized him made him all the more skittish in his operations on the *Smart Set*. He sounded a warning to his story writers to keep their characters well clothed. Contributors believed that he would not tolerate such a sentence as "She went home with him"; and for the same reason he rejected some of Sherwood Anderson's "Winesburg, Ohio" stories. In other ways, too, his nerves began to play tricks on him: he became, in his own words, "a skeleton at the feast"; and his doctor advised him, somewhat irrelevantly, to get more exercise.

## [ 3 ]

If Mencken suffered during this critical period, Nathan did also, with recurrent attacks of neuralgia. But outwardly he was more relaxed and resilient than his fellow editor; and when Mencken joined him every third week in New York, inevitably he set the tone of the visit. The two men put in a leisurely day in the office from 10 to 4:30 with a three-hour intermission for lunch at Monetta's or Delmonico's, and in the evening they went the rounds of the cafés or attended grandiose parties "which the ancient Romans might have envied," with show girls in abundance, liquor served in gallon jugs, food consumed until 3 A.M.

Meanwhile, with many allusions to the Italian playwright Pirandello, Nathan reminded his partner that all life was an illusion and nothing in it mattered very much, including the *Smart Set* itself. "Why bother ourselves with questions of 'availability' and the like?" Nathan asked one day. "More magazines have been wrecked by this search for availability than by anything else I can think of, save it be too much money. And what is the point of editing the magazine if we don't get any fun out of it?" To which Mencken replied approvingly, "You have reached such a stage of cunning that you can put my own ideas into such ingratiating phrases that they convince even me." In the ensuing interaction between Nathan's aesthetic snobbery and Mencken's resurgent clownishness, something new and unique was added to the magazine.

In the first place, when the editors were forced to move out of the Knox Building into cheaper offices, they exchanged the thick red carpets and gold cigar lighters of an earlier era for all the props of a three-ring circus. On the walls they hung a huge French placard warning of the deleterious effects of absinthe on the liver, a scarlet souvenir banner from Atlantic City, a Victorian tapestry showing a large Newfoundland dog holding a baby in its mouth, a streamer emblazoned with the words "God Bless Our President," and life-size chromos of Follies girls. Upon the bookcase they placed a yellow tidy woven out of thousands of silken cigar bands, purportedly sent to Mencken by a secret admirer; on his desk Mencken kept a portrait of William Shakespeare personally inscribed to him. Their most cherished object was a spittoon; and when their publisher objected to it, Mencken assured him that it would be covered with cretonne whenever poets came to call.

Again, in conference with the editors a visitor could no longer tell precisely where he stood. When Harry Kemp, the *Smart Set*'s favorite Greenwich Villager, complained that Nathan had mangled one of his stories by resetting it in France, they silenced him with a phony French fan letter. If an author protested that he was underpaid, Mencken would agree with him, but would tell him that Nathan's parsimony was at fault and that nothing could be done about it. "If I go to Nathan with such a demand as you make, it will kick up the very row we must now avoid." When this failed, they instituted an authors' free lunch service with pickles, pretzels, and cold ham on ice at all times, and finally, after Prohibition, paid bonuses in Maryland Brewery Company bonds in $1000 denominations, which were, of course, worthless. One poet was so insistent that the editors had no alternative but literally to buy him off. They agreed to purchase and print one of his poems on condition that he never contribute another manuscript and never set foot in the office again.

What dazzled a visitor most of all, however, was the ridicule with which they smothered each other. At the least provocation, Nathan would say that "Heinie" dressed like Jim Morgan in *Ten Nights in a Barroom*, that his hat looked like an Allentown, Pennsylvania, cuspidor, and that whenever he saw him loping along Fifth Avenue, he was reminded of a Rube Goldberg cartoon dramatized by Harry Kemp with music by Eric Satie. In reply, Mencken would declare that clothes simply did not interest him, that he had no more desire to become a Beau Brummell than to become a vestryman of St. Bartholomew's, for he was already pretty enough, and that if he owned twenty-five overcoats, as George did, he would be overwhelmed by women. If that was the trouble, Nathan countered, why did he insist upon making violent love to all the *Smart Set*'s lady authors? Mencken denied that these lady authors interested him in the slightest. True, he said, he had gone out to see Lilith Benda, one of the loveliest of them all, but on that occasion he had spent most of the evening eating clams with her father. And so it went. Each partner, it seemed, was obsessed by the foibles of the other. But the more they haggled over their differences in small matters, the more they advertised their agreement in the large ones, and at the same time their joint superiority to the herd.

Of itself this literary vaudeville did not save the *Smart Set*. But in its time and place, it was highly infectious, and under its spell, all the very real problems of the magazine seemed to dissolve. At the completion of the pump-priming operation at the end of 1916, the debt was retired and a sustaining fund created for several years' further operations. Under the joint editorship (Mencken often worked with authors through four or five unsuccessful drafts), a new school of writers was brought into being. Most of its early members self-consciously imitated the sophisticated style of the *Smart Set*'s European contributors, Max Beerbohm, W. L. George, and later, Aldous Huxley. But a few later ones were far more than imitators and destined to become literary personages in their own right, notably, F. Scott Fitzgerald, Thyra Samter Winslow, Ruth Suckow, Ben Hecht, Julia Peterkin, and Eugene O'Neill. Thus the editors became saucier than ever. They let it be known that they had "cadged" $50,000 in the sale of the "louse" publications (they never revealed the actual sum), and they expanded their vaudeville act into several new departments. Soon, too, they would boldly exhibit their names on the front cover, along with the two sinous S's, the masked devil and the other hallmarks of the *Smart Set*.

CHAPTER 6

# How Dreiser Was Managed

## [ 1 ]

FROM HIS EARLIEST DAYS on the *Smart Set*, Mencken had recognized that as a critic he was essentially a parasite—that in the long run he would make his fortune not by deploring the hollowness of the current letters, nor by whacking Nathan with a slapstick, but by attaching himself to some neglected author who was "bound to win out" in the end. He had not far to seek. During Mencken's nonage, Theodore Dreiser, his journalist friend, had written a novel, technically inept, but morally so plain-spoken that it had not been released to the American public until 1907. Despite its weaknesses, Mencken later told Dreiser that this was precisely the novel that he himself had wanted to write, if only he had possessed the necessary compassion. But "imagine *Sister Carrie* written by someone without that capacity—say Nietzsche. It would have been a mess." Which was another way of saying, "I, too, would have botched it." Repeatedly after their first meeting, Mencken had urged Dreiser to provide the rising generation of rebels with another *Sister Carrie*.

To the workaday world outside of Hollins Street, the completion of Dreiser's second novel, *Jennie Gerhardt*, in March 1911, would pass unnoted. But to the thirty-year-old Mencken it was perhaps the single most important event of his critical career. No other contemporary work of art would ever mean so much to him. Forty years later his eyes would dilate to saucer size at the mention of it. One can imagine him, then, with his glasses slightly ajar on his nose, his rounded shoulders, his attention concentrated upon the manuscript under the lamplight. After a five hours' sitting, well beyond midnight, he collects the loose pages and, so stirred that he cannot sleep, impulsively turns to the typewriter to pound out the following letter of appreciation:

*When "Jennie Gerhardt" is printed it is probable that more than one reviewer will object to its length, its microscopic detail, its enormous painstaking—but rest assured that Heinrich Ludwig von Mencken will not be in that gang. I have just finished reading the ms—every word of it, from first to last—and I put it down with a clear notion that it should remain as it stands. The story comes upon me with great force; it touches my own experience of life in a hundred places; it preaches (or perhaps I had better say exhibits) a philosophy of life that seems to me to be sound; altogether I get a powerful effect of reality, stark and unashamed. It is drab and gloomy, but so is the struggle for existence. It is without humor, but so are the jests of that great comedian who shoots at our heels and makes us do our grotesque dancing.*

*It is difficult, just rising from the book, to describe the impression I bring away. That impression is of a living whole, not of a fabric that may be unravelled and examined in detail. In brief, you have painted so smoothly and yet so vigorously that I have no memory of brush strokes. But for one thing, the great naturalness of the dialogue sticks in my mind. In particular, you have been extremely successful with Gerhardt. His speeches are perfect; nothing could be nearer the truth. I am well aware that certain persons are impatient of this photographic accuracy. Well, let them choose their poison. As for me, I prefer the fact to fancy. You have tried to depict a German of a given type—a type with which I, by chance, happen to be very familiar. You have made him as thoroughly alive as Huck Finn.*

*These are random, disordered notes. When the time comes, I'll reduce my thoughts to order and write a formal, intelligible review. At the moment I am too near the book. I rather distrust my own enthusiasm for it. Perhaps I read my own prejudices and ideas into it. My interest is always in the subjective event, seldom or never in the objective event. That is why I like "Lord Jim." Here you have got very close to the very well-spring of action. The march of episodes is nothing: the slow unfolding of character is everything.*

*Here and there, I noted minor weaknesses. For one thing, it is doubtful that Jennie would have been able to conceal from so sophisticated a man as Kane the fact that she had had a child. Child-bearing leaves physical marks, and those marks commonly persist for five or six years. But there are, of course, exceptions to this rule. Not many readers, I suppose, will raise the point. . . .*

*But I go back to the effect of the book as a whole. That effect, believe me, is very powerful. I must go to Hardy and Conrad to find its like. David Phillips, I believe, might have done such a story had he lived, but the best that he actually wrote, to wit, "The Hungry Heart," goes to pieces beside "Jennie." I mean this in all seriousness. You have written a novel that no other American of the time could have written, and even in England there are not six men who, with your material, could have reached so high a level of reality. My earnest congratulation. By all means let me see that third book. "Jennie" shows immense progress in craftsmanship. As a*

*work of art it is decidedly superior to "Sister Carrie."*
*Reading this over it seems damned cold. What I really want to say is just—"hurrah!" You have put out a truly big thing.*

Long before the publication date, Mencken had written his *Smart Set* review. He had another panegyric ready for simultaneous appearance in Wright's Christmas Book Section of the Los Angeles *Times* and the Baltimore *Evening Sun,* and still others for any organ that would print them. He persuaded his pulp-writer friend, Bronson Howard, to do one for the New York *Telegraph.* After a second reading of the novel, it was his considered opinion, "hot from it," that "*Jennie Gerhardt* is the best American novel that I have ever read, with the lonesome, but Himalayan exception of *Huckleberry Finn.*" Harper Brothers used the line in their advertising. But he was not sure that he had effectively stated the case. "It is much under the mark I set," he told Dreiser, "but a rotten cold in the head must take the blame."

Dreiser was bewildered by this ardent championship; he thought the critic's kindness had got the better of his judgment. "It looks to me," he wrote, "as though your stand on Jennie would either make or break you." But soon Huneker and other critics swelled the chorus, and though the book was no great popular success (it sold five thousand copies in the first month), it was clear by the end of the year that Dreiser was at last being heard.

Meanwhile the two principals had kept in close touch with each other. Mencken had entertained Dreiser in Baltimore at a Thanksgiving dinner (he had promised him accommodations in the Cathedral and a personal introduction to all the brewers in town), and whenever he was in New York he paid his respects, sometimes in company with Wright or Nathan, sometimes alone. In return, Dreiser gave him a choice of his original manuscripts (Mencken chose *Sister Carrie*) and, in preparation for further engagements, designated him officially his literary executor and unofficially his agent and manager.

[ 2 ]

How important Mencken's services were at this stage, nobody knew except Dreiser himself. A few years before, as editor of the Butterick publications and founder of the National Child Rescue League, with pince-nez perched over his deep-sunk eyes, Dreiser had passed as a highly successful man of affairs. Now that he had left his high offices (hastened on his way by an office romance), his artistic temperament had reasserted itself. Though he had planned an ambitious program of novel writing, including a trilogy based on the life of Charles T. Yerkes, the streetcar magnate, midway through the first volume he lost heart. "I sometimes think my desire is for expression that is entirely too frank for this time," he told Mencken. Even the excitement over *Jennie Gerhardt* did not sustain him. In one breath he talked about launching a new magazine; in another he urged Mencken to propose him for the Nobel Prize.

Mencken, of course, did not share Dreiser's confusion. He urged him to forget all such whimsical alternatives and to proceed with his original program. And as Dreiser produced his successive volumes, roughly at the rate of one a year, he applied his "eagle eye" to the manuscripts. Among other things, Dreiser lacked a sense of artistic proportion; he described things that needed no description and left undescribed things that were essential. In a criticism of *The Financier*, the first volume of the trilogy, Mencken called his attention to this. "Why give the speeches of the lawyers in full?" he asked. "Why describe particularly the architecture of the jail in which Cowperwood spends his five days? It is not that you have laid on too much detail—I am in favor of the utmost detail—but that you have laid on irrelevant detail." Dreiser was slightly stunned by these direct, forceful statements, but he heeded them. "You always see a thing as a whole, which is God's blessing," he said.

Another flaw in Dreiser's armor, according to Mencken, was the vagueness of his philosophy. In his youth Dreiser had been profoundly moved by two of Mencken's masters, Herbert Spencer and Thomas Henry Huxley; and in his maturity he had arrived at the same general conclusion: "that men should give no countenance to the theory that their fate is determined by the arbitrary moods of the gods." Yet how differently this conclusion had affected the outlook of the two men! Where it had intoxicated Mencken with joyous skepticism, it had left Dreiser morose and disillusioned, a renegade from the Catholic Church. Where it had made Mencken the champion of the strong and the prophet of the superman, it had made Dreiser the historian of the weak and the ill-fated. Above all, where it had answered all Mencken's questions with conviction and finality, it had left Dreiser dissatisfied and vulnerable to all other programs for human salvation.

In 1909, while managing the *Bohemian*, Dreiser had

told Mencken that though he disapproved of organized religion, he considered the religious impulse a good thing, and, with this as his starting point, had written a sympathetic study of spiritualism. " 'The Matter of Spiritualism,' " Mencken remarked candidly, "arouses my unholy horror. I wish you would read an article on the editorial page of the New York *Sun* and then tackle some of the late treatises on biology. I think that would land you in the German camp of violent unbelievers. The notion that the soul is immortal seems to me utterly gratuitous and abhorrent." Shortly afterward, Dreiser had expressed interest in the current Socialist agitation. Mencken again belabored him, advising him to read and master his own Nietzsche book.

Dreiser was not impressed with "Nietche [*sic*]," whose philosophy seemed to him nothing more than a "confused and warmed over" version of Schopenhauer. Yet under the spell of Nietzsche's foremost American apostle, consciously or unconsciously, he adopted it as his own. In 1914 he issued a public pronouncement that might very well have been dictated for him in Hollins Street. He declared that what this country needed was "an intellectual aristocracy"; that "the idea that all men are created equal is one of the fundamental errors of our system of government"; that America is the laughingstock of Europe because we discard "the opinions of those at the highest point of the intellectual scale for the prejudices and stupidities of the mob."

Thus, for four years, the two men labored together with mutual profit and pleasure. But since Dreiser was extraordinarily sensitive and since Mencken was extraordinarily blunt on occasion, it eventually occurred to the novelist that his manager (ten years his junior) was taking advantage of him. He was amused, no doubt, when Mencken threatened that a dead cat would approach him at terrific speed if he ever mounted a lecture platform. But he suspected that the purport of this buffoonery was to make him look ridiculous. Again, he knew that it was partly through Mencken's criticisms that he had made *The Titan*, the second volume of his trilogy, far more dramatic and thrilling than the first. But, at this late date, could Mencken help him by denouncing the earlier book as a total loss—"loose, tedious, vapid and exasperating"?

Finally, when Mencken applied the same adjectives to the manuscript of *The "Genius,"* Dreiser told him flatly that henceforth he would stand on his own two feet. The scene was Dreiser's heavily curtained, candlelit apartment in Greenwich Village; the time, the winter of 1915; the dramatis personae, Mencken, Dreiser, and the latter's actress friend, Kirah Markham. According to Mencken's account of it, "Kirah Markham, apparently horrified at the thought of two Christians murdering each other, rushed out of the house. But 'The Genius' [*sic*] was not cut."

The truth was, however, that Dreiser was still too deeply implicated in the anti-Puritan war to dispense with Mencken's services; and soon after the publication of *The "Genius"* in October 1915, he realized his error. The newspaper critics descended upon him like hounds upon a wild beast. The Chicago *Tribune* called him "the tom-cat of American letters"; the New York *World* admonished him for continuing "world without end, filling thick volumes with the emptyings of his passion." The publishers were frankly afraid of him. A year before, Harper had balked at publishing *The Titan* after it was already in print, and had it not been for J. Jefferson Jones, the American agent of the English firm, John Lane Company, this masterpiece might not have been published at all. Even Jones was not wholly reliable. When *The "Genius"* fell under the ban of the New York Vice Society, he promptly impounded the book, and Dreiser, at his wit's end, recalled Mencken to conduct a counterattack more far-reaching than any previous one.

[ 3 ]

Under ordinary circumstances, Mencken would have regarded this as the opportunity of a lifetime. But the circumstances were not ordinary. With World War I entering its third year, righteous organizations of all sorts, including the Vice Societies, had been heartened by the popular revulsion against the unrighteous activities of the German *Wehrmacht*, and Mencken's several interests had suffered accordingly. His Baltimore "Freelance" column had been suspended; his "louse" magazine, the *Parisienne*, had barely escaped extinction at the hands of the same organization that had suppressed *The "Genius."* Nor did he believe that Dreiser had any more chance against them than he had. Suppose, he asked, Dreiser should defy the censor's ban and take his case into the courts? The judge, the jury, the press—all would be infected with the anti-German mania. If only because of his German name, they would convict Dreiser of everything that had been charged against him.

In short, Dreiser had no alternative but to compromise.

After all, Mencken said, the passages in *The "Genius"* that the censor had complained about were trivial in the extreme: seventy-four "lewd" scenes of kissing, hugging, and seduction, one essay on the female breast, and eight profane oaths, such as "Jesus Christ" and "God damn." Dreiser could cut some or all of these; the book would again be circulated, and nobody would know the difference. At the same time, he assured the novelist that this period of compromise and humiliation would not last forever. "My whole life, once I get free from my present engagements, will be devoted to combating Puritanism. But in the meantime, I see clearly that the Puritans have nearly all the cards. They drew up the laws now on the statute books, and they cunningly contrived them to serve their own purposes. The only attack that will ever get anywhere will be directed—not at the Puritan heroes but at the laws they hide behind. In this attack, I am full of hope that shrapnel will play a part." In his next letter, he added: "There is very heavy work to be done once the war approaches an end and you are one of the many who are in duty bound to help do it."

But all such strategic considerations were wasted on the impulsive Dreiser. Nothing could dissuade him from the showdown, not even the possibility of a jail sentence; and in lieu of Mencken, a group of Dreiser's radical friends organized a Committee of One Hundred for the defense. Outmaneuvered, Mencken promptly changed his tune. "It goes without saying," he declared, "that I shall be delighted to join," and on his next trip to New York he completely forgot the inhibitions of the week before. He enlisted Nathan and Wright, pushing Wright into a debate with the Vice Society spokesman. "With your handsome stand of whiskers," he said, "you can mop up the floor with him." He pleaded with Jones to submit the case to a court test. Then, working through Harold Hersey, the assistant to the secretary of the Authors' League, he pressured that powerful organization to declare itself for Dreiser and, having accomplished this, wrote the *Sun* an editorial congratulating them for their courage. As yet, the newspapers were almost uniformly hostile to Dreiser ("they are run by cads," Mencken said). Hence the novelist had to rely almost exclusively upon Mencken for his artillery support.

In itself, the lifting of the ban against *The "Genius"* did not interest him very much. The book, he believed, was the poorest of all Dreiser's novels, "flaccid, elephantine, doltish, coarse, dismal and wearisome." But once the smoke of battle was in his mouth, it was psychologically impossible for Mencken to wage a small war or to confine himself to the issues. It now occurred to him that *The "Genius"* would make a very convenient nettle for the embarrassment of the deans and bishops of the polite world of letters. Why not, he asked himself, draft a formal Protest against the censorship, circulate it among all these dignitaries, and force them to declare themselves publicly pro-Dreiser or anti-Dreiser? As an author of realist novels, Dreiser would receive few votes; but as a martyr—as an exponent of the freedom in which all literary men obviously had a stake—he would be virtually irresistible.

In theory, Dreiser was delighted with the plan, but in practice he did not understand it. More particularly, he did not understand that henceforth he was to cut himself off from the intellectual underworld of Greenwich Village, including the Committee of One Hundred, and conduct himself like a true literary dignitary. On September 5 he blandly wrote Mencken that they both had been invited to speak at a meeting of the Liberal Club in a McDougall Street restaurant. Mencken replied hotly that if his name were heard ever again in connection with the Liberal Club, he would sue for libel, and that if Dreiser himself attended the meeting, he was an "ass." Yet, in October, Dreiser offended again, and even more seriously, by inserting into a published extract of the Protest half a dozen names of characters out of this intellectual underworld.

This enraged Hersey, who complained to Mencken, who exploded outright in Dreiser's face. "Let me say once more," he wrote, "that I think this is damnably silly, perverse and dangerous policy. You are making it very hard for Hersey, who has already imperilled his job in your behalf and spitting into the eyes of the rest of us. Just what satisfaction you get out of this course I'll be damned if I can see. Why start a fight in the trench while a bombardment is going on? All of these jitney geniuses are playing you for a sucker. They can't advance your reputation an inch, but you make a very fine (and willing) stalking horse for them."

In reply, Dreiser analyzed Mencken's charges as dispassionately as possible. He assumed that the "tenth-rate village geniuses" were Floyd Dell, Max Eastman, and some of their associates. Sardonically, he noted that "compared with the other names approved by you and never before heard of by me, they may be tenth-rate." He denied they were his friends.

But at the same time he could see no reason for Mencken's "harsh and dictatorial" tone. Never before, throughout their relation, had Mencken shown his hand so openly;

and Dreiser remonstrated with him in the same terms. "Although I have privately said to myself and here and now state to you that it is really none of your business, anymore than your private or public friendships are to me, still you persist. Have I tried to supervise your private life or comment on any of your friends, or deeds? What's eating you anyhow? . . . I owe you too much to turn on this or any occasion and say the few ugly things we can say when hurt. . . . Your letter smacks of something I do not like and if you have any real downright grievance come across."

Mencken apparently knew that he was in the wrong, but he made no apology except to deny that he ever had any "secret grievances." Meanwhile a cable had arrived from England, announcing the support of Arnold Bennett, H. G. Wells, W. L. George, and Hugh Walpole. It was the most impressive endorsement that could have been hoped for; at once, whatever stature Dreiser may have lost by the signatures of Max Eastman and Floyd Dell was restored to him and with additional cubits to boot. The Protest moved smoothly down the list, one eminent partisan bringing another, until there were four hundred of them, including Winston Churchill (the novelist), Booth Tarkington, Gertrude Atherton, Ida Tarbell, Ellery Sedgwick, Clayton Hamilton, and Lawrence Gilman. As Mencken had predicted, the martyred Dreiser was irresistible; even the *Saturday Evening Post* fell into line.

When the list was closed on October 18, Mencken took stock of the new alignment of forces. On the one hand, he had mustered—or rather blackmailed—his first significant group of converts, a potential "league against the Puritans with plenty of money to fight them," and he anticipated "some pleasant sport during the next few years." On the other hand, some of the foremost exponents of the polite school were missing—W. D. Howells, their eighty-year-old "Dean"; William Lyon Phelps of Yale; Joyce Kilmer, the young tree-poet, whose career would soon be gloriously ended on the Marne; Edith Wharton, who had never read a Dreiser novel; and Hamlin Garland, himself a forerunner of American realism, but now a pillar of the Academy. These holdouts he had in part expected, and since the list was so conspicuously small, he knew just what to do with it. He had a hundred copies of it printed and circulated among his friends and he carefully preserved all the pertinent documents in his files. Here again, he anticipated "some pleasant sport during the next few years."

If Mencken was heartened by the success of the Protest, Dreiser was even more elated, and he celebrated it by making his final declaration of independence from his Baltimore manager. In November and December of 1916, he wrote *The Hand of the Potter,* a four-act play about a sex pervert who violates an eleven-year-old child and then kills himself. Mencken protested this literary outburst, on strategic grounds as well as artistic. "You stand in serious danger through this play, of being definitely labeled as a mere shocker of boobs. . . . Fully half of the signers of the Protest, painfully seduced by all sorts of artifices, will demand that their names be taken off." And he reminded Dreiser that with or without the Protest, *The "Genius"* was still legally under the ban and would probably remain so for a long time (1923 was the actual date of its release). To this Dreiser replied: "When you tell me what I can or cannot put upon the stage . . . you may be well within your critical rights but my answer is that I have more respect for my own judgment in this matter than I have for yours." A few weeks later, when Mencken returned to New York as a war correspondent en route to Germany, Dreiser attended his farewell dinner at Lüchow's. But if Mencken had not threatened him with a "German command," and if women had not also been present, it is very doubtful that he would have come.

Thus the final settling of debts between the two men was necessarily postponed until Dreiser had been securely established in the position that Mencken had carved out for him. In November 1920, Dreiser forgot all his grievances. "Except for your murderous assaults and onslaughts in my behalf," he told Mencken, "I should now be little farther than in 1910." Mencken modestly demurred. "You greatly overestimate my services to you. You were squarely on your legs before I came into contact with you or wrote a line about you, and you would have made the same progress if I had been hanged in 1902, perhaps more." Three years later, however, when Dreiser, by a slip of the tongue, declared that he had fought the battle of *The "Genius"* singlehanded without aid from any quarter, Mencken was furious. "With all due respects," he wrote, "you lie like an archbishop. Young Hersey sweated for you like a bull and there was a critic in Baltimore, who, as I recall it, laid out $300 in cash to round up the authors of the United States on your side. Most of them, true enough, ratted but that was surely not his fault."

*CHAPTER 7*

# Between Wilson and the Kaiser

## [ 1 ]

THE BLEAKEST CHAPTER of Mencken's life was begun with a brief and ill-timed tour of duty as a war correspondent for the Baltimore *Sun* and the New York *World*. En route from New York to Copenhagen by Danish steamer, he faced Atlantic storms, German submarines, and the British North Sea patrols, and after these ordeals he crossed the Baltic on an unstable railroad barge. Safe at last in Germany, he proceeded to the battle front, where, deep in Lithuania, with the temperature at 40 degrees below zero, he heard a German field commander explain the operations of the *Wehrmacht*. Despite all its discomforts, the spectacle of war entranced him. He was just beginning to settle down and enjoy himself when he was interrupted by a diplomatic rupture between the United States and Germany. Regardless of how the other correspondents would interpret and discuss this development, for him its meaning was clear. The United States would soon be in the war, and he would have to leave Germany as expeditiously as he had entered it.

Back in Berlin, however, he found himself trapped. By order of General Ludendorff, an eight week cooling-off period was prescribed for all newspapermen returning from the front line—a period during which, presumably, whatever they had learned would lose its military importance. The prospect of two months—perhaps more—of enforced idleness, drinking Martini cocktails at the Adlon bar, appalled the restless Mencken. He presented his case at the Military Bureau. He was informed that no one could make exceptions to the rules except General Ludendorff himself, and Ludendorff was a very busy man.

Desperately he initiated an application. It was given formidable endorsements on its upward course. The Bureau officials testified that he was a man of high integrity. A member of the Reichstag swore by him. Even some of the more dispassionate members of the American press corps worked in his behalf, declaring that of all the American newspapermen who would come out of Germany, he was the one most likely to tell the truth. "On the morning of the 4th," he later recounted, "I was hauled out of bed by a telephone message from the Military Bureau. Come at once! I went—shivering, breakfastless, frostbitten—and behind the door I heard the Awful Name [of Ludendorff] again. Excellenz had stooped from his Arctic Alp. I was free to go or to stay; more, I was a marked and favored man. All the way to Zurich I paid no fare."

He rode with Ambassador Gerard and his staff on the "last train" from Berlin to Switzerland, and thence to Paris. When the Ambassador became hopelessly bogged down in the French capital, Mencken, with less baggage and less respect for formalities, continued on by himself. He negotiated with a hotel porter, who got him tickets on a southbound train. He reached Madrid, and there with the same dispatch booked passage on an outbound steamer. He was on the high seas fully a week ahead of the diplomatic party.

What he thought during this precipitate flight we learn from a letter dispatched from Madrid: "It is the carnival season here, and the war seems infinitely remote. When I got to Biarritz the other day, and saw the clear blue sky, and sniffed the warm caressing air, it seemed almost too good to be true. At San Sebastian the private car of the King of Spain was attached to the train, so I came down to Madrid in state, between two rows of soldiers presenting arms. I am sorry I can't spend a couple of weeks in Spain, but my orders are to proceed home by the quickest route, and the quickest is by the Alfonso XIII via Havana. The number 13 bemuses me. No doubt it will give encouragement to mines and U-boats."

One day out from Havana, he received a wireless message from the *Sun* ordering him to disembark in Cuba and make sense out of the latest Cuban revolution. Havana seemed to be in a state of siege, though the nearest armed rebel was 180 miles away. American correspondents on the job could not break the government censorship. They could not mention names or dates, or present the case of José Miguel, the leader of the revolutionary junta, even if they could discover it. All they had to work with was highly rhetorical and unreliable communiqués. But three days after his arrival Mencken understood the ins and outs of this vest-pocket war; and within a week he felt sufficiently confident to write the history of Cuba. Moreover, with the complicity of an old friend, Captain Asmus Leonhard, he managed to bootleg his dispatches out on a packet boat to Key West, whence they were freely relayed to Baltimore.

Buoyantly, Mencken returned to Baltimore. He had survived the Arctic cold and the tropical heat, the menace of mines and U-boats, and proved his capacity to cope with the war-fevered bureaucrats of many nations. Yet he would have to muster additional reserves to face the perils of life of a pro-German on the home front. It was the Ides of March. His fellow townsmen were waiting for President Wilson to launch them on a great crusade, and in the interim they were inclined to be restless and hysterical. There was rioting in the streets. A pacifist rally was interrupted and disbanded by a free-fisted mob.

Even in times of peace the notorious Mencken could command but little tolerance from these people, and now his situation was incomparably worse. The story of his exit from Germany had come with him. It was known that General Ludendorff, in the midst of serious duties, had found time to give him a special dispensation to go home; hence it seemed reasonable to believe that he had come back on some highly subversive and incendiary mission. Even the German-Americans believed it, and they inquired what decorations the Kaiser had promised him for the performance of his underground duties. Soon after his return he was expected in New York at the *Smart Set* office, but he postponed the trip. He would not leave his mother and sister alone, unprotected. He was afraid that when war was actually declared, there would be window-smashing and other "delicate heroics."

[ 2 ]

Mencken had arrived at this nightmarish predicament not simply by the entangling events recounted here, but by the course of his lifelong dissent from the American creed. On strictly logical grounds, he might have confined his dissent to abstract ideas without having impaled himself on the issue between America and Germany. But Mencken's development was not logical, and his almost native German partisanship had tinctured the whole fabric of his creed. Even during his formative years he had remarked that most of his intellectual gods were of German nationality—Nietzsche, Ibsen ("more German than Norwegian"), Hauptmann, and Sudermann—and that the sweetest sound which came to his ears was the music of the great German composers. Hence he had slipped easily into the conviction that the *Kultur* which could produce such genius was necessarily the foremost *Kultur* of the world.

In 1914 the march of the Kaiser's armies had brought the German complexion of his thought militantly to the fore. Nor did the possibility that Germany's interests might be inconsistent with American interests detain him. The victory of the Reich, he believed, would unify Europe and ensure the peace of the world for one hundred years. Thus, in his "Freelance" column he had singlehandedly exposed the "snarling, puling, hypocritical" propaganda of the British press agents. Debating the issues of the "rape of Belgium" with the local Belgian consul, he ridiculed the consul's plea for "justice" and upheld the

German doctrine of military necessity. On May 7, 1915, when the *Lusitania* was sunk by a German submarine commander with a loss of 1100 civilians, including 124 Americans, a tidal wave of moral indignation swept the Anglo-Saxon world. But Mencken stood against it in his little bailiwick, as G. B. Shaw (for different reasons) did in his much larger one. He plunked solidly for the submarine commander. "The English challenge," he wrote, "has been boldly accepted. . . . The Germans, you may be sure, will not stop with the *Lusitania.* They will not stop until the iron ring is squeezed so tightly around John Bull's neck that he gasps for breath and begs for mercy." Mencken could hardly wait until the German armies had occupied Paris and gutted London. "The war is in its last stage," he cried almost once a month. "Deutschland über Alles!"

For such partisanship as this, the local German-American societies had looked to him as to a patriarch, and the Germania Männerchor, among others, had made him an honorary life member. The ceremony was performed amid choral renditions of "Deutschland über Alles" and "Die Wacht am Rhein." Mencken was acclaimed as a "literary Uhlan," as invincible in his way as General Hindenburg. But he was embarrassed by his new responsibility. If he had had his way, he would have stood as a minority of one rather than be intermixed with a minority of fifty thousand. His allegiance was, after all, to a Germany that existed in its pure state only in his mind, and it was highly distressing for him to be reminded how much the German-Americans resembled other Americans. "In the whole lot of them," he wrote later, "I can think of but a score or two who could name off-hand the principal works of Thomas Mann, Otto Julius Bierbaum, Ludwig Thoma, or Hugo von Hofmannsthal. They know more about Mutt and Jeff than they know about Goethe."

But now he swallowed his prejudices. The German-Americans, himself among them, were being tried to the breaking point; they could find neither sympathy nor understanding outside their own ranks. "This is the testing time," he told the Männerchor. "Soon or late, our rights, and the rights of all non-British elements in the American Republic, must be settled." Publicly he confronted them with a vision of a triumphant finale, but privately he did not believe it. "Let us pay strict attention to our religious duties, during the next month or two," he whispered to one of the leaders. "I believe that both of us will be killed by patriots within six months."

Yet, with the actual declaration of war, nothing happened. The German-American community was humbled by a city ordinance transforming German Street into Redwood Street, and with that the patriots were apparently satisfied.

At this juncture a less bellicose man would have given thanks to God for His mercy. He would have recanted as gracefully as the circumstances permitted; he would have decorated his home and his person with red, white, and blue bunting and rallied to the flag. But how, Mencken asked himself, could he support a government that had for three years been so dishonestly neutral, that had entered the war at favorable odds of four to one, and that was now wasting public money, persecuting all opponents and critics, bribing labor, manufacturing false news, robbing enemy civilians, hunting spies, floating public loans by a process of blackmail, and, in general, abandoning all decency, decorum, and self-respect? On the one hand, he resolved to say and do nothing to contribute to this insane crusade; he would not even buy war bonds. On the other, he did not propose to put himself at the mercy of a hostile mob. He was no martyr. In all the bloody history of martyrdom, he could think of no man who had ever gone down for a doctrine that was true. As he conceived them, his convictions were rooted in scientific fact, not in religion, poetry, or political idealism. Galileo, the greatest scientest of them all, had gainsaid the truth in his hour of trial, well aware that his suffering would not add to the argument one way or another and that the truth could not be suppressed forever.

[ 3 ]

Naturally, Mencken's policy did not elicit much sympathy from patriotic Americans. In October 1915, recognizing the futility of any further plea for the German cause, he had abandoned his "Freelance" column, declaring, "I do not believe that mutiny on the quarterdeck should be tolerated." Since then, he had contributed occasional literary articles to the *Evening Sun.* His report on Germany (fifty thousand words written during the ten days of the Atlantic crossing) the *Sun* printed in part, but it gave him no further assignments. After all, the paper had a serious role to play in the war effort. There were bonds to sell, and it was planning a patriotic pageant to be called "Over There." The *Sun* had nothing to gain and everything to lose by continuing to print articles by the patriarch of the German-Americans. Even without printing them, it still had to contend with the echoes of his former crusade, for readers were constantly demanding that he be made to repudiate what he had written before.

In the fall of 1917, John Cullen, the managing editor of the New York *Evening Mail,* took up Mencken's torch where the editors of the *Sun* had dropped it. Cullen could not forget that Mencken had helped boost him out of Baltimore journalism into his present job, nor did he think that a writer as great as Mencken should ever be denied a platform. He persuaded Mencken to sign a six months contract for a series of three weekly articles. At the same time, knowing that the Nietzschean still doffed his hat whenever he passed Lüchow's restaurant, and hence was still capable of sedition, he warned him to confine himself strictly to humorous matters. For further safety, he alternated Mencken's articles in the same space with articles by the Catholic sage, Monsignor John A. Ryan. The *Evening Mail* had been the most ardently pro-German of all New York dailies, and Cullen wanted it to live down its past.

Mencken performed on the *Evening Mail* with admirable restraint. Only once did he stray, submitting an article on the Irish revolution with an implicit criticism of British imperialism, and when Cullen rejected it, he took the rebuff without complaint. Otherwise, he concerned himself with a rich variety of subjects, with the "Virtuosi of Virtue" (that is, the Prohibitionists), with "Penology: A Sick Science," with "Poetry and Other Vices." He expounded his proposal that New York be detached from the Union, and he concocted a purely imaginary history of the bathtub. The bathtub, he wrote, was invented in Cincinnati in the 1840's; it was first installed in the White House by President Fillmore; its use was opposed by eminent doctors of the time as contrary to sound principles of health. Mencken had intended to make this hoax perfectly transparent, but his air of scholarship was so convincing that even Cullen swallowed it. Most of the *Evening Mail* readers did likewise. Thereafter the story was circulated, with or without credit lines, in newspapers, magazines, and Y.M.C.A. lectures, and was incorporated eventually in an encyclopedia article. Some eight years later, Mencken thought that the hoax had gone far enough; but no confessions on his part could possibly stifle it. By accident he had struck a mainspring of human credulity. And as of 1949, the item promises to become as immortal as any newspaper feature article can be.

Meanwhile the *Evening Mail* was being shot out from under him. In July 1918, Edward Rumeley, its publisher, was arrested and jailed by federal agents on charge of having received financial aid from the Wilhelmstrasse. Mencken had only a formal acquaintance with Rumeley. He had no connection with the *Evening Mail* except as a contributor of signed articles; and he was as surprised by the scandal as everyone else. But it enveloped him nonetheless. In New York he was trailed for four days by reporters and sleuths of various sorts. When the *Evening Mail* came under new management, one of their first acts was to break Mencken's contract, ostensibly as an economy measure, but more likely because they regarded him as too notorious to be of any use to them. Mencken, however, was uncoöperative. He threatened a lawsuit for breach of contract. Then, having frightened the management into a more considerate frame of mind, he compromised for back payments of his articles, a settlement of $250 on a $450 debt, and agreed without regret to sever all relations with the paper. The work, he told his friends, was "intensely unpleasant." By long experience, Mencken had become convinced that the gods were on his side. The next year, when the *Evening Mail* disappeared, he was not surprised.

The only one of Mencken's platforms that served him throughout this period was the *Smart Set*. Nathan did not wholly share Mencken's views: politically speaking, he was neutral. Germany's invasion of Belgium had left him cold. Had Belgium been the aggressor, he would have been equally unconcerned. Editorially, however, these differences were easily reconciled. The magazine made no mention of Wilson, Creel, Pershing, Foch, or Lloyd George, nor did it give any indication, by fiction or nonfiction, that a quarter of the manhood of America had been uprooted and dispatched upon a great crusade. In their book and theater departments, Mencken and Nathan continued to refer admiringly to German art. They adorned their rhetoric wherever possible with German words and phrases, such as *Polizei, Katzenjammer, Gelehrten, Privatdocent,* and *Backfisch*. In short, they left no doubt as to their detachment from the current hysteria. Yet when German agents had proposed either to purchase the *Smart Set* or to employ Mencken as editor of a pro-German review, he would have nothing to do with them. According to his version of the story: "I remember being approached in 1914 by one Revere with a proposal to set up an independent review. I demanded $1000 a month and absolute control, and he vanished. I thought at the time that Revere was a stock speculator."

Charming as this policy was, it was, in its time and place, seditious, and as such was heatedly discussed. The book page of the Toronto *Mail and Empire* was given over to prolonged debate between rival zealots on whether it was possible to admire the *Smart Set* and, at the same time, profess loyalty to the British Empire. The *Smart Set* was bombarded by letters of protest and demands for official investigation. "There must be at least 1,000,000 detectives at work in the United States," Mencken speculated, and it seemed that a good fraction of them had assigned themselves to his case. Fortunately, there was one man on the magazine, Warner, the publisher, who was in good standing with the spy-hunters and who could defend his two editors at critical moments. He showed Mencken the kind of charges that were circulating against him: that Mencken was an intimate friend of "the German monster, Nitzsky" (that is, Nietzsche, then dead seventeen years), and that Mencken was in wireless communication with Captain Paul Koenig of the U-boat *Deutschland* (a deduction from the fact that he had entertained Koenig during the *Deutschland's* visit to Baltimore in 1916). It was at Warner's suggestion, moreover, that Mencken wrote a memorandum on himself for the files of the Justice Department. He depicted himself as "an American patriot of the highest virulence."

[ 4 ]

In the fall of 1913, Mencken had expanded his literary circle to include Ernest Boyd. A young Irishman in his middle twenties, Boyd had come to Baltimore as the new

British Vice Consul. He was a gifted linguist, literary critic, and conversationalist whose allegiance ran more to the "German camp of violent unbelievers" than to the British camp of moralists. Almost immediately a friendship sprang up between the two men. At least once a week Mencken entertained Boyd and his wife Madeleine at dinner in Rennert's basement cafeteria. On hot summer evenings, he and his mother took them motoring through the Maryland countryside in his new automobile. And while Mencken and Boyd on the front seat discussed the American language or the perfidy of British rule in Ireland, on the back seat Mrs. Boyd told Mrs. Mencken that a marriage should be arranged between Henry and Ernest's sister in Dublin. Mencken encouraged Boyd in all his extracurricular activities: he found a publisher, the John Lane Company, for Boyd's first book, *Contemporary Drama of Ireland,* and on several occasions took him to New York to meet Wright, Nathan, and Dreiser. Unfortunately, Boyd's literary debut was ill-omened, not only for Boyd himself, but for the entire circle as well.

In October 1916 he received orders to proceed to Barcelona. Perhaps, Mencken thought, some echo of Boyd's pro-German associations had reached London. Not long before, Roger Casement, another Irishman of the Foreign Service, had been caught in actual negotiations with German agents and been hanged with few preliminaries; Mencken had visions of his red-bearded friend suffering a similar fate. The two men put their heads together. Should Boyd resign from the consular service, and if so, what would he do for a living? Mencken was apparently more concerned about the danger even than Boyd himself. He had the publisher of the *Sunpapers* recalled from his yacht, and arranged that Boyd be employed as an editorial writer. Then suddenly Boyd changed his mind: he had begun the war in the service of Britain and would continue there till the bitter end. The publisher was furious at the confusion of plans, but Mencken remained as sympathetic to his friend as before. At parting, he loaded him with books, magazines, and all the material essential for the continuation of his literary work and implored him to return to the United States as soon as possible.

A year later it was Wright's turn. His stenographer at the *Evening Mail* office had made a nuisance of herself, complaining of the unpatriotic tone of his book reviews and rifling his correspondence. Suspecting that she was a stool pigeon, he dictated a letter addressed to the Washington correspondent of the *Evening Mail,* loaded with alarming and highly imaginative details—among others, references to conversations with the German ambassador. Before he completed his dictation, the girl tore the letter from the typewriter, fled into the street, and handed it to the nearest policeman. Thus, in effect, Wright had been caught in his own trap. For days he had been subjected to the most intensive investigation. And though he had cleared himself, the affair had been made public, and he had lost his job.

In relating the story, Wright expressed no regret except that he had to throw himself once more on Mencken's bounty. Mencken was infuriated not only with Wright but with himself for having indulged this irresponsible protégé these many years. "I regard the whole affair intolerably idiotic," he wrote Boyd. "To put such burdens upon innocent friends in such crazy days as these is an unforgiveable offense. It is impossible, in the circumstances, to have anything to do with him. A man as silly is a public menace. . . . There is no personal rancor in the matter; I myself was not mentioned but what he did [to the Washington correspondent] in his childish folly he might have done to any of his friends." For his part, Wright soon abandoned his appeals to Baltimore. He retired to Los Angeles, and Mencken heard no word from him until he had come East again as S. S. Van Dine, the author of a new-style detective story. In 1928 Mencken received a check from him settling a prewar debt of several hundred dollars. Mencken genially acknowledged its receipt, saying, "New York is full of reports that you have made a great hit." He suggested that Wright exploit his success by reissuing his prewar books, but he did not suggest a resumption of the old intimacy.

Mencken's circle was now reduced almost by half, and to relieve their boredom the remaining members played rather cruel jokes on each other. At midnight, after four or five seidels of beer at Lüchow's, Mencken and Nathan would suddenly decide to call on Dreiser; they would clatter their way down West Tenth Street and pound on his door. Dreiser was always out—that is to say: if he was out, there was no answer; and if he was in, there was no answer. But the visitors were prepared with their calling cards. In his mailbox, according to Nathan's version, they left "small American flags accompanied by scrolls issuing Black Hand threats, letters ostensibly written by the President urging him to come at once to the White House for a confidential talk, menus of Armenian restaurants affectionately inscribed to him by Robert W. Chambers, Elinor Glyn, and Harold Bell Wright, frankfurters tied with red, white and blue ribbons, beer bottle labels, photos of the Czar bearing the inscription, 'To Theodore, gentleman and scholar—well anyway scholar.'"

Though Mencken could ill afford to alienate another friend at this point, he ignored all Dreiser's protests. He could not remember having taken part in any night raids on West Tenth Street, he said, after the first one, and if he had actually done so, he must have been in his cups. "Let this episode teach you a lesson. Rum is a serpent. I am too far gone, but from the depths of a drunkard's grave, I beseech you to take warning by my folly." Dreiser warned him that he had given "strict orders to the janitor to sound 'lights out' whenever editors, publishers, critics and managers appear in this vicinity." But again Mencken pressed his advantage. "Why not simplify all that guard," he countered, "by employing a one-legged soldier to stand at the door? He is welcome to my medals. Besides he will be in fashion. Pretty soon, the whole country will be flooded with damaged veterans. When I was a boy there were still 7,000,000 remaining from the Civil War."

Thus, in the last phase of the war, the only available members of the inner circle were its founders, Mencken and Nathan. As editors they had managed to ignore their "patriotic duties," but as private citizens no pretense of expatriation could save them from the call to arms. On September 13, 1918, in the third and last draft of the war, Mencken registered without enthusiasm along with thirteen million "human blanks." Nathan was subject to the same indignity; but when he appeared for his medical examination, he was summarily dismissed, for he weighed little more than 129 pounds and his sparkling brown eyes were too weak for military work. Mencken was far more vulnerable. He was a 38-year-old bachelor, contributing nothing to the war effort, and despite a rich collection of medical curiosities on his person—asthma, piles, tongue trouble, hay fever, alcoholic liver, weak heels, and dandruff—he was as sound as a red apple. On August 9 he wrote Boyd: "I expect to be called up for military service on September 5. What job I'll be assigned to I don't know. My experience fits me for the medical department, but that is already overcrowded, so as a bachelor I'll probably draw the infantry. Picture me with my weight, digging ditches and learning the goose-step! After all there are some humors in war."

On October 16 he reported in a more serious vein: "If the war stops by the end of the year, I'll be passed over. But if it goes on, I'll be conscripted." Meanwhile an influenza epidemic had given him a foretaste of the actual battlefield. Nathan's brother died of a virulent form of the disease; Nathan himself suffered an attack. When Mencken returned from the New York office, arriving at Union Station in Baltimore, where fifty coffins were piled up in the train shed, he noted, "Today, for the first time, I feel wobbly myself." For weeks thereafter he dwelt among horrors. One of his Saturday Night Club friends, a young professor at Goucher College, died in a Maryland training camp. He watched the procession of undertakers' wagons file past Union Square, directly under his window. Yet once more the Hollins Street household was spared. On the day before the Armistice he was sure the war and its attendant evils would continue for a long time. On November 13 he breathed easily again: "All drafts seem to have been called off here, and so my military duty vanishes. As soon as the din ceases, I shall start on a new book."

[ 5 ]

On several occasions during this period, when all other palliatives had failed him, he had talked about moving to Munich "as soon as I can shake off my obligations." Four years later, however, when he finally got around to visiting Germany again, he made it but one stop on a four months vacation tour of England and Central Europe, and he was very much disappointed with it. Physically the country was unchanged, with his ancestral streets, churches, and universities looking very much as they had in the eighteenth century—but the heart had gone out of it. His opposite numbers among the German literati were destitute: if he had not given them several hundred dollars, some of them would have had no coal for the following winter. Still worse, the "intellectual aristocracy" that had ruled Germany during the war years had been ousted by a Camorra of "democratic mountebanks" just as bad as those at home.

One night in Berlin, eighteen authors called at his hotel to give him "an old-fashioned Christian welcome with wine." As they all got "stewed" together, he declared in bad German that he was "a monarchist of the fourth dimension." Later, in Prague, he passed up an invitation to the Czech White House. He told President Masaryk's secretary that the invitation must have been a mistake, for he had no acquaintance with that distinguished democratic statesman, and as quickly as he could, he slipped out of Prague and down to Pilsen. There he accepted a hospitality more to his taste. At the hands of the chief brewer, he sampled a brew that is rarely seen or tasted. He exclaimed that it towered as far above ordinary Pilsen, as ordinary Pilsen above ordinary horse piss. Between drinking sessions, he slumbered like an innocent.

Earlier the editors of the Baltimore *Sunpapers* had urged him to interview the survivors of the German royal family. It was a difficult assignment. Hitherto both the former Kaiser and his son, the former Crown Prince, had made themselves inaccessible in remote castles in Holland. But since Mencken was now more palpably interested in Europe's past than its present, he was determined to have a look at them, and in this he was assisted by Dr. Henry Wood, former Professor of German at Johns Hopkins, now living in retirement at Berchtesgaden. The professor's wife was a German countess; through her connections at the exiled court, she arranged that all drawbridges be lowered for him.

When he arrived at Wieringen the Mayor was on hand to greet him, and shortly thereafter he was ushered into the presence of William, the former Crown Prince. Mencken spent the day with him and penetrated his ugly exterior to discover an alert mind and a broad culture. "He is no intellectual," Mencken reflected, "but compared with any American general, he seems like Aristotle." As the interview came to a close, Mencken had enough material for a highly revealing dispatch to the Baltimore *Sun*. Afterwards, he might have moved on from Wieringen to Doorn, where the Kaiser himself was prepared to receive him, for the latter was then, or would soon become, the most ardent Mencken admirer in all of

Europe. But somehow Mencken had got it into his head that the Kaiser had mismanaged the Empire in its last days; hence, his reticence. During the ensuing years, the Kaiser often wrote to Mencken, expressing his disappointment that he never came to see him. But the Baltimorean would not relent. He was satisfied that he had two photographs of the Kaiser in his full regimentals, inscribed and tinted with crayon by the Kaiser's own hand.

CHAPTER 8

# Bid for Immortality

## [ 1 ]

MENCKEN had been devoted to his "Freelance" column as the most exciting of all mediums. He loved to dream up "offensive wheezes" against the "Baltimoralists" of one variety or another, to preside over their publication, and to observe at close hand the confusion and indignation that almost invariably followed. Indeed, had there been no war to deprive him of it, he might have gone on indefinitely, dissipating his annual torrent of three hundred thousand words in this more or less futile way. Since *The Philosophy of Friedrich Nietzsche* in 1908, he had written no full-length book. Even as late as 1916, his *Book of Burlesques* and *A Little Book in C Major* were simply collections of *Smart Set* epigrams and buffooneries. Yet now that he no longer had his column, he returned to the creative life, to the life of "hard, steady striving with a definite goal in sight," with joy heavily intermixed with regret. The demagogue drug was still in him: at least once a month he would visit the *Sun* office, partly out of habit and partly out of curiosity—just to see what the "Anglo-maniacs" were up to.

Throughout the summer and fall of 1916 he labored on a magnum opus in literary criticism to be called *A*

*Book of Prefaces.* Its composition, he found, was even harder than he had expected. Though he narrowed its compass from eight chapters to four, it was still difficult to keep it abreast of the changing scene. Where it dealt with the lives of Huneker and Dreiser, he had his subjects themselves check the facts in the rough draft. At Christmas he took time out for his brief adventure as a war correspondent. Returning in March 1917, he rewrote the manuscript "from snout to tail" and in a final two week stretch polished it until he had changed "all intelligible English into fantastic and mystical balderdash." In June he sent it to the printers, making no greater claim than that "there is some very good stuff in it."

Next he turned to *The American Language.* This ambitious volume had already been drafted once in the winter of 1915–1916. But again he had grown in knowledge and technique, and again he found it necessary to revise the manuscript "from snout to tail." "It is," he remarked, "a superb piece of punditry, shaming the college professors. But you can imagine what a job it is to coordinate the material." At the halfway mark, in the fall, he was becoming adjusted to his new regimen. His files were choked with the plans and outlines of seven more books: *A Book of Prejudices, In Defense of Women, The Anglo-Saxon under the Terror* (a scholarly study of jingoism in the universities, later abandoned), and a series of small aphoristic volumes on Democracy, War, Puritanism, and Sex. Eagerly he looked forward to at least six or seven years of detached creative activity.

At eight every morning he arose and collected his wits with a cold shower. After a light breakfast he retreated to the little room on the third floor that constituted his office. He assured himself that there was a fresh black ribbon in the flyweight typewriter and plenty of copy paper (secured gratis from the *Sun* office) in his desk drawer. Then, chewing on a cigar (he did not smoke it, because he disliked ashes falling on his clothes), he set to work. He clacked away with two fingers. Each sentence was thought out in his head from start to finish before he committed it to paper, and one followed upon another in rapid sequence with few mistakes. He had long since acquired a reputation for infallibility. Indeed, the copyreaders at the *Sun* office had lately stopped correcting his errors for fear that what they took for error was actually a new or obscure usage of American English. Yet to achieve such infallibility he demanded solitude. His door was closed against all visitors, including the members of the household and Tessie, the black and tan terrier.

At noon he would lunch at the Rennert basement cafeteria with one of his cronies, most frequently with Al Hildebrandt, the music shop proprietor, whose sole interest in literature was to read articles about Mencken. Late in the afternoon he would stretch out for a brief cat nap on his chintz-covered couch, and promptly at six he would dine with the family. His workday continued until ten, after which he underwent a process of emotional decompression. It was one of his rules of thumb that he never accepted a drink by day, nor refused one by night; so now, for an hour or so, he drank a few seidels of beer in the living room or in town with his friends. At eleven he retreated to his bedroom. Propped up with pillows, he read at the rate of two hundred pages an hour the novels later to be reviewed in the *Smart Set*, until at one he fell asleep.

In Hollins Street he could not, of course, shut himself off entirely from the war, but because of his perversity the war provided an atmosphere highly favorable to his art. In the first place, the patriotic platitudes bored him so much that he worked harder than ever to make his prose glittering and epigrammatic. Secondly, his books were now subject to the wartime censorship, and to evade it he developed his flexibility and subtlety to a high point. Finally, as his public reputation reached its nadir, his hidden resources came welling to the surface, and by good luck he was physically and intellectually in condition to make the most of them. According to his own testimony, "I was wisest at the age of 35 [that is, during the first year of his retreat], and since then I have been going down hill. At the age of 20 a young man is admittedly an idiot—not that he is ignorant but that he knows so many things that are not true. At 35 he is pretty well emptied of these delusions. But the antitoxin for ideas, having got into his veins, keeps on working after its usefulness is past, and its subsequent prey is not error, but truth. Thus the fellow is slowly submerged in a scepticism that leaves him, in the end, almost *non compos.*"

Women, he insisted, played no part in his creative life, but undoubtedly, both in New York and in Baltimore, they stimulated some of his wittiest utterances. It delighted him, he wrote, to lie stretched out on a divan, within arm's length of a good-looking, intelligent woman (not too young), vaguely to listen to the chatter of her soft, low-pitched voice, to admire the "fine sheen of her hair, the glint of her white teeth, the graceful curve of her arm and then alternately to sleep and be aroused from sleep." "The sensation of falling asleep," he exclaimed, "is to me the most exquisite in the world. . . . Well, here is sleep poetized and made doubly sweet. Here is sleep set to the finest music. I match this situation against any that you can think of." In painting this scene, Mencken bowdlerized it by referring to a divan rather than a bed and by omitting the name of the woman, but it was accurate enough to evoke a protest from her. She had wept many a tear for Mencken when he was off with the German armies; hence she was not pleased at this display of romantic grossness.

Under these influences, Mencken brought his peculiar art to its finest flower. On February 1, 1918, at the suggestion of a publisher, Philip Goodman, he commenced *In Defense of Women;* six weeks later it was completed. As with most of his other books, his problem was somewhat simplified by his backlog of magazine and newspaper articles on the subject. He believed that a good phrase or a good paragraph did not suffer from repetition: on the contrary, it was only by repetition that it was grasped at all. Yet it had been no mean feat to collect his random paragraphs and give them continuity and coherence.

The argument of *In Defense of Women* was, in brief, that women are more competent than men; and by implication, that men (particularly American men) are boobs with "shoddy souls." It was not original. "Blow the froth off Mencken," one critic remarked, "and you get Shaw; skim the scum off Shaw and you get Nietzsche; drain off the lees and settlings of Nietzsche's melancholy brain and you get Schopenhauer." But the froth was the central merit of the work, and certainly none of Mencken's prototypes would have been embarrassed by it. He set a fast pace for himself in his opening paragraph: "A man's women folk, whatever their outward show of respect for his merit and authority, always regard him secretly as an ass, and with something akin to pity." Then, by an inspired sophistry, he leaped from point to point high up above all restraints of plausibility. Looking at random, one could find such remarks as these: "[A woman in military uniform] looks like a dumb-bell run over by an express train. Below the neck by the bow and below the waist astern there are two masses that simply refuse to fit into a balanced composition."—"A man never really sees his wife—that is, as God is supposed to see her, until they have been married for years."—"To tell a man flatly that his wife is not beautiful, or even that his stenographer or manicurist is not beautiful, is so harsh and intolerable an insult to his taste that even an enemy seldom ventures upon it. One would, relatively speaking, almost caress him by spitting into his eye."

The stuff was so good that even Mencken was dazzled by it. And by the spring of 1919 he was convinced not only that he could solve the problems in his own art form, but also those in a form that had previously been beyond his reach—namely, the drama. The inspiration came one evening at dinner with Nathan in Roger's restaurant at Sixth Avenue and Forty-fifth Street. It was not the first time that the two men had spoken of a venture in this direction. They had but recently translated and revised *Moral* by Ludwig Thoma, a witty German playwright, and though their version was not produced, they had learned the mechanics of playwriting from a master. Also, a few days before, a pioneer movie company, "The Famous Players," had bought the rights to some *Smart Set* epigrams for use as fillers between featured reels. The purchase price was astonishingly high. "There is no justice in the world," Mencken remarked. "Playwriting is the easiest of all literary enterprises, and the most gaudily rewarded." Nathan nodded in agreement. "Why, there is nothing in it," Mencken continued. "All you need is a bag of stale tricks, a transparent psychology, some platitudes. The plot—pish-posh. I have an idea. Take the most disreputable character you can think of—say, a Roman emperor, like the one in Edgar Saltus' 'Imperial Purple'—married to a lady Y.M.C.A. secretary."

"Why not try it?" Nathan ventured. "I'll help you."

Mencken set to work at the first opportunity. Despite a heavy docket of other work, he finished the first draft in five weeks and sent it to his partner. Nathan found various organic faults, which were subsequently corrected, and to Mencken's lines added many of his own. The fruit of the collaboration was *Heliogabalus.* It was certainly no masterpiece of theater, but, to his own satisfaction, Mencken had proved his point: in a little over a month, he and Nathan had turned out a three-act farce that was not only readable but probably playable as well. In the first act, there was a water tank in which quack doctors were dunked—a steal from Corse Peyton's tank dramas at the old Holliday Theatre in Baltimore (circa 1905); in the third act, there was a fan dance. But in the second act there was a device hitherto never attempted on the burlesque stage—a bed large enough for twelve Follies girls. Upon it a marital courtship was conducted, interrupted at intervals by knocks on the door.

Theatrical managers agreed with the playwrights that *Heliogabalus* had the makings of a very amusing production; but they added that it was far too bawdy to be tolerated by the police. Undaunted, Mencken and Nathan had their play published in a limited edition of two thousand and a de luxe edition of sixty. When their devotees immediately bought out the printing and when Broadway columnists began seriously discussing it, the producers realized their error. Negotiations were reopened, this time with the playwrights holding the cards. One producer followed them all evening from bar to bar and then back again to Nathan's suite in the Royalton Hotel: he offered to buy all rights to the script without even having read it. The late Will A. Page, Mencken's oldest friend in the theater, offered $10,000 in addition to the usual royalties. But by this time the literary dignity of the two partners had been affronted beyond repair. Producers, they declared, who would not produce a play until its success was assured them were not worthy of *Heliogabalus;* nor would the authors offer it to the American theater again until the country became "civilized" up to it.

Instead Mencken tried to launch himself as a dramatist in Europe. He sent the play to impresarios in all the European capitals from Copenhagen to Rome. On January 26, 1920, he noted: "Max Reinhardt's New York agent has bespoken the Continental rights, and is having the play translated into German and Hungarian at once. He says he thinks he can get an early production in Budapest. He probably lies." Other producers nibbled at it. Charles A. Feleky had a German edition published at his own expense; but the staging of the play was beyond the resources of the impoverished German theater of the time. Three years later *Heliogabalus* was still unproduced and Mencken believed that he and his partner had smarted themselves out of a highly profitable venture. By way of consolation, he had printed in the Paris edition of the New York *Herald* a fabulous item, datelined Munich, Germany. It announced that *Heliogabalus* was being played at the Munich Municipal Theatre, that on the opening night it was greeted with "gales of laughter," that the chief Munich critic predicted a run of a thousand performances, and that at the same time Eugene O'Neill's *Anna Christie* fell dead in the Deutsches Theater in Berlin.

[ 2 ]

At some point during these closeted years, the hand of destiny beckoned to Mencken. He did not expect a wide sale of his books, nor could he be certain that their publication would be followed by great rewards of fame and fortune. But he was astute enough to foresee that great opportunities would open up after the war, possibly even "a transvaluation of values." Whatever the outcome, he now felt an irresistible urge to "compel the attention and respect" of his equals and to "lord it over" his inferiors. In *A Book of Prefaces* he made it very clear who these people were. He ranked himself slightly below Joseph Conrad, equal to Huneker and Dreiser, and above practically all other authors, domestic and foreign. The "Prejudices" book was dedicated in large part to a slaughter of all personages who had any distinction that Mencken might have desired for himself.

Was Thorstein Veblen, the idol of the college boys, the "American Voltaire"? After reading the entire shelf of Veblen's works—that is, after examining the most original contribution to social thought ever made by an American—it was Mencken's opinion (1) that Veblen had "an unprecedented talent for saying nothing in an august and heroic manner"; (2) that the theory of conspicuous waste was "one per cent platitude and ninety-nine per cent nonsense," because Veblen had ignored the effects of cows' excrement in discussing why Americans don't keep cows in the city; (3) that Veblen's basic premises are simply "Socialism and water." Was H. G. Wells one of the most potent intellectual figures of the modern world? He should have stuck to the novel, Mencken argued, for he had no facility as a "Great Thinker." At the same time, Irvin S. Cobb was accorded a terrific whacking, his offense being that he was widely hailed as the "Heir of Mark Twain." The highest compliment that Mencken could pay him was to say that one of his stories had merit on the order of "a slice of Smithfield ham between two slabs of store-bread."

Most challenging of all was the towering figure of George Bernard Shaw. Shaw, it will be remembered, had taught the boy Mencken his profession; in 1906 Mencken had acclaimed him as "the premier scoffer and dominant heretic of the day." But what could be more appropriate now than to give him a swift kick in the "pantaloons" and to inform the world that a new and bolder scoffer had arrived? Mencken had been rehearsing the deed since his unfavorable review of *Androcles and the Lion* in the *Smart Set* in 1914. Now he stepped back and swung his leg with all his might. Shaw, he said, was the "Ulster Polonius," a great windbag full of platitudes, and "it is his life-work to announce the obvious in terms of the scandalous." Moreover, Shaw was not a heretic at all, "but an orthodox Scotch Presbyterian of the most cock-sure and bilious sort—in fact, almost the archtype of the blue-nose."

Clearly, as Cobb himself remarked, Mencken was "drunk with the power which he has found in his pen." Moreover, if he had not been hitting so many bull's-eyes in his war with the Puritans, he would not have been permitted such license against his literary kinsmen and particularly against Shaw. For whatever the differences between Shaw and Mencken—the one a vegetarian, a Socialist, a dramatist, a fountain of changing and variegated ideas; the other a beef-eater and beer-drinker, a reactionary, with a considerably smaller range—they were both iconoclasts, as intolerant of human folly and as devoid of human sentiment as mortals weaned on mammal's milk could be. In 1923, when *Collier's* magazine called on a jury of eighteen authors to give judgment on Santa Claus, this pair cast the only two votes against him. Mencken, breaking another lance at the same time, added: "I am glad to hear that the American Legion has spoken out boldly against Kris Kringle. The old man was a Prussian and must be put down. He used alcohol. Thank God that we have brave and patriotic men among us!" Finally, in 1930, in a more sober mood, he freely acknowledged that Shaw was the most charming stylist and the most successful of all intellectual demagogues. Nor did he deny any longer that both he and Shaw were "working the same side of the street"—that is, "stating the obvious in terms of the scandalous."

Even in the fury of the "Ulster Polonius" assault, Mencken could not wholly conceal a schoolboy admiration for the other, and eagerly he awaited Shaw's response. On a trip to England in 1922 he walked the streets of London within easy reach of Shaw's flat, but he hesitated to pay his respects. Frank Harris, or some other intermediary, had told him that G.B.S. was very angry. Nor did Mencken have it in him to make the first gesture. In his youth he had shyly stood apart during a *Sunpapers* reception for Mark Twain, and in his maturity he was still unwilling to intrude upon his heroes. Two years later, Shaw broke the impasse with some remarks on American letters. "I am obviously and ridiculously out of date," he confessed in the *Fortnightly Review*. He had never heard of Willa Cather; he thought Cabell was a Senator. But inevitably he had read Mencken and, what is more, found him to be "an amusing dog and a valuable critic." Here was a gesture indeed, but unfortunately not quite warm enough to invite familiarities. During the ensuing years the only correspondence between the two men was an exchange of notes on a business basis. Mencken asked Shaw for permission to insert a Shavian tract into *The American Language*. Shaw replied, "Yes, and you may go the limit."

## [ 3 ]

In the spring of 1917, when word got about that Mencken was writing books again, there was a little flurry in the publishing business. Within one month, he received offers from four different firms, the most interesting and the most tempting from Philip Goodman. Goodman, a successful advertising man, proposed to buy the current works of Mencken and Nathan, put them into mass production, and sell them across every drug counter in America—in short, to make them the spearhead of a revolution in the publishing business. Mencken was captivated—in part by the daring of the plan, in part by the gusto of its originator—and his judgment went askew.

It is doubtful that even an experienced publisher could have cracked the drugstore market at this time; two decades later it would still be virgin territory. But Goodman had no outside capital for his proposed venture, no circulation facilities, and, despite a critical eye and a passion for perfection, permitted his own name to be misspelled on one of his title pages. As an advertising man, he staked everything upon a sensational approach. He would have issued *In Defense of Women* under the title *A Book for Men Only* if Mencken had not objected, and he did in fact, after a long argument, issue a collection of Mencken's short essays under the startling title *Damn*. Within six months, it was evident that the plan would not work. The woman book, under other auspices, was to sell in tens of thousands and undergo eleven reprintings in so many years, but Goodman with difficulty sold less than a thousand copies.

If Mencken had not been so blinded by irrational factors, he would have known that his publishing problems had, in fact, already been solved. Four years before, Alfred Knopf, then a factotum in the house of Doubleday, Page and Company, had come to see him about a uniform edition of Joseph Conrad. In the ensuing conversation, however, this ambitious young man had overplayed his hand: he had talked much about Conrad and little about budgets and paper costs; and he had impressed Mencken as too idealistic ever to make his mark in the publishing business. Nor did Mencken easily shake off his first impressions. He was skeptical in 1915 when Knopf had established a firm of his own in the back room of his father's office. He had looked doubtfully at Knopf's first list of ten obscure European authors. Yet every year thereafter the Knopf firm expanded, not only in the European field, but also in the American, gathering in such serious authors as Carl Van Vechten, Alfred Kreymborg, Max Eastman, and Joseph Hergesheimer, and from Hergesheimer, Mencken now received highly favorable reports upon it.

By the summer of 1917 Mencken was willing to entrust Knopf (or "Noff" as he called him) with *A Book of Prefaces*. True, he had already promised the manuscript to Jones of the John Lane Company. But Mencken thought Jones had bungled the promotion of *A Book of Burlesques*, and he was not eager to continue the association. Artfully, he inserted into the text a paragraph denouncing William J. Locke, the best-selling author on Jones's list. When Jones saw it, he responded as expected. "If I print that passage," he told Mencken, "I'll lose my job." Mencken replied, "I sympathize with you fully, but I cannot touch a word. I must stand on my literary dignity." Then, with his contract broken, Mencken removed all references to Locke and delivered the manuscript to Knopf.

If Mencken had any remaining doubts about Knopf's competence in his chosen field, he had only to watch how tenderly Knopf cultivated the market, and how promptly he brought out a second printing of the *Prefaces* as soon as the first was exhausted. It was solicitude which he had never before enjoyed. Knopf, he told his friends, "gets out good-looking books, not abortions; he pays royalties promptly, and he is a good drummer." Also,

Knopf was willing to take a chance on many of Mencken's and Nathan's undiscovered authors. And when Nathan himself became a Knopf author, the two editors were launched, each in his own right.

At first, perhaps, Mencken was abashed by his new dignity. But when his publisher asked him to adopt some mark of distinction to be stamped upon the bindings, he chose the ancient Mencken coat of arms, two roebucks rampant under a linden tree, which his father had registered as a trade-mark back in 1875. This, he admitted, was the "noblest act of Philistinism that even America can show." He assured his friends that "the animals supporting the tree" were nothing more than "common hounds."

*CHAPTER 9*

# The Battle of the Books

## [ 1 ]

SAMUEL BUTLER once said that the extraordinary man never worries about rising to the occasion; he does it naturally. This was the case with Mencken. By force of circumstances rather than by design, he had written the three or four most important works of his career. And he had written them at the exact moment when the educated public was best prepared to receive them.

Had the war been fought "to make the world safe for democracy"? In Paris the Allies were squabbling like highwaymen over the loot of their late enemies; at home our citizens were breaking strikes, ostracizing alien and dissident groups, shutting down bars and saloons. Within the space of two years the secure, self-righteous, optimistic prewar world had been exchanged for a wasteland of sordid realities; the continuity of the democratic tradition had been broken; and in the ensuing disillusionment, the rising generation no longer felt itself bound by the precepts of its elders. "The older generation had certainly pretty well ruined this world before passing it on to us," declared one disheartened young man. "They give us this thing knocked to pieces, leaky, red-hot, threatening to blow up and then they are surprised that we don't accept it." "Eat, drink, and be merry, for tomorrow we die," cried the heroes returning from the battlefields of France. Young girls ("flappers" they were called) were equally defiant and even more demonstrative. They adopted short skirts, flesh-toned stockings, bobbed hair, and face paints, and forced their way into male society on equal terms—smoking, drinking, and discovering sex.

Under the changed circumstances, Mencken could no longer be dismissed as a "circus critic," a "cheap-jack journalist," "an irresponsible cynic." "We need a public scold—a Bernard Shaw, a G. K. Chesterton, a George Moore, and a John Galsworthy," wrote a columnist in the Detroit *Journal* in November 1918; and he urged Mencken to "taunt the nation to the point of madness." Similar sentiments were expressed in other quarters. And as they increased both in volume and in intensity, it became apparent that Mencken's following was growing from a cult into a crusading army and that everywhere, from the batik-curtained studios of Greenwich Village to lonely Minnesota farmhouses, disaffected youth were rallying to his banner. Ironically, his progress was slowest in Baltimore, where he had been writing newspaper articles for two decades, and fastest in Chicago, where he was just beginning. There a literary society met regularly around a table in Schlogl's restaurant, planning how best to further the cause. One member was Burton Rascoe, the 26-year-old critic of the Chicago *Tribune;* in November 1917 he had written the first full-length study of Mencken. Others were Ben Hecht, Sherwood Anderson, Harry Hansen, Floyd Dell—contributors or would-be contributors to the *Smart Set.* And when Mencken, in his turn, acknowledged their help, he made them feel, as Anderson later put it, as though they were being knighted by a king.

By the same token, more books were now being written according to the Mencken critique; in fact, since *Jennie Gerhardt* almost a decade before, he had accumulated a shelf of some thirty-odd volumes exposing in part "the gross, glittering, excessively dynamic, infinitely grotesque, incredibly stupendous drama of American life." It was, as might have been expected, an eccentric list, as remarkable for what it excluded as for what it included. In the realm of poetry, Mencken took no notice of all the revolutionary bards who loomed so large during the period—of Amy Lowell, whose reputation, he believed, derived solely from the fact that her brother was the president of Harvard; of Ezra Pound, "Abelard in grand opera" but the "best of the revolutionaries"; of Vachel Lindsay, the "chautauquan"; nor even of Robert Frost and E. A. Robinson. His list was restricted to Lizette Woodworth Reese, Edgar Lee Masters, Sara Teasdale, and John McClure, an obscure *Smart Set* poet. In biography he included not *The Education of Henry Adams,* but Frank Harris's *Oscar Wilde* and Paine's *Mark Twain.* Of eighteen novels on the list, two were works of uncontested merit—namely, Edith Wharton's *Ethan Frome* and Mary Austin's *Woman of Genius.* Almost half were works that appealed to Mencken and to few others. *One Man,* by the pseudonymous Robert Steel, for example, was a sordid true confession of a Christian prodigal. Almost singlehandedly Mencken had edited it, published it, and acclaimed it. For the rest, he picked a handful of fiction writers then relatively obscure, who were destined to become the foremost exponents of his school—Willa Cather, Ring Lardner, Joseph Hergesheimer, Sherwood Anderson, and James Branch Cabell.

At this point it must be reiterated that Mencken was a cynic, and no cynic has ever qualified as a truly professional critic. His critical code was broad enough to comprehend the enduring elements of a Dreiser or a Mark Twain, but not penetrating enough to expose the synthetic elements of a Cabell or a Hergesheimer. And when it was applied over the whole range of literature, it produced judgments utterly grotesque. He had never read *Alice in Wonderland, Moby Dick, Pilgrim's Progress,* the novels of Victorian England, of George Eliot, George Meredith, Bulwer-Lytton, nor the great Russians, Dostoevski and Turgenev. He did not look to Homer, Dante, Shakespeare, Milton, and Goethe as the fixed stars of the literary universe. If he enjoyed the lush imagery of Shakespeare in fitful moments, he was either bored or revolted by the other titans, even by Goethe, the chief exponent of German *Kultur.* As early as 1914, he had decided that the drama was by nature a democratic art, saturated with platitude and buncombe. He was just as impervious to great poetry as to great drama, yet he continued his annual poetry circuses in the *Smart Set,* revealing his weak underpinning. Lewisohn later remarked that Mencken could write of music as no other American, "with beauty, with fire, with a love that creates wisdom," but outside of music "he is intellectually lost."

Nevertheless, in the eyes of the disillusioned "Young Intellectuals," he was, as Edmund Wilson put it, "the civilized consciousness of America . . . realizing the grossness of its manners and its mind, and crying out in horror and chagrin." And in this capacity he became more cocksure and more bellicose than before. The day of reckoning was at hand—the final and decisive battle with the Puritan enemy. He recalled the many indignities that he and his friends had suffered at their hands—the pathetic funeral of Percival Pollard, the censorship of the *Smart Set,* the martyrdom of Theodore Dreiser, the hostile reviews of his books. For years he had put up with such things, his protests virtually unheard. But now, at last, he could face his tormentors on more or less equal terms. Nor did he doubt for a moment that justice was on his side. Once he had cleared the reviewing stands of Puritan bluenoses, he believed, American letters would come alive. Masterpieces would be written comparable to those of Joseph Conrad and Anatole France; writing would become as respectable as nail manufacturing; and America would at last take her place among the civilized nations.

[ 2 ]

If Mencken could have stage-managed the ensuing battle, he would have picked as his antagonist the preeminent literary scholar in America, Paul Elmer More, known to his fellow Puritans as the "Bishop" of American letters, just as Howells was known as the "Dean." From 1909 to 1914, More had been literary editor of the *Nation;* then he had retreated to a professorship at Princeton, ostensibly to bring up his children in an "English-speaking community." For, oddly enough, he was as contemptuous of the age in which he lived as was Mencken himself. He hated the mob rule of democracy. He despised the sentimentalities of the market place. With Irving Babbitt of Harvard, he was one of the founders of a Humanist movement—a movement metaphysically so subtle that few of its supporters fully understood it. With such phrases as the "inner check," "the individual's responsibility to God," the Humanists advocated a spiritual discipline more rigorous than anything known to Americans. More himself lived in an intellectual cosmos of Platonic purity that was but slightly removed from Catholicism.

Mencken was not equipped to exchange syllogisms with More. But he was anxious to try the effectiveness of his chosen weapon, the "horselaugh," against such a learned and unworldly man. "To rout him out of his armored tower, to bring him finally to the wager of battle—this would be an enterprise to bemuse the most audacious and give pause to the most talented," Mencken wrote; and to that effect he applied every stratagem he could think of. He fell upon one of More's kinsmen, a minor but prolific poet, with exceptional malice, thinking to bring the scholar flying to the rescue. He advertised the fact that More had given his great name to the Comstocks in the "*Genius*" case. Yet More could not be aroused from his world of dead giants. He had already disposed at length of Nietzsche as a hideous and despairing nihilist, and he could see no point in exchanging unpleasantnesses with Nietzsche's bastard offspring, or "the wolf," as he called him.

Meanwhile, a deputy had stepped into the arena. He was Stuart P. Sherman, a professor of English at the University of Illinois, one year younger than Mencken. He was at this time little known, yet he was one of the most promising of the newer Puritan spokesmen. As a graduate student at Harvard, under Babbitt, he had written a doctoral dissertation reputed to have been the most brilliant work of its kind. Later, for More's *Nation,* he had learned to write book reviews with a clear and fluent style. As Sherman made his way, it became apparent that he was more conventional in his views than his masters, and also more belligerent. As early as 1916 he saw that the challenge of the "vulgarians" would have to be faced. "We cannot shut out the new nation of writers," he told Ellery Sedgwick, editor of the *Atlantic Monthly.* We must become their singing master "with a little cordiality and a great deal of catholicity and patience." In place of the old stiff, snobbish Puritanism in frock coat, he urged a new dynamic Puritanism in khaki. And Sedgwick, who had helped Mencken to find himself circa 1905, urged Sherman on, believing him to be the other's Nemesis.

Thus, in November 1917, when Sherman settled down to review Mencken's *Book of Prefaces* for the *Nation,* he realized the great opportunity that lay at hand. We can well imagine that his face flushed, that there was a choking sensation at his throat, that his hand was unsteady on the pen. At any rate, he abandoned all pretense of cordiality, catholicity, and patience, and assaulted Mencken with the latter's own "waspish" weapons. Ironically, he referred to him as "a sensitive intellectual aristocrat," pointed to his "unfailing good taste," and exclaimed that "the sheer loveliness of writing like this can never pass away." And then the *coup de grâce* deep under his opponent's skin. The reader must decide between them, he said—between Mencken, a self-professed German, possibly a secret agent of the Wilhelmstrasse, and himself, Sherman, a typical American critic, a native "whose blood is not so richly tinctured with Saxon, Bavarian, and Hessian elements."

Four or five years hence, when the anti-German hysteria had subsided, Mencken would proudly assume the stigma of his foreignness, pointing out that without such "foreigners" as Huneker and Dreiser the native culture of this country would be almost totally sterile. But the author of this assault he would forever ignore. The stage was set for an extremely dramatic, if not very illuminating, duel. Sherman's opening sally was regarded in some quarters as the finest piece of ironic writing ever done in America. The public demanded more. Repeatedly through the years, Sherman invited Mencken to exchange blows with him. But Mencken kept his distance. Once he wrote casually that Sherman was "too American. One inevitably sees in him a *reductio ad absurdum* of his fundamental theory—to wit, the theory that the test of an artist is whether he hated the Kaiser in 1917, and plays his honorable part in Christian Endeavor, and prefers Coca-Cola to Scharlachberger 1911 and has taken to heart the great lessons of sex hygiene." But this, according to Sherman, did not constitute a rebuttal. "It is his turn to strike," he remarked to Henry Seidel Canby. "But that is not the same thing as emptying the contents of his garbage bucket on my side of the fence. I don't see my part in that sort of Teutonic harlequinade."

In explanation of his forbearance, Mencken was somewhat evasive. First of all, he had made no secret of his pro-Germanism before or during the war, and it was common practice in those days for writers to discuss each other's racial backgrounds. Secondly, in point of honor, he could not complain of the manner of the attack—that is, the appeal to mob prejudice—for he, too, occasionally slipped on this ground, as when he remarked of certain writers that "they think in Yiddish and write in English." Somewhat feebly, he told his friends that he objected to Sherman's denunciation of Dreiser. "Dreiser was not in politics, and it was certainly unfair fighting to get the patriots upon him, especially in view of the fact that he was already beset in those days by the Comstocks."

However this may be, Mencken's excommunication of Sherman was absolute and final. Nothing would make him change his mind. Once, at a luncheon at the Brevoort for Sherwood Anderson, the two men stood under the same roof, and indeed in the same room, though in opposite corners, while Carl Van Doren, the *Nation* critic, a former colleague of Sherman's and a Mencken admirer, attempted a *rapprochement*. Van Doren asked Sherman if he would be willing to cross the intervening space and shake the hand of the Anti-Christ. "Sure," Sherman said. Van Doren then approached Mencken and asked if he had any objections to the introduction. He fully expected Mencken to reply, "Nonsense. Bring him up and let me confound the fellow and all his works." To his astonishment, Mencken stiffened and said, "I'd rather pass into heaven without the pleasure of his acquaintance. He is a dirty fighter."

In the spring of 1919, with the publication of *The American Language*, an unnatural calm settled over the battlefield. Twenty-five years later the critics would look back upon this as a landmark in "a new era of American linguistic studies." Between 1919 and 1944 more books and articles would be written on American English than in the hundred and thirty years preceding, and *The American Language* would be linked with the works of Professor Louise Pound as a prime mover of the movement. In 1919, none of the academic critics could have foreseen this. Yet, in view of what had gone before, they were remarkably sympathetic. Brander Matthews, a philologist and Puritan critic of even greater authority than Sherman, called *The American Language* "interesting and useful." "It is a book to be taken seriously," he declared cautiously; "it is a book well planned, well proportioned, well documented, and well written." Professor J. R. Hurlbert in *Modern Philology* said that he could have filled pages with Mencken's errors, but he would nonetheless recommend his book for the general reader and the undergraduate.

If Mencken enjoyed this era of good feeling, he did so apparently because it gave him the opportunity to renew hostilities in a particularly offensive way. While he remarked privately that he was "tickled that the academic idiots are all taking it [*The American Language*] seriously," he said publicly that their interest was hypocritical. Would these gentlemen, he asked, have approved *The American Language* if they had not read an article in the *Mercure de France* describing me as "the first American critic after Edgar Allan Poe . . . as peculiarly American as pumpkin pie or a Riker-Hegeman drug store"? And if so, why had they never seen the merits of my earlier books? "In order to put an end to this new respectability," he explained to Boyd, "I am inserting some rat poison in the *Prejudices* [First Series]." In November, shortly after the publication of the *Prejudices*, he added gleefully: "I hear that my old friend, Prof. Dr. Sherman, is denouncing it in the New York *Times* as German propaganda. Well, maybe it is."

Needless to say, the era of good feeling terminated as abruptly as it had begun. "Will he never learn to keep himself out of his books?" asked the academic critics bitterly. "Will he never stop sneering at Americans who were active in their enmity to Germany and Austria? How can he expect to get good reviews if he continues to insult his reviewers?" Sherman surpassed all his previous performances, declaring that it was the flappers and second-generation Americans who constituted the bulk of Mencken's audience. Two months later, with the approval of many of these same critics, the New York Vice Society declared Cabell's *Jurgen* to be obscene and indecent; and as the book disappeared from the nation's book counters, Mencken in his turn began to sulk. What kind of debate was this, he asked, with the censors and the police always intervening against him? How long would the Puritan tyranny endure? How long would this benighted America remain hostile to its masterpieces? When he tried to "stir up the animals," both publicly and privately, he could get nowhere. For every man willing to do something for Cabell, he found fifty glad to see Cabell in difficulty. In February he informed the poet Louis Untermeyer that he was secretly "revolving a scheme for a small but effective organization of American authors, a defensive and offensive alliance." It would include, besides the two correspondents, Dreiser, Cabell, Hergesheimer, Nathan, and Abraham Cahan. Francis Hackett of the *New Republic* was also proposed—"if an Irishman can be trusted"; and Aldous Huxley, who, Mencken noted, was the grandson of his boyhood idol, Thomas Henry Huxley.

[ 3 ]

Nothing ever came of it. The postwar shake-up on the principal New York newspapers and magazines was still in progress with a new generation of critics quietly infiltrating into their book departments: Edmund Wilson on the *New Republic,* Carl Van Doren on the *Nation,* Ernest Boyd (Mencken's prewar intimate, now safely returned from his European wanderings) on the New York *Evening Post,* Burton Rascoe on the *Herald* "Books." None of them had yet made much of a splash in the literary world, but they all subscribed more or less to Mencken's anti-Puritan doctrines, and some of them had adopted his style as well. Of the latter group, the 35-year-old Van Doren remarked: "In his [Mencken's] hands, the style is supreme, but in the hands of his copyists it becomes mere flubdubbery. Some of it is atrocious." Ben Hecht, then editor of the Chicago *Literary Times,* carried this imitation to such an extreme that he was hard pressed at times to prove his own identity. Nevertheless these "Young Intellectuals," as they were loosely called, constituted powerful shock troops. And though Mencken had discounted them in his earlier appeals, they were soon taking the offensive into their own hands.

Like Mencken, they hailed *Jurgen* as a masterpiece and its author as a genius: for what other American had ever, or could ever, reach such heights of sophistication as Cabell in his imaginative kingdom of Poictesme? Soon afterwards they threw up at the reading public two more masterpieces out of the Mencken critique: Sinclair Lewis's

*Main Street,* which revealed how the intellect was tortured in a small Minnesota town, and F. Scott Fitzgerald's *This Side of Paradise,* a novel based upon the author's intellectual confusion and liberated sex adventures. Under this barrage, shockingly written and shockingly championed, the Puritan influence in American letters gave way like a gutted fort, revealing that at the very moment when it appeared strongest, it was in fact weakest. Despite the censorship, *Jurgen* was bought on the black market and Cabell was suddenly elevated from one of the most obscure American authors to one of the most famous. Despite all the usual objections *Main Street* and *This Side of Paradise* were the first novels, at least since the turn of the century, that were at once first-rate works of art and best sellers. At the same time, a play out of the Nathan critique, Eugene O'Neill's *Beyond the Horizon,* was shown successfully on Broadway. It was an easy and an intoxicating victory. This, declared the "Young Intellectuals," was the Renaissance—the dawn of a new and more civilized era; and they celebrated it with an orgy so intemperate, so ill-considered, so preposterous, that most of its survivors are embarrassed to recall it.

It was no doubt an important occasion: if not the Renaissance, then at least a turning point in the life of the nation—the final, long-delayed liberation of the American artist. Since the time of Emerson our best writers had been deploring the catchpenny materialism of the American public, and since the 1890's, as we have seen, this revolt had been extended to the whole Puritan code. By the turn of the century, observers had foreseen that this Puritanism was doomed, that in our development from a spinning-wheel frontier community into a metropolitan world power, we had outgrown it. Even so, there was no reason why the final liberation could not have been celebrated more decorously and more constructively. If Henry Adams had lived long enough; if the learned Van Wyck Brooks or the philosophical George Santayana had been more assertive; or even if Eugene Debs, the Socialist leader, had been a man of greater resource, perhaps it would have been. But Mencken had not given them a chance. And because his followers were, at bottom, not born cynics like himself, but frustrated idealists, they covered their confusion by settling old scores even more recklessly than he did.

They shouted down "Dean" Howells as a "stuffed shirt" and "Bishop" More as "a pompous ass." Saving only Poe, Mark Twain, and Whitman, they toppled all the saints of the American literary tradition. Then successively they desecrated the shrines of great men across the length and breadth of history. One of them ranked Nietzsche above Plato and Aristotle; another held Picasso above Raphael; still another elevated Charlie Chaplin into the immortal company of Shakespeare and Leonardo da Vinci. As to themselves, the "Young Intellectuals" were confident that they could hold their own against any age and any race. Was not Cabell the equal of Anatole France, Dreiser the equal of Zola, Lewis the equal of Meredith, Fielding, or any of the English satirists? And when the English critics who at first had been sympathetic to the movement reverted to their "fatuous" theory that a third-rate English work of art was better than a first-rate American work of art, they broke the last cultural ties with the mother country.

Meanwhile, on the domestic front, the Puritan critics

were broken and demoralized. It is no use talking of "beauty on the landscape, heroism in the people, or the promise of a greater American life," wrote William Allen White in the first year of the regime of "Nietzsche and Mencken and God." "We only show our green eyes when we lift them in supplication to a providence that has been junked by our youngers and betters. 'We who are about to die salute you.' " Thereafter, they were but rarely heard from. In 1922, Fred Lewis Pattee of Pennsylvania State College took vengeance on the modernist leader by depicting him in a textbook as the "Mussolini of American Letters"; in 1923, Henry van Dyke of Princeton assured an International Conference of British and American Professors of English that the language of the United States was English and not American. "The natural style of the persons who gravely make the proposal [for an American language] gives rise to frightful dreams of the kind of new language they probably would make if they were let loose on the job." But in 1924 Stuart Sherman, the most eloquent of them all, not only abandoned the fight but tacitly, at least, joined the opposite side. Leaving the University of Illinois campus for the editorship of the New York *Herald Tribune* "Books," he found traces of "immortal yearnings" in Mencken's soul, mixed in with the "two-fisted grobianism," and rightly proclaimed *An American Tragedy* a masterpiece when Mencken wrongly denounced it as a failure.

Yet even in defeat the Puritan professors found no peace. For the Mencken terror was now raging behind them as well as in front of them. It was, of course, not the first time that the students had become disaffected: in recent years they had rallied in great number behind the

Socialist spokesman Scott Nearing. But this revolt differed from all previous ones in that it was directed at the academic authorities themselves. At the University of Michigan a boy Mencken in 1921 denounced his professors as "asses," demanded that sex and atheism be incorporated into the curriculum, and urged the coeds to discuss frankly "things that would curdle the blood of a Sunday-school superintendent."

For a time the Michigan authorities ignored him; but when fisticuffs broke out on the campus, they took preventive measures, denying him the use of campus publications and refusing him a diploma. Yet, like the Renaissance in its larger sphere, the more sternly this revolt was suppressed, the more it flourished. From Michigan it spread to Smith College, Brown University, Johns Hopkins; on all the campuses, the students spent more time with Mencken and Eugene O'Neill than with Carlyle and Shakespeare. In 1923 the *Nation* reported that young Socialists had become virtually extinct on college campuses, that the prophet of the intellectual youth was Mencken, not Marx. Three years later a professor declared that his colleagues had completely lost control over their students: they could no longer train them properly as community leaders, and sooner or later the country would face the consequences.

All the veneration that was withheld from the older gods was now heaped upon Mencken. His authority was acknowledged from the New York *Times* and the *Bookman* on the conservative front to the *Freeman* and the *Dial* at the advanced outposts. He was quoted more widely than any other living critic—more widely even than Matthew Arnold, the ranking voice from the tomb. Novelists licked his boots by mentioning his name in their masterworks. Publishers displayed his "blurbs" on the dust jackets of their current lists. Book dealers rounded up every available copy of his prewar shelf, pushing him marketwise above Dreiser, Theodore Roosevelt, Henry James, and Joseph Hergesheimer, and almost as high as Mark Twain and Herman Melville. And because it was widely but erroneously believed that he was ashamed of it, his book of poems, *Ventures into Verse,* became a collector's item at $300 per copy.

# PART THREE

## *The Dean*

*CHAPTER 10*

# Within the Court

## [ 1 ]

IN HOLLINS STREET, the "Sage of Baltimore," as Mencken was now often called, received the news of his rising fortunes. He read his press clippings and pasted them into large bound volumes, dating each item with his own hand. But he refused to be dazzled by them. Of the excessive praise that was heaped upon him, he told Dreiser, "A man knows deep in his heart that he doesn't deserve it. When he sees all his petty bluffs and affectations accepted seriously, the sole result is to make him lose respect for the victim. . . . I have learned more from attacks than from praise. In even the most vicious of them, there is a touch or two of plausibility." When Knopf sent him his semiannual royalty check in January 1920, he expressed no regret that his income (roughly $6000 a year) was not keeping pace with his notoriety. "In 1919 my books earned more than $1200," he noted. "This fills me with amazement. The most I ever got in any single year before that was $200." Thus, under many distractions, Mencken remained as ever—a curious compound of an outward worldling and an inward ascetic, a rollicking Gargantua and an uncompromising Diogenes.

With no pause for a change in his routine, he continued

to produce articles and books in his third-floor office. It looked now like a literary rolling mill, orderly in its arrangement but swollen with unprocessed materials. He sat at his desk, his back to the window, and an unlit corncob pipe in his mouth. On his left was a pile of books to review, a bound copy of the *Smart Set*, an encyclopedia; on his right, a heap of manuscripts under an old iron hook, a product of his Polytechnic days; in front of him, a cigar box for collecting worn-out pencil stubs and broken rubber bands; at his feet on the Oriental rug, prepared envelopes for his outgoing correspondence. Every available space was utilized. There was but one hint that this room was the headquarters of a literary movement. He had requested and received inscribed portraits of Hergesheimer and Cabell, and these now hung beside a sketch of Carl Sandburg and the eighteenth-century prints of the Menckens of Leipzig.

Towards his well-wishers, Mencken displayed in part the affection of a rebel leader for a new recruit and in part the politeness of a merchant cultivating his market. No fan letter was ever received that was not answered or at least acknowledged by return mail, and in replying to these missives, he cut short his letters to his close friends until the two types became almost indistinguishable. The replies in either case were one-page affairs. They were crisp and compact, with a show of cordiality, yet with an evasion of intimacy. There was a deft dispatching of current business in the first paragraphs; a hope for a meeting or reunion in the next; then an exclamation of cosmic despair over the irritations of the literary business ("I am constantly tempted to buy a dog house and live on $100 a month"), over his forthcoming book

("I am suffering like an elephant dancing the mazurka"), over his hay fever ("I am never able to work during September and October"); finally, a characteristic flourish ("Yours in Christ," "All is lost, including honor," "God save all honest men, if any").

In January 1919 it occurred to him—apparently for the first time—that his new admirers were taking advantage of him, particularly in the matter of autographs. "According to an article by Guido Bruno in Pearson's," he told Dreiser, "there are grafters who make a business of them to sell. On the other hand, it seems ungracious to refuse a man who may be a very sincere and useful reader. Today I had a letter announcing a shipment of all my books, whatever that may mean. It will take 15 or 20 minutes to unpack them, inscribe them and repack them. And it will take almost as long if I merely tie up the package unopened, readdress it to the sender and take it to the parcel post office. Probably the best solution would be to demand a contribution to some charity. But I don't know any charity worth contributing to."

Soon, however, he was confronted with another problem, even more exasperating. Daily from 9 A.M. to 10 P.M., he received twenty or thirty telephone calls—calls from ladies announcing a charity drive, from insurance salesmen, from amateur poets demanding a hearing for their poems, from authors requesting publicity, and from tourists inquiring how most profitably to spend two days in Baltimore. Worst of all were long-distance calls. The only phone in the house was located on the first floor, and with each interruption the Sage had to go down two flights of stairs from his third-floor office. While he waited impatiently for the operator to check all the connections on the intermediary switchboards between Baltimore and New York, he reflected bitterly that no business had ever been transacted in this fashion that could not have been equally well transacted in a letter delivered by oxcart. At such times, he cursed his notoriety—or at least cursed the invention that had proved such "a boon to bores."

Once in the midst of an exacting labor, he left the receiver off the hook, but he was conscience-stricken when the telephone company wasted the time and energy of one of its trouble shooters to discover why outsiders couldn't reach him. Yet he rejected the simplest of all solutions to the problem, the withdrawal of his name and number from the phone book. Though he might be driven out of his mind, he would not cut himself off from the few strangers who really had something to say to him.

[ 2 ]

Meanwhile his mother and sister looked after him, saw that his clothes were in order, his office clean, his books arranged, and that he looked presentable when he went out. It was a standing joke of the household that he was "an extremely careless and hoggish fellow"; but in fact he was very neat, and as dutiful as could be expected in the discharge of his household duties. He not only kept the house in good repair but continually made improvements, replacing the coal furnace with an automatic gas heater and installing a handsome colonial doorway outside the vestibule. By constant care, including several extractions of teeth, he had kept the family dog, Tessie, alive well beyond her allotted years. And whenever his niece, his brother Charlie's girl, was brought down from Pittsburgh, he spent the afternoons with her, rolling the dice, exhibiting picture books, and deploying a menagerie of rubber elephants. Once, reflecting upon his success with the little girl, he remarked, "What a father was spoiled when I dedicated my life to learning."

The faded silver-coated plaque on the door, announcing this house as the residence of August Mencken, the Sage's deceased father, also announced by implication that this was the family reservation, separate and inviolable. The Sage never asked his mother to provide shelter for itinerant literary men; he reserved rooms for them at the Stafford Hotel and entertained them usually at the Saturday Night Club. With the advent of Prohibition, when the club itself was driven out of the restaurants into the members' homes, Mencken entertained the members in his turn, yet with the utmost consideration for the ladies of the house. At these times his sister withdrew at 8 P.M., and after listening to the music for a while, his mother also. But no matter how long the meeting, the Sage always cleaned up afterwards. He swept the ashes off the carpets, adjusted the furniture, washed and dried all the crockery. It was 2:30 sometimes before he went to bed.

On the other hand, Mencken had now come to look upon the Saturday Night Club itself as a kind of extension to his family circle and had gone to great lengths to ensure its survival through the hazards of this period. During the war, he had maintained the morale of its members by sending them birthday presents, visiting them when they were laid up in the hospital, attending their funerals and charming the federal agents who had come looking for "enemy aliens" among them. After the war, and on the eve of Prohibition, he had gone one step further, selling his automobile (which had become a nuisance to him anyway) and investing the proceeds in a large stock of gin, vermouth, bottled beer—fifty dozen bottles in all—for their benefit. This he had stored in a cellar vault made of wooden frames and reinforced with concrete. The vault was designed to withstand floods, earthquakes, air raids, and to frighten off even the most determined poachers. Its door was padlocked and upon it was posted a warning notice, decorated with skull and crossbones, saying that after false entry chlorine would be released under 250 pounds pressure. It was so formidable a bulwark that the Sage himself would shudder when he looked at it.

As the year rolled by, however, he found that his stock was dwindling faster than expected (under heavy inroads by such guests as Sinclair Lewis). Indeed, at the prevailing rate of consumption, the club would soon run aground in a desert, as yet unrelieved by bootleggers. In desperation, he began to experiment with some hops sent to him by a Michigan dealer. The members took heart again, knowing that the Sage, among his earliest enterprises, had acquired a considerable knowledge of chemistry. They would not have been so enthusiastic if they had known, too, that he could no longer follow a chemical formula or even a recipe.

Years later they would recount, perhaps with some exaggeration, how, when they entered his cellar, they found bottles exploding and glass flying through the air, shattering against the concrete abutments. Hemburger, the coolest head of them all, was asked to take charge and to contrive some means of getting at the brew safely.

At his suggestion, a blanket was dropped over the bottles, and young August Mencken gingerly stepped into the mined area. His hands protected by an old pair of automobile gauntlets, he removed two or three whole bottles intact. But when he pulled the corks, the brew proved so gaseous that much of it fizzled off.

Gradually each member of the club acquired a brewing outfit of his own. The obscure process by which Mencken had introduced this art to his fellows gave way to a more simplified one ("as easy as having a tooth pulled," Mencken said), with the malt purchased from commercial distributors. The Sage continually worked to improve the beer, borrowing a microscope at one point so that he could better select his yeast strain; and if the members complained of hang-overs, he prescribed the cure—a variety of Epsom salt that had been recommended to him by a physician. The members, however, could no longer take seriously his scientific pretensions. When he dangerously garbled the proportions of the Epsom salt, James M. Cain, then a Maryland journalist and an honorary member of the club, drew up a document denouncing him as a quack. It was signed by all the members and sealed by a notary public, and for a time it hung on the walls of the Knopf offices.

Thus Prohibition, far from wrecking the club, added new piquancy to its social activities. It was in this era that the members worked their greatest prodigy—the rendition of seven of the nine Beethoven symphonies in one sitting, from 4 P.M. to 5 A.M. Again, it was in this era that they admitted Dr. Raymond Pearl, Professor of Biometrics at the Johns Hopkins School of Hygiene, who was to become Mencken's closest confidant on his home ground.

[ 3 ]

When Mencken boarded the train every third Monday morning and settled down in his Pullman chair with an armload of manuscripts, he looked forward without enthusiasm to his round of duties in New York. Behind him was his delightful provincial seat where he enjoyed a mode of life fashioned after his heart; ahead of him was "Totentanz," "a place fit only for the gross business of making money." Actually it was not his work that depressed him, but the city's fast-moving, self-conscious, glittering multicolored atmosphere. And it was his policy to endure it by revolving in a narrow, circumscribed orbit, subject to few modifications. With so many of New York's culture-conscious hosts and hostesses anxious to have him at their parties, his personality was felt and discussed everywhere, but his actual person was almost never seen.

He invariably put up at the Algonquin Hotel on Forty-fourth Street, opposite the Royalton Hotel, where George Jean Nathan was in permanent residence. He had settled upon this hostelry back in 1914. It was then handy to the *Smart Set* office, and its clientele had attracted him—a curious and unclassifiable mixture of actresses, Hindu princes, Arctic explorers, and Salvation Army captains. More recently, however, it had become the headquarters of the Round Table—a group of witty dramatists and drama critics, including George S. Kaufman, Robert Sherwood, Franklin P. Adams, Marc Connelly, Harold Ross, Robert Benchley, Heywood Broun, and Alexander Woollcott. And though Mencken was often mentioned as a member, the truth was that he regarded all literary societies except his own as composed of "childish gossips and idiots." Woollcott, particularly, impressed him as a bad critic and a rude exhibitionist. Many times, when he saw Woollcott, extravagantly dressed, at the Round Table, he was tempted to tell him what he thought of him, but out of loyalty to Alec's brother Willie, a Baltimore friend, he generally restrained himself. Once, however, he blurted: "How can you parade yourself around like this, when your poor brother Willie can't afford to buy a clean shirt?"

At his office he received hundreds of invitations for personal appearances—from friends and foes alike, from college fraternities and women's clubs, from American Legion conventions and Rotary Clubs. To all of them he replied in the same vein: that he had "sworn a dreadful oath upon the Evangels of Almighty God to refrain absolutely from public speaking." When the Authors' League announced in April 1925 that their fund-raising extravaganza at the Hotel Roosevelt would be attended by "every famous author and artist in the country, together with theatrical stars," a reporter asked the Sage whether he too would be on hand. "No," replied Mencken, "not unless carried there by the police, and not unless I am hit over the head with an axe and dragged in unconscious." A lecture agent, during the period, offered Mencken and Nathan $30,000 to make a six weeks tour of the American lecture platforms. Mencken countered with a qualified acceptance. They would make the tour on condition that they be allowed to refuse invitations to dinner from the literary women of each community, and that after their performances they be permitted to drink beer with companions of their choice. Fortunately, the agent interpreted this as refusal, for later Mencken confided to Nathan, "We might get to like it and then we would be ruined."

The one regular appearance which Mencken made during these years was conducted very much according to this specification. It was his annual lecture at Goucher College in Baltimore, delivered in a private home and without publicity before a selected group of English students—a lecture that was no lecture at all, but a series of answers to questions from the floor, terminating with a few remarks on how to win a husband. In this setting, Mencken was to meet his future wife.

Nathan managed to get Mencken listed as a member of the fashionable Fifty-eighth Street Club and of the even more fashionable France-Angleterre Club. But the Sage made a point of steering clear of them, as he did of musical concerts, plays, and most other social functions. On one occasion Nathan and John Williams, a theatrical producer, induced him to attend the worst play of the season by telling him beforehand that it was a remarkable translation from the Italian, indeed the best thing since Ibsen. They saw to it that he came out in full dress; they sat him conspicuously in a box and kept him there throughout two acts by telling him that the author would come to greet him in person after the show. He suffered through it all, decrying the "pish-posh," wondering whether his friends had become imbeciles or whether he had lost his critical wits. But in the end the hoax backfired and thereafter Nathan found it harder than ever to get him out of his shell.

The truth was that though Mencken was by rights the

center of any social gathering, he was awkward and ill at ease whenever he entered a room full of strangers. His technique was to drop anchor in one spot beside a congenial friend (most often, of late, Philip Goodman, his onetime publisher and now a successful theatrical producer), and then by the vigor of his monologue to draw in, one by one, the passing ships into his anchorage. If none came, he might very well drop off to sleep.

Women were also something of a problem to him at this period, so many being now available, he complained, that he was hard put to choose among them. "I get little enjoyment out of women, more out of alcohol, most out of ideas," he said. In his more serious affairs he had switched every couple of years—from a Socialist to a Christian Scientist and now to a society girl. With none of them obviously did he find any abiding companionship. Moreover, he was far more vocal about his sexual defeats than about his conquests. When he returned from his tour of the political conventions in 1920, he revealed: "I consorted with a virgin and she is a virgin still. But that is simply because I was very tired and she was very amiable." Mencken made much of the charm of this girl. In April 1921, John Macy, the critic, spread the report that Mencken was either on the threshold of a marriage or had been secretly married for several years, thus further complicating the Sage's life. "It has played hell with my chances with a certain fair creature," he told Hergesheimer. "She won't listen to my denials. After all, it is hard to prove that one is not married. I'll have to hand her lawyer transcripts from every parish register in the United States since the year 1886, when I attained to puberty."

[ 4 ]

In 1914 Hergesheimer had written to him taking issue with his criticism of *The Lay Anthony;* more recently he had found Mencken to be "vastly encouraging, illuminating and stirring." Sinclair Lewis introduced himself on the eve of *Main Street* by declaiming in his circus barker style the principal speeches of his characters; but until Mencken had read the book for himself, he was convinced that "of all the idiots I've ever laid eyes on, that fellow is the worst." Soon Sherwood Anderson, F. Scott Fitzgerald, Carl Van Vechten, Edgar Lee Masters, and many others were circulating in his vicinity, and the more intimate they became with the Sage, the more vocal they were in admiration of him. Fitzgerald told him, "I'd rather have you like a book of mine than anyone else in America." Lewis went Fitzgerald one better, telling him, of the forthcoming *Babbitt*, "If you don't like the book, nobody in the entire Vereinigen will."

As luck would have it, the older Mencken-Nathan circle had by now almost evaporated. So there was plenty of room for the newcomers. Characteristically, he welcomed them with bulletins of the Michigan Authors' Society, advertisements of Kosher Chinese restaurants, announcements of the Second Coming of Christ with a note attached, "This is urgent. Pass it on to Percy Hammond," or a Gideon Bible inscribed "With the compliments of the author." In 1922 it was reported that Mencken had stolen fifty-eight Bibles, twenty-seven from the Hotel Astor alone, for this purpose. Fitzgerald, more

Nathan's discovery than Mencken's, was initiated into the circle with five copies of the *Berliner Tageblatt* sent to his home at Westport, Connecticut, designed to stir his neighbors to the suspicion that "Fitzheimer," as Mencken called him, was harboring a German spy on the premises. Sometimes, too, a new author was nominated to the American Institute of Arts and Letters (Colored) by the hand of the Reverend Hannibal S. Jackson, A.B., A.M., Ph.D., LL.D., D.D., Chancellor and Financial Secretary, on the Institute's especially engraved stationery.

The form of this initiation was, of course, frivolous, but its moral was deadly serious. Mencken could not conceive of a literary society that was not patterned after his former one—a rebel band, united not only against the hostile "democratic mob," but also against the conventional establishment of letters. Admittedly the circumstances of his group had changed. On all sides, doors that had hitherto been closed were being opened to them—the drawing rooms of rich Babbitts, Hollywood and the *Saturday Evening Post* (with their high remuneration), the National Institute of Arts and Letters. But according to Mencken's creed, such distinctions were the result of a "meretricious rage" and no self-respecting artist would be interested in them.

In this, Mencken certainly should have given a special license to his old master, James Gibbons Huneker. Huneker was between sixty and seventy (nobody knew his exact age); he had fought the cause of modernism before Mencken was born and, until recently, had received little recognition for it. Yet, when he mentioned in his autobiography that he had been entertained by Theodore Roosevelt at Oyster Bay and that he had assured the ex-President of his wartime loyalty, Mencken ridiculed the old man unmercifully. In a lengthy *Smart Set* review, he recalled the Huneker of the nineties, the disciple of Chopin, de Goncourt and Huysmans, a man "steeped in all sorts of savory pots," in "endless babble about the seven arts," and committed to an "heroic revolt against the professors and their superstitions." Was Roosevelt so powerful a rabble-rouser, he asked, that he could fetch even Huneker? Or was it the Pilsner shortage? "A Huneker emptied of Pilsner was a Huneker denatured and not himself."

Huneker was pained but, like all the other Mencken admirers in similar situations, he turned the other cheek. "Naturally, I'm sorry you don't see it, but what's a book review between pals? You forget that *Steeplejack* is a book of the past, not dealing with the present. However, no bones are broken. You have been so kind to me for years that I blush to write you the above. . . . I shall have some fun in the *World* next Sunday over your review simply to stop the mouths of condoling friends who seem to think we are at loggerheads. It makes me ill, the smallness of people."

Shortly afterwards, Huneker again offended the Sage, this time by accepting membership in the National Institute of Arts and Letters—and what was worse, accepting it side by side with Stuart Sherman. What possible explanation could there be for this betrayal of the alley cats? And if Huneker could explain it, how could he explain his wearing the Institute button? No reprimand could ruffle Huneker's temper. Mencken was mistaken, he wrote. That button was conferred on him by the Bürgermeister of Vienna on tour in London during the war. "If I ever have the luck to see you in the flesh again, I must show you my Chopin book in the German edition." The next and last meeting was a luncheon at Sherry's. Huneker, a dandy to the end, wore a cutaway morning coat and a pearl-gray Homburg adorned rakishly with a green feather. In their turn, Mencken and Nathan appeared in full regalia, wearing the pendants of the Order of Chastity, Third Class, decorations which had been especially designed to shame Huneker for his apostasy. At the end of lunch they crowned him with "an amorous warming pan" for the care of bladder troubles.

The Sage did not schoolmaster Sinclair Lewis as he did Huneker. The two men did not see each other very often; being monologuists, they found it so difficult to converse that much of their correspondence was conducted through two mutual friends, Philip Goodman and Paul de Kruif. Yet of all the rebel band, Lewis was the most exemplary. In 1926 Lewis rejected the Pulitzer Prize for *Arrowsmith,* and in explanation of this startling act gave reasons with which the Sage could find no fault: "Between the Pulitzer Prizes, the American Academy of Arts and Letters and its training school, the National Institute of Arts and Letters, amateur boards of censorship and inquisitions of earnest literary ladies, every compulsion is put upon writers to become safe, obedient and sterile." Four years later, Lewis would be offered the highest distinction known to the literary profession, the Nobel Prize. Again, the Sage would be prepared to reinforce Lewis in a magnificent act of defiance. But it was too late: by that time the spell of the Mencken circle had been broken beyond recall.

Frequently when Mencken had important business to

discuss with his followers, he would take them over to the Alt Heidelberg in Union Hill, New Jersey. After three years sampling of speakeasies throughout the length and breadth of Greater New York, he had found what he was looking for, this relic of Teutonic *Gemütlichkeit,* serving real beer and adorned with a picture of Heidelberg Castle by moonlight. Here, on one occasion or another, he drank with Dreiser, Anderson, Rascoe, Boyd, Edgar Lee Masters, and Philip Goodman. Looking around the table, Mencken reflected, at times, that though this circle was more dazzling than the one in Baltimore, it was also far less substantial. Few of these "literati" had the deep-rooted solidity which he found essential for enduring friendship. In 1924 he wrote: "Of the men I knew best when I first began going to New York, twenty-five years ago, not one is a friend today. Of those I knew best ten years ago, not six are friends. The rest have got lost in the riot, and the friends of today, I sometimes fear, will get lost in the same way."

*C H A P T E R  1 1*

# Launching the *Mercury*

## [ 1 ]

A YEAR EARLY, in April 1923, the Seven Arts Club of Chicago opened the 1924 Presidential season by choosing Mencken as its nominee. The occasion was celebrated, according to the Chicago *Literary Times,* by a half-hour demonstration during which $20,000 was pledged for Mencken's campaign. A month later, many "Young Intellectuals" in New York joined the band wagon; house parties were converted into political conventions, and critics vied with one another for the Cabinet posts. In June, Mencken formally accepted the nomination. He declared that, if elected, he and Nathan—his running mate —would liquidate all homely woman politicians and all members in good standing of the New York stock exchange; bring the Kaiser to America and make him Governor General of West Virginia; give the Liberty Bell to the Turks; make a replica of the *Mayflower* at the Norfolk Navy Yard, load it with all the living descendants of the Pilgrim Fathers, and employ it, until sunk, as a target for battle practice of the North Atlantic Fleet.

From start to finish, the Mencken candidacy was a jest. But at the same time his followers could see no flaws in its logic. Mencken had liberated American letters, as

Nathan had liberated American drama, they asserted. Why then couldn't these two buccaneers do something equally remarkable for American politics? And ever since the Armistice, Mencken (this time without any encouragement from Nathan) had asked himself the same question.

For one thing, his career as a literary critic had been a "biographical accident": he had not asked for the job on the *Smart Set*—it had been thrust upon him. He had always looked upon himself (potentially, at least) as a great political force. True, he had nothing to offer his countrymen except the destruction of their religious and patriotic delusions, including their belief in democracy. Nor could he see very clearly what would emerge from his campaign: his only issues were the dignity and freedom of "first-rate" men like himself. Yet in the prevailing atmosphere all the more constructive writers, like Walter Lippmann and Herbert Croly, were confused or disillusioned, while never before had the opportunity for a destructive critic seemed so bright.

On April 28, 1919, less than six months after the Armistice, a bomb had mysteriously appeared in the mail of the Mayor of Seattle. The next day another bomb had turned up at the home of the Senator from Georgia, and soon thirty-six of them had been intercepted en route to such public figures as Attorney General Palmer, Postmaster General Burleson, and Justice Holmes of the Supreme Court. Some bystanders were injured by the explosions, but none of the addressees. There was no evidence that this was an organized conspiracy by the Bolsheviks. In the imagination of most Americans, however, a million heavily-armed and bewhiskered Bolsheviks were now about to storm the Capitol (though they had as yet hardly established themselves in Russia); and in the pursuit of these phantasies, many cherished American liberties disappeared. On May 1 a mob of soldiers and sailors entered the offices of the Socialist newspaper, the New York *Call*, wrecked the furniture, and severely beat the members of the staff. On New Year's Day, 1920, the Attorney General rounded up six thousand alleged Bolsheviks in their headquarters and held them, citizens together with aliens, incommunicado pending their deportation to Russia. The next year, with the bomb blasts still ringing in their ears, the Massachusetts authorities convicted two Italians, Sacco and Vanzetti, of perpetrating a payroll murder, with no conclusive evidence against them except that they were foreign-born anarchists.

If Mencken had any doubts about launching his political campaign before the red hysteria, he had none afterwards. In his own words, he felt "an irresistible impulse to rush out and crack a head—in other words, to do something for common decency." But outside of the *Smart Set* (which was properly a literary magazine, not a political one) no organ of the press could then contain him. On his right, the editors of the Tory press were magnifying the "red menace" beyond all reasonable proportions. On his left, the editors of the radical weeklies were struggling against great odds to defend the rights of Max Eastman, Eugene Debs, Sacco and Vanzetti, and their other martyrs. Between the two camps, he believed that the radical editors, in point of "intellectual honesty and courage," were far superior to their rivals: they constituted not only the "most intelligent sector of the press" but also "the only one that was telling the truth." In the uncertainties of the moment, he wrote for the *New Republic,* and later accepted an honorary position as contributing editor of the *Nation.* Yet, as a skeptic, he could not tolerate their "delusion" that they knew the cures of the nation's ills. Hence he was not comfortable as their ally.

In the fall of 1919, Mencken received an invitation to return to the Baltimore *Sunpapers.* He was, of course, delighted, but he made a show of resistance appropriate to his new position in the world of letters. "I doubt that they could either stand the doctrine or pay the price," he told his friends. "I shall not make any arrangement that does not include absolute freedom on all subjects and very good pay." For their part, the management knew precisely what they were up against. Harry Black, now the principal director, had given the Sage his first freedom as the "Freelance" columnist, and Paul Patterson, the new president, had worked with him closely for almost ten years. They assured him that he would suffer no repetition of past indignities—and that, in collaboration with him as a consultant and staff writer, they would inaugurate a new era in *Sunpaper* history. No further argument was necessary. Without cavil, Mencken accepted the $50 a week that Patterson offered him, and in the same spirit later accepted a raise to $100.

When Mencken joined Black and Patterson at the Black estate, he threw himself into the deliberations as though the *Sun*'s welfare had always been his greatest love and nothing had ever blighted it. He held up before his collaborators a conception of newspaper greatness that they had never dreamed of. No reporters anywhere were too good for appointment to the new *Sunpapers;* nor was any new departure beyond its range. He proposed that the

*Sun* publish a national weekly on the order of the *Manchester Guardian* and thus enter into competition with the *Nation* and the *New Republic.* Sometimes, perhaps (as in this last case), his proposals proved impractical, but they were always stimulating and always boldly argued. In the midst of a discussion about a change in typography, he swore, "Black, that's the god-damnedest stupidest idea ever heard of," and by way of solution proposed, "God, let's roll the dice, and whatever the outcome, go to it." He made Patterson pace the floor so much that soon one of Mrs. Black's prize Oriental rugs was worn through. Under similar circumstances in February 1922, he conceived fifty new terms, all based on the root "boob," two of which, "booboisie" and "Homo boobiens," became fixed in his vocabulary.

Meanwhile, down in the *Sun* office, John Haslip Adams, the editor in chief, waited anxiously for the results of the conference. An ardent Wilsonian, he had for almost a decade kept the Mencken opposition within reasonable bounds and, despite the change in bargaining positions, was determined to keep it that way. Naturally, he disapproved Mencken's current small talk: that "Wilson's ideals for two years the marvels of Christendom are now seen to have been mere buncombe," and that under Wilson "Americans at home are being reduced to the state of Irishmen in Ireland." And when Mencken incorporated such remarks in his articles, Adams applied his blue pencil to them. Theoretically, he believed in the maximum freedom of speech; but in practice he could not understand how such things would appeal to the public. For Mencken was an outspoken antidemocrat; and so far as he could see, "only an insignificant fraction of the public is hostile to the democratic theory."

On the whole, Mencken accepted this opposition with good grace. He was so delighted to be back on his old stamping grounds that, for the moment, he affected not to notice it. In April 1920, Adams suppressed three of his articles in a row. Mencken sold one to the *Freeman* magazine, edited by his fellow cynic, Albert Jay Nock, and made "quiet inquiries" about the others.

In June he joined Adams, Patterson, and virtually the whole top echelon of the *Sunpaper* staff at the Republican National Convention in Chicago. Here he enjoyed himself immensely covering the nomination of Warren G. Harding, and when Patterson, Adams, and the other editors returned to Baltimore, he enjoyed himself even more. Proceeding on to San Francisco, he put in a couple of hours each day watching the Democrats, in effect, repudiate Woodrow Wilson, the nominal leader; and at night and during the early mornings, he caroused with the poet George Sterling, the two of them alternating as dinner hosts, drinking "grappo" and going the rounds of the Bohemian quarter.

At this point, nothing could have been further from his mind than his feud with Adams. Back in Baltimore, however, Adams could not forget it. This time, oddly enough, it was not Mencken's current activities that galled him, but an article that he had himself passed and printed about a month before. Discussing President Wilson's explanation of why we had refused to take Armenia as our share of the peace settlement, Mencken had declared: "His own accounts of such transactions are never to be taken seriously. . . . His statements, transcending mere mendacity, take on a sort of fourth dimensional preposterousness." If Adams had found Mencken's other remarks objectionable on political grounds, this one he found objectionable on moral grounds as well; for clearly no responsible journalist would call the President a liar. For weeks he had brooded upon it, and some of his associates, including John W. Owens, did likewise. Finally they took their case to Patterson. "You cannot stop this man and you cannot reason with him," Adams declared. "If you don't fire him at once, you can have my resignation and the others will resign with me."

Patterson listened to the argument of his editors; he may even have agreed with them that Mencken's language was intemperate. But he stood his ground. "I have given my word to Mencken," he told the rebels, "that he is perfectly free to write what he wants. I will not break my word now. I think you are getting yourselves stirred up over a small matter, and if you make a decision in this mood, you will regret it. Think it over a few days before you commit yourselves."

Mencken did not hear about the *Putsch* until his return to Baltimore, by which time it had completely subsided. Nor was he very much distressed by it. "Suppose," he reflected, "Patterson decides there isn't room enough for me and the editors on the same paper. If I go, I can always get a better job across the street. If they go, they'll only do worse." At any rate, when he bounded into the office, he shook hands with Adams and the others and told them that the slogan for the Democrats should be: "All is lost, including honor." He felt sorry for them for being stuck with such unlikely candidates, he said; for his part, he would work for a third-party coalition of all disaffected groups—the Germans, the Irish, the I.W.W. Syndicalists; a coalition, incidentally, that was achieved four years later around the candidacy of Senator Robert La Follette.

Thus beaten, Adams was forced to face the consequences. By the terms of the reorganization, he was allowed to continue as editor in chief of the morning paper, but the evening paper was taken from him and operated under a more or less independent command. Mencken took a hand in naming the new editors—first, in late 1920, Stanley M. Reynolds, then, in 1922, Hamilton Owens (no relation to John Owens), both men of puckish disposition and both highly sympathetic with his general outlook. The result was almost immediately apparent: the *Evening Sun* followed the Sage in his pioneering (and at the moment almost hopeless) battle for repeal of Prohibition; and as time went on, it supported most of his other causes as well. It "howled" against all oppressive institutions, including government bureaucracy, the Ku Klux Klan, and the Methodist Church in so far as the latter was the "secular arm" of the Klan. It changed its label from "liberal" to "libertarian"; it renounced Woodrow Wilson and professed admiration for George Washington, Thomas Jefferson, Grover Cleveland, and Prince von Bismarck—all out of Mencken's Valhalla of "honorable men."

If Adams had really believed that Mencken's doctrines were unsalable, he was now shown to be a bad prophet. Governor Albert C. Ritchie, a Democrat of aristocratic background, not only paid lip service to them (as incorporated in the *Evening Sun* platform), but also made them into the guideposts of his long administration. He did everything he could to prevent local enforcement of Prohibition, and refused point-blank to co-operate with the Harding Administration in crushing a coal strike. The same rebellious spirit also infected the electorate. As early as 1922, the "Maryland Free State" (as Hamilton Owens had rechristened it) was notorious as the sauciest, hardest-drinking, most irreverent state in the Union—and also one of the first to shake off the postwar hysteria.

[ 2 ]

Mencken's *Evening Sun* articles were often expanded and reprinted—first in the *Smart Set,* then in his successive "Prejudices" books; often too, they were quoted in the radical, freethinking press. But at best, this was a makeshift system, incommensurate with the scale of his potential audience. So far as he could see, there were thousands —perhaps tens of thousands—of Americans who supported his new campaign, and they comprised not only the "Young Intellectuals" but also the "leading men of science and learning and the more imaginative business men"—in fact, the whole "civilized minority" of "normal, educated, well-disposed, unfrenzied, enlightened citizens." Years before, he had dreamed of serving this group in a great national magazine. The project had lapsed. Yet its logic was now so compelling that when his publisher, Alfred Knopf, confided his own ambition along this line, it suddenly came alive again. In a three-way conversation among Mencken, Nathan and Knopf, in the fall of 1922, it was given a thorough airing.

Of the three, Nathan's was the only voice of moderation. In the past the *Smart Set* had admirably served his purposes both critical and editorial; it still did so; and though he did not object to Knopf's taking over its management, he urged that its essential features, if not its name, be preserved. Mencken, on the other hand, insisted that the *Smart Set* be abandoned outright. Since the war, he had tried in various ways to accommodate it to his new interests, and Nathan had done "what I felt I reasonably could to keep him happy." The magazine's formula was altered in the direction of less fiction and more nonfiction. The masked devil was removed from the cover and a device of artistic abstractions substituted. Instead of reviewing all the new novels, Mencken had turned his book department into a sounding board for his political views. But now many readers found the *Smart Set* more incongruous than ever—a hodgepodge of current events, belles-lettres, and literary vaudeville. Nor was it at this date any more solvent than in 1914, having survived by pump-priming operations such as the postwar launching of the *Black Mask*.

As a result of the conference, Nathan was outvoted 2 to 1, and, for the first time, the Mencken-Nathan partnership was in jeopardy. The editorship of the new review had been offered to Mencken alone; he was strongly tempted to take it. At the same time, he could not forget that under similar circumstances about nine years before, when the decision had been Nathan's, Nathan had stuck by their partnership. Nor could Mencken conceive of editing any magazine without the other's participation. After a debate that extended throughout the fall and winter of 1922–1923, Nathan resigned himself to Mencken's ambition. As an experienced editor, he still did not believe in what he called the "Messianic" aspects of the new review. As a friend, he "amiably agreed to string along."

In the summer of 1923 the *Smart Set* was on the block, but without its editors nobody would buy it. Months passed while William Randolph Hearst, like a great buzzard, wheeled uncertainly back and forth over the cadaver. Mencken was so doubtful of the outcome that he surrendered his holdings to Nathan. And when Hearst finally settled down, as Nathan knew he would, Nathan surprised Mencken by returning them *in toto.* The sale price was $60,000. Of this, Mencken and Nathan each received a fourth part and also $40 a share for their bonds, which they had originally purchased at $15 a share. Thus, what might have been a sentimental leave-taking was converted into a highly profitable bit of jobbery. And Mencken hardly paused long enough to explain its historic significance. For fifteen years, he wrote in his farewell editorial, the two editors had fought to break down the barriers that stood in the way of "imaginative authors." Having accomplished this, he said, they were eager to spread themselves beyond belles-lettres into the "whole field of American life."

By this time Samuel Knopf, the publisher's father, and himself a highly successful businessman, had been appointed business manager of the new review; and in the ensuing conferences at the Knopf office its vague outlines were taking shape. Its name was picked from a pretentious list. *The Blue Review* (which had been the name of Wright's abortive weekly) was dismissed as too arty;

*The 20th Century, The Capitol, The Sovereign, The Regent, The Chancellor, The Athenaeum,* were all discarded before Nathan hit upon *The American Mercury.* Mencken objected that the London *Mercury,* with which the new organ might be compared, had set a precedent of stuffiness. But he was convinced by the others that "*Mercury*" was in fact the perfect name, dignified like "*Harper's*" and "*Atlantic Monthly,*" yet non-committal. The same considerations were uppermost in the selection of the cover. It was bright green, with a border of whorls and a handsome monogram in Garamond type designed at great expense by Elmer Adler, the typographer.

In the framing of the editorial policy, Mencken boldly took the initiative. He wanted to print the facts about American life and recent American history that no newspaper and no other magazine would print; he wanted to conduct, according to his lights, a realistic investigation of the "whole gaudy, gorgeous American scene." In this endeavor and with Nathan's help, he would mobilize "all the best people." For literary glamor and authority, he counted upon such personages as Lewis, Fitzgerald, Cabell, Anderson, and all the others of the Mencken-Nathan circle. For factual exposés, he had at his command the editorial staff of the Baltimore *Sunpapers* and a host of allies on the other newspapers. But for the more thoroughgoing analysis that was now his chief concern, he was forced for the first time into the academic groves. And he exercised all his diplomacy to surround himself with an advisory faculty of first-rate pedagogues: in law, Zechariah Chafee of Harvard; in biology, Raymond Pearl of Johns Hopkins; in psychology, John B. Watson (the father of behaviorism); in anthropology, Robert Lowie of California; in architecture, Grant La Farge; in medicine, Morris Fishbein; in philology, Louise Pound of Nebraska and George Krapp of Columbia.

Knopf fixed the editors' salaries at $5000 a year, which was to be paid during the first year by shares of stock in the American Mercury, Incorporated. Also, he provided them with space in his suite in the Heckscher building—a bare businesslike inner sanctum and a decorous reception room with an Oriental rug, heavy hangings, and shaded lights. Though Mencken derisively referred to this room as "the Undertaker's Parlor," both he and Nathan understood that in such decorous surroundings their buffooneries would no longer be tolerated, that henceforth they must conduct themselves, privately and publicly, as responsible editors. Accordingly, they dropped the curtain on the Mencken-Nathan literary vaudeville, and also on Major Owen J. Hatteras, D.S.O., the *Smart Set* straw man. Their "Répétition Générale" department with its cursory observations on life was transformed into the more formal "Clinical Notes." The elements of the *Smart Set* formula that survived were the "Americana" collection of national absurdities, Nathan's theater department, and Mencken's book department, now known simply as "The Library."

In September 1923, when Dreiser was told about the new magazine, he objected at once that it would be much too tame and respectable. The Sage advised him not to be deceived by appearances. "What will go on inside the tent is another story," he wrote. "You will recall that the late P. T. Barnum got away with burlesque shows by calling them moral lectures."

[ 3 ]

In the inaugural issue the editors made it clear that they were not now, and in fact never had been, members of the literary "advanced guard" which included the Gertrude Stein expatriates and the "Greenwich Village obscurantists." And as if to emphasize the differences between the two groups, Ernest Boyd in the same issue painted a devastating composite portrait of them. The "Aesthete: Model 1924," he said, was the product of a half-baked Harvard education, was the master neither of grammatical French nor of intelligible English, and was susceptible to any literary fad so long as it emanated from Paris.

On Friday, December 28, 1923, two hours after the trucks had delivered this dynamite at the newsstands, almost every struggling poet or art theorist in Greenwich Village had read or heard of the article. Individualists though they were, they were united as one man in the face of a common assailant. Within a few hours many of them had crossed their northern frontier, gathering ammunition en route, and deployed along East Nineteenth Street outside Boyd's flat. There, according to Rascoe's report, for three days they pinned down the red-bearded critic under a full-scale siege. They hurled their insults at him by telephone calls, telegrams, and ingenious use of a radio loud-speaker. They jammed his doorbell and dropped stink bombs through his kitchen window. When he tried to make his escape, they fired at him with ripe fruit and vegetables. Rascoe also reported that during the first ten hours of the siege, the *American Mercury* had sold out on every stand in the Village, and that soon afterwards it was virtually unobtainable anywhere in New York.

Mencken could laugh at this explosion among the "advanced guard," but he could not laugh at the disaffection that prevailed within his own circle, now sometimes referred to as the "middle generation of letters." For, contrary to the general opinion, the *Mercury* was not even literary enough to please them. Cabell would not discuss Calvin Coolidge in the new magazine because, he said, he knew and cared nothing about any Coolidges. Fitzgerald had nothing to contribute except the suggestion that the Sage collect all the *Mercury's* political articles and print them in book form under the title, "Can It Be As Bad As All This?" Lewis, in London, was fertile with proposed contributions, among them a critical essay that would condemn all literary schools as damned nonsense and end all literary strife forever; but he was slow to oblige. Aldous Huxley, one of the few foreigners on the first list, had nothing in his files but an obscene poem that had been rejected by the *New Republic.* Behind the scenes there were even deeper signs of discontent. Some of the Knopf authors—Willa Cather, for example—predicted that the *Mercury* would be bankrupt within a few months and advised Knopf to abandon the enterprise entirely.

In Nathan, his fellow editor, this discontent was not only deep but of the most critical importance. As he faced Mencken across their double-ended desk in the *Mercury* office, he was confounded at the transformation that had come over his old "corpsbruder." Nathan had observed the terrors of the war and the postwar reaction with calm, indifference, and perhaps even boredom. "The beauty of the world diverts me," he told his friends. "The problems of the world are of utterly no interest to me. I have never voted; I shall never vote. An art gallery is more important to me than Vice-President Dawes. I have always been that way and I probably always shall be that way. It is not a pose. It is the way I am made." In this state of mind, he could not "stomach" what Mencken was about. According to the Mencken-Nathan myth, he and his partner were indissolubly bound by the conviction that life is an illusion and indignation a folly. Sooner or later, he thought, "Heinie" would see the absurdity of his political rages.

Mencken had also been victimized by the Mencken-Nathan myth. Publicly and privately, he had declared his amazement that a man as brilliant as George should confine his talents to the theater, and predicted that eventually George would become as political-minded as himself. It was not long, however, before he discovered his error. George would not abandon his aesthetic principles or compromise them one whit: he rounded up Eugene O'Neill's *All God's Chillun Got Wings* (written especially for him and printed prior to a Broadway showing), an interview with George Moore, a pen portrait of Lillian Gish by Hergesheimer, Carl Van Doren's study of Stephen Crane, and enough other such works to keep the magazine in fifty-fifty balance between letters and politics. Mencken could not deny the quality of such articles, but so far as he was concerned they did not illuminate the workings of the American democracy, and hence did not belong in the magazine. Worse, George would not handle the traffic with authors who wrote about the "drool method" in history, the "fallacy" of disarmament, the "failure" of higher education in America. All articles political and sociological Mencken had to solicit and edit himself.

In the fall of 1924, after a year of this regimen, Mencken was ready for a showdown. Nor was he dissuaded any longer by considerations of affection or loyalty. "Loyalty," he believed, "is the virtue of a dog." Bluntly, he forced Alfred Knopf to choose between the two editors. "I'm going nuts," he said. "One or the other of us must leave. You can be sure that if you fire me it will not oppress me in the slightest. Besides, if Nathan has his way, you will probably sell more magazines and make more money." Knopf, it is true, was not wholly sold on the political mission of the *Mercury*. Still, Mencken had been his original choice as the editor, and at this critical moment he stuck by him, giving him permission to manage the dissolution of the partnership as he saw fit. The issues at the bottom of it neither of the two men ever disclosed; for a decade their separation would remain a celebrated mystery. All that was known was that on February 19, 1925, Nathan retired as co-editor to become contributing editor; that for the next five years he also conducted his theater department and "Clinical Notes" without Mencken's collaboration; that in 1930 he severed all connections, selling back his share of *Mercury* stock.

Thus in the end Mencken had his way, but now he had to pay for his ruthlessness by the temporary loss of his oldest and closest friends. Though Nathan still had his desk in the *Mercury* office, the two men could no longer confide in each other with their former intimacy, and in the evenings they generally parted company. Boyd remained a *Mercury* contributor, and even wrote a friendly critique of the editor, but his sympathies were naturally on Nathan's side; henceforth Mencken rarely dined at his apartment. As to Dreiser, he not only joined the opposition but told Mencken bluntly just what he thought of him in his latter-day role. In January 1926, out of long habit, he had let his friend read his masterpiece, *An American Tragedy,* prior to publication. And Mencken, also out of long habit, was quite candid in his reaction to it—perhaps too much so. "I think the trial and execution of Griffiths goes beyond anything you have ever done," he told the novelist. "But the first volume made me shed some sweat." Dreiser, bitterly disappointed, replied, "As to your critical predilections, animosities, inhibitions—et cet. Tosh. Who reads you? Bums and loafers. No-goods." On this, Mencken had no comment and the two men did not correspond again for eight years.

In 1932 Nathan and Boyd would carry this opposition to a belated but logical conclusion. They rounded up such alumni of the former Mencken-Nathan circle as O'Neill, Anderson, Dreiser and Cabell, and founded the *American Spectator,* a "real monthly literary newspaper." Unstated but implied was their purpose to prove that the *Mercury* had misrepresented the aims of the literary Renaissance; and during their success with the paper, they took a satisfactory slice out of the *Mercury*'s circulation. By this time, however, the Sage's conscience had got the better of him. When Boyd prodded him into expressing an opinion about the new paper, he said that it was pretty good, but that it would have been better if the editors had written all the contents themselves. As to the notion that he was lying awake and beating his breast about it,

"What could be more fantastic?" he wrote. "I forget what was in my last communiqué, but if it did not end with Christian sentiments, then I must have been in my cups when I wrote it." The truth was that the Sage regretted the imperatives that had separated him from his old "booze-companions"; hence he took his punishment without enthusiasm, but also without bitterness.

The immediate effects of the reorganization, however, were not so clear. The *Mercury*'s format remained unchanged; and some members of its original circle, including James M. Cain, Jim Tully, Miss Winslow, Miss Suckow, and Edgar Lee Masters, continued occasionally to contribute to it. Meanwhile Mencken dedicated himself to the development of a new school—more journalistic than the old one and better equipped to explore the social scene—of whom Louis Adamic, Marquis Childs, John Gunther, Max Lerner, and I. F. Stone were destined to make their mark in the following era. Many were drawn in by Mencken's personal magnetism; others he discovered through his omnivorous reading. Any writer anywhere, professional or amateur, who could command the "hot flush" and the "hostile snort" essential to a *Mercury* author, he invited into the fold. By the same token he installed Charles Angoff, a recent Harvard graduate, as his New York office manager. Angoff had come to him seeking his recommendation for a job on the Baltimore *Sun* and had been "shocked out of a year's growth," as Mencken observed, when suddenly appointed assistant editor of the *Mercury*.

Despite these changes, oddly enough, the *Mercury* continued to grow. Neither Mencken nor Nathan had ever dreamed it would command more than 30,000 readers.

Yet in their first year, it had grown from its first experimental circulation of 10,000 to 42,000. And in the second, at 60,000, it outsold the liberal weeklies, while *Harper's* and the *Atlantic Monthly* had to renovate their format to keep up with it. College boys collected its issues, number by number and volume by volume, exhibiting them on their bookshelves along with the classics. Flappers read it on trains; self-consciously cultured families placed it conspicuously about the house; village atheists doted on it. Thus, by mid-1925 Mencken had become a journalistic, if not a political, force to be reckoned with, and though by this time most of his original "chopping blocks," the war and postwar patriots, had subsided, there were still plenty of other heads for him to crack in the name of "common decency."

## CHAPTER 12

# War with the South

### [ 1 ]

When Mencken first projected himself into the national arena, he studied the situation "North, East, South, and West" to discover which was the most civilized part of the country and which the most barbaric—to be determined, of course, by the distribution of "first-rate" men. At first, for sentimental reasons, he had been inclined to leave the South out of consideration. His grandfather, like many Baltimoreans, had been a Southern sympathizer, and Mencken himself had the same tendency. He openly admired the half-Southern gentlemen who owned the Baltimore *Sunpapers*. They possessed an "urbane instinct and an aristocratic manner" not found in other American types. Moreover, the civilization in which they had their roots was a civilization "of manifold excellences"—"perhaps, the best that the Western Hemisphere has ever seen"—better by far than the New England civilization of "shop-keepers and theologians."

For the task that he had set himself, however, he had to look at the facts as they were, not as they might have been. And the facts were that the Old South had long since passed away, and in its place had arisen a New South of lynchings and hookworm, Georgia crackers and Kentucky mountaineers, "moron Baptists and Methodists."

In his opening attack, he gave the South credit for one novelist, James Branch Cabell (he might have added Ellen Glasgow), two *Smart Set* poets (now forgotten), and some charming but faded Virginia architecture. Otherwise, he wrote, the region had no critics, composers, painters, historians, sociologists, philosophers, or scientists of any significance. "For all its size and all its wealth and all the 'progress' it babbles of, it is almost as sterile artistically, intellectually, culturally, as the Sahara Desert. There are single acres of Europe that house more first-rate men than all the states south of the Potomac; there are probably single square miles in America. If the whole of the late Confederacy were to be engulfed by a tidal wave tomorrow, the effect upon the civilized minority of men in the world would be but little greater than that of a flood in the Yang-tse-kiang. It would be impossible in all history to match so complete a drying-up of civilization."

Having thus disposed of the South, the Sage might very well have passed on to less vulnerable regions. But the Southerners, in addition to their other deficiencies, were extraordinarily sensitive about themselves. "The Sahara of the Bozart," which first appeared in the New York *Evening Mail* in November 1917, was expanded for the *Smart Set* and again expanded for *Prejudices: Second Series* (1920), in each case to the accompaniment of a gathering storm of recriminations. It was true, of course, that Southern newsstands carried only token quantities of the *Smart Set;* that their diminutive bookstores traded mostly in best sellers, for which category the "Prejudices" did not qualify; that literary events were rarely discussed in their newspapers, none of them providing any regular space for book reviews. Yet the eyes and ears of Southern spokesmen were so sensitively attuned to bad reports that all the normal barriers of communication were transcended and "The Sahara of the Bozart," which might have been passed over as an amusing literary jibe, pricked Southern skins from Richmond to El Paso. In Arkansas, particularly, the people could think of nothing else.

In one of the many sequels to the "Sahara," Mencken remarked: "I know New Yorkers who have been in Cochin China, Kafiristan, Paraguay, Somaliland and West Virginia, but not one who has ever penetrated the miasmatic jungles of Arkansas." On or about August 1, 1921, Virgil C. Pettie, president of the Arkansas Advancement Association, wrote to his Congressman in Washington, urging him to call all Southern Congressmen into conference for legislative action against the Sage. Concretely he suggested that Mencken be deported. It could be arranged, he said, whether Mencken was an enemy alien, a naturalized citizen, or even a native son. "Fur will fly when the Congressmen buy up the available copies of the *Smart Set,*" he promised.

Pettie had public opinion almost unanimously behind him. The *Arkansas Democrat* assured him for a fact that "Mencken is a former subject of the German Kaiser." The Lions Club approved the action by formal resolution. In a letter to the Little Rock *Daily News,* a half-educated but highly rhetorical rustic defended the "good people of the South" against "one of those silly New York magazines that caters largely to a clientele of nincompoops and mollycoddles." "Poor, ignorant misguided fool," he chided, "Robert E. Lee towered so far above your vision that it were like a bull gnat gazing at Mars and expecting to bring the planet in his range of vision for a man like you to attempt to get a vision of Robert E. Lee." Among the cultural leaders of the community, the editor of the *Arkansas Writer* demanded that the "menace of Herr Mencken" be brought to the attention of every newspaper, pulpit, and civic organization in the South.

Two weeks later the Arkansas Congressman wrote back that since Mencken was a native Baltimorean, he was exempt from deportation. Accordingly, the *Arkansas Democrat* made a correction of its former charge and sounded a general retreat. It observed that the patriots of Arkansas had pushed the counteroffensive with excessive vigor and had thus lent themselves to Mencken's master plan of publicity. It implied that there was an unseen and vicious force behind his anti-South propaganda. As for Mencken, "let him stew in his own obscurity." On September 5 the editors found that everybody had forgotten about "Mencken's sewage." Summing it up, they admitted that Arkansas could be improved in its schools, opera houses, health facilities, and its roads, though other states in America were also at fault and almost equally in arrears in these matters.

The effects of the "Sahara" were considerably more far-reaching than "everybody" now believed. Emily Clark of Richmond, among other writers, had received it not as an insult but as a most powerful stimulus to action; and as evidence of her good faith she had sent Mencken a prospectus of her new review, to be known as the *Reviewer*.

Miss Clark made no great claims for herself. She was socially prominent but very young and in modest circumstances. She had no experience with magazine make-up.

She did not believe that she would ever master the art of proofreading. Potentially, however, she was a highly resourceful editor. For publication, she was the master of an urbane style after James Branch Cabell; face to face with literary greats, she affected a girlish helplessness; and one thing taken with another, she was irresistible. Already she had enlisted a group of literary godfathers, including Cabell himself, Hunter Stagg, a leading Richmond aesthete, and Mencken's good friend Joseph Hergesheimer. Why shouldn't the Sage himself join the group, she asked? By a happy accident, his *Prejudices: Second Series,* containing the "Sahara" article, was published just in time to be reviewed in the *Reviewer*'s first issue, February 1921: it was cited as the most telling statement of why such magazines as the *Reviewer* were necessary.

Mencken welcomed the *Reviewer* as "a violet in the Sahara." "The South," he told Miss Clark, "is beginning to awake from its old slumbers. You have a capital chance to lead the way." But when she asked him just how that was to be done, he was for a time uncertain. In his first directive, he advised her that it was "far better to move away from the conventional criticism of the South gradually than to run amok" like a similar group editing the *Double Dealer* in New Orleans. However, he was not pleased with the excess of moonlight and magnolia blossoms that filled the second issue, and in a rapid turnabout he shifted the line to the opposite extreme. "It will be useless to attempt a compromise," he now declared. "You must arm yourself and take to the highroad, ready to cut throats whenever it is necessary. The thing must be done boldly and in order to get a crowd, a bit cruelly." Unfortunately, Miss Clark was not equipped to take to the highroad. In July 1921, Mencken told Hergesheimer: "The *Reviewer* seems not to be long for this life. The gals are too timorous." Four months later, he and Hergesheimer paid a visit to Richmond to see what could be done about it.

The occasion was a coming-out party for Cabell's step-daughter. But Mencken had made it clear beforehand that he was as intolerant of Southern swank as of Southern patriotism. "The dance rather appals me," he had written. "I stopped dancing when the minuet and varsovienne went out." He spent the first evening paying homage to Cabell (who rarely left Richmond and whom he had never met before), engaging him in a sociological discussion of the decline of the First Families of Virginia. The next evening, at a reception in the Clark home, he and Hergesheimer performed together like a couple of burlesque troupers. Mencken warned his hostess that Joe was a leg-pincher and in the midst of a polite discussion the two men left the room together to drink mountain whiskey on the terrace. But on a tour of Richmond's shrines the following day, the Sage was so tame and appreciative that Miss Clark wondered whether he had completely forgotten about his mission.

For three years thereafter, the *Reviewer* made great strides, introducing with Mencken's aid such significant writers as Mrs. Julia Peterkin of South Carolina, Gerald W. Johnson of North Carolina and Frances Newman of Georgia. Yet in the development of Southern civilization, its success was overshadowed by an even greater success of the opposing forces. In the midst of the "Sahara of the Bozart" furor, the Southern Baptists had renounced the

Mencken heresies, reaffirmed their faith in the authority of the Bible, and agreed upon a course of counteraction—a campaign to prohibit the teaching of Darwin's evolution in the nation's public schools. William Jennings Bryan was drafted as torchbearer, and among their organizers were many veterans of the Ku Klux Klan. The movement spread rapidly. By 1925, the Fundamentalists, as they were called, had prevailed in Oklahoma and Tennessee, and looked forward to easy victories in Mississippi and Arkansas. At much the same time, the *Reviewer* was encountering financial difficulties, and after a change of locale under the aegis of Paul Green, the Chapel Hill dramatist, disappeared entirely.

In facing these reverses, Mencken might easily have lost heart. But, as always, the more intense the conflict of forces, the better he liked it. In the first place, it brought him the allegiance not only of the South's literary people but of its liberal educators and newspaper editors as well. In the second place, the Fundamentalists in many ways were the most vulnerable of all his latter-day "chopping blocks." By insisting that "God created the universe during a single week of the year 4004 B.C.," the Southern theologians were opening themselves up to widespread ridicule. By marching down from the mountains of the "Bible Belt" for a "jehad against what remains of American intelligence already beleaguered in a few walled towns," they were converting a local issue into a national one. Half a century before, his Victorian precursor, Thomas Henry Huxley, had met a similar challenge from the foremost English bishops. Now Mencken could fill the Huxley role and under far more dramatic circumstances.

[ 2 ]

In the spring of 1925, a 24-year-old biology teacher was willing to defy the Fundamentalists in their own territory. He was John Thomas Scopes of Dayton, Tennessee. Aroused, perhaps, by Mencken's Jeremiads, he blandly violated the state anti-evolution law, was arrested, and then waited quietly while the famous partisans of both sides converged on Dayton for his trial. For the defense, the American Civil Liberties Committee took the field with Clarence Darrow, the nation's pre-eminent trial lawyer, assisted by two lawyers of almost equal forensic power, Dudley Field Malone and Arthur Garfield Hays. Bryan himself joined the opposing counsel. Clearly, it would be a contest of titans, a front-page story for every American newspaper, and Paul Patterson of the *Sunpapers*, having one of the most notorious of them on his own payroll, prepared to make the most of it.

He advanced $500 for Scopes's bail. He dispatched his best writers, Frank R. Kent and Henry M. Hyde, and his cartoonist, Edmund Duffy, to Dayton. Then he approached the Sage, urging him to join the others and to write about whatever aspects of the Dayton scene interested him. Mencken balked: because of the heavy burden of *Mercury* business, he said, he would be unable to attend. It was, of course, simply a piece of stage business; on the face of it, it was inconceivable that "civilization" could be tried anywhere in the United States without Mencken's participation. Nevertheless, he kept Patterson on tenterhooks until the last moment.

On July 8 Mencken took quarters in a Dayton hotel, sampled the four quarts of Scotch that he had picked up en route from his *Mercury* "customers," then went out to see the town. The trial had not yet begun; hot-dog stands were going up on the main street and telegraph instruments were being installed in a grocery store. As Mencken passed the offices of the prosecution lawyers, he saw Bryan standing on the steps, surrounded by a crowd of local admirers. Affably, Mencken introduced himself and chatted with the Commoner on the neutral ground of technicalities. Mencken repeated the thesis that he had advanced two weeks before in the *Nation,* that the anti-evolution law was constitutional by every known precedent. Bryan was delighted with what Mencken told him. "This Mencken," he said, straining his once-melodious voice so that everyone could hear him, "is the best newspaperman in the country." In the same spirit, Mencken expressed admiration for Bryan's pongee shirt, sleeveless and cut low at the neck, and Bryan informed him that it was made by his wife.

A few hours later, Mencken told a reporter from the Chattanooga *Times* that he was amazed at Bryan's sportsmanship. "I never knew Christian people before to disagree without hating each other," he said. Dayton itself seemed to him "a most charming human habitation." "Everything is here that a sensible man wants or needs. There are no roof gardens, but what sensible man goes there?" He made but one recommendation: that the townsfolk burn down the blast furnaces. These furnaces were eyesores, and they brought the town no profit since their owners lived elsewhere, spending their money upon fat women on the Riviera.

Though he said nothing about it, Mencken had also taken note of the large number of itinerant evangelists in the town and he was mixing affably among them. One night he attended a camp meeting of Holy Rollers out in the hill country. Unobserved, he crept from the outer fringe of seats to the center, falling under the spell of the presiding evangelist and (according to one version of his story) twitching and moaning "Glory be to God" like the hillbilly dervishes. He was "converted" (according to the press) six times within four days, several times by the white-haired Reverend T. T. Martin of Mississippi, a leading figure of the anti-evolution lobby and author of *Hell in the High Schools.* Then, trying his own hand at the game, he hired a boy to distribute a thousand handbills proclaiming the arrival of a new Fundamentalist preacher, Elmer Chubb, LL.D., D.D.

These circulars had been conceived and drafted weeks before by the Sage's good friend Edgar Lee Masters. They promised that Chubb, among other things, would be bitten by poisonous snakes and imbibe large quantities of poison; they were so plausibly done that among the testimonials printed upon them was one by Mencken himself, saying "Chubb is a fake." Unfortunately, the handbills made no impression whatsoever upon their readers. In this lush religious atmosphere even miracle workers were more or less taken for granted. On the other hand, when Mencken advised the evangelists that a gang of Bolsheviks was coming from Cincinnati to "butcher" Bryan, the news spread instantly from one end of the town to the other. The Dayton police were alerted; they provided Bryan with a special armed escort, and they arrested an innocent young man (a Y.M.C.A. secretary, Mencken believed) as he stepped off the train from Cincinnati.

Horrified, Mencken wrote to Dr. Pearl: "This is far worse than you could imagine, even under the bowl. Every last scoundrel in sight is a Christian including the town Jew. I begin to realize what life must have been in Judea 1925 years ago. No wonder the Romans finally bumped off the son of Joseph. After an hour on the main street, listening to the bawling, I feel like loading a cannon with the rejects of adjacent hogs (sus sorofa) [*sic*] and letting fly. The thing is genuinely fabulous. I have stored up enough material to last me twenty years."

In the courthouse, Mencken talked frequently with the three luminaries of the defense, Darrow, Malone, and Hays. Before the trial, at Malone's solicitation, Mencken had laid out their grand strategy, advising them not to defend Scopes, who was legally beyond help, but to expose the backwardness of the South and to plaster Bryan as a "jackass." Darrow, for one, had been reluctant to do this, for in his youth he had been one of Bryan's most ardent admirers. But now, in the hot, tense courtroom, he forgot all his inhibitions. Openly he declared his purpose "to show up Fundamentalism . . . to prevent bigots and ignoramuses from controlling the educational system of the United States," while Bryan declared it his contrary purpose "to protect the word of God against [Darrow] the greatest atheist and agnostic in the United States!"

As the debate continued, Mencken was silent, but he could not be ignored. His reports to the Baltimore *Evening Sun* were reprinted in the Chattanooga *News* and read among the conflicting parties. Even as a spectator, his whole being was so poised that he was almost eloquent. Mrs. Haldeman-Julius reported: "He listened to practically the entire trial standing with several other journalists and a movie man or two, on a table in a corner of the court room. He faced the pleading advocates and incidentally the audience. Mencken's most usual expression when a member of the prosecution spoke was one of delighted incredulity. He has the most amazing china blue eyes that survey the world with a sort of 'Where-did-you-come-from-baby-dear,' surprised, ingenuous look." In this fashion Mencken stared at Bryan. Bryan, in turn, stared at him, but with eyes that were "blazing points of hatred," glittering "like occult and sinister gems"; they made Mencken wince as though he had come under fire.

Now, casting off all pretenses of objectivity and geniality, Mencken denounced the Fundamentalists with complete abandon. He wrote of "the degraded nonsense which country preachers are ramming and hammering into yokel skulls," of the turnout of "gaping primates" and an "anthropoid rabble" in Bryan's claque, of the spinelessness of the educated Tennesseans. To see themselves thus described, the Daytonians bought out the available copies of the Chattanooga *News;* and those who couldn't or didn't buy the paper caught the gist of Mencken's reporting at second hand. The townsmen were more incensed by what Mencken said of them than by any of Darrow's orations. Leading divines of all denominations rose to protest this "cheap blatherskite of a pen-pusher with his rattling gourd-seed." On July 16 the citizenry gathered in stores and on the street corners; cries of "Take him into an alley," "Run him out of town," re-echoed from one group to another.

That afternoon one of the bailiffs at the courthouse took Mencken aside, warned him about the seriousness of the situation, and suggested that he meet with a committee of representative citizens at Robinson's drugstore. Mencken readily agreed. After the court session, he and the bailiff kept their appointment; but for some unaccountable reason the citizens did not. He chatted with the bailiff for ten minutes, twenty minutes, thirty minutes, and still there were no citizens.

Meanwhile his adversaries were assembled in a general store nearby, planning what to do with the Sage when they met him. By chance, A. P. Haggard, the local bank president, entered the store in the midst of their deliberations. One of the citizens approached him and bent over his ear. "You must come along with us," he said, "to keep the boys from going too far. We don't mean to do more than ride him out of town on a rail and tell him to stay out. But there's no telling what the boys will do in a case like that!" Haggard nodded. Then, mustering the full authority of his position as Dayton's leading citizen, he told the group: "I don't like the things Mencken is writing any more than you do, and I want him to know it. Mencken is dead wrong about Dayton. He has never met any of our real people here. He spends his time in the back alleys, and he judges us by the hillbillies from East Tennessee. But this is not the way to set him straight." Haggard continued earnestly in this vein, and in the end he persuaded the citizens to abandon their bloody mission and go home.

When Mencken left Robinson's drugstore, he had no inkling of what had passed in the other meeting place. He remarked to the bailiff that the citizens had been frightened off by the impending thunderstorm. Somehow he could not take seriously the possibility of mob action.

With his sloping shoulders and his 180 pounds concentrated at the midriff of a short frame, he lacked the physical resources of a Lone Ranger. He carried himself with assurance, nonetheless, striding along with his slightly bowed legs well to the front of him. What he lacked in might, he made up in integrity. He was popular among his newspaper colleagues, and their esteem added to his armor. If the mob went beyond muttering, the reporter from the New York *World* assured him, a league of two hundred battle-hard reporters would spring to his defense.

The next day he departed for Baltimore. His friends knew that he had not altered his schedule one way or the other. But that night the hotspurs of Dayton gathered around the foot of a flagpole at the junction of Main and Market Streets, blocking traffic and celebrating Mencken's departure as a victory for local valor. "We may be ignorant," one speaker said, "but none of us has ever been arrested for disloyalty in wartime; and none of us is so highly educated that he feels it his duty to substitute the red flag for the American flag or to dispose of his Bible." On July 19 Bryan held another valedictory meeting in nearby Pikeville. He did not mention Mencken by name, but what he said about newspaper reporters generally could apply only to Mencken. "These men who come from another state to call you yokels and bigots, I wish I had them here, to set them face to face with a humanity they cannot imitate. But in the end every critic you have will be rotted and forgotten." Bryan himself had not long to live. The next day he faced Darrow's cross-examination, in the course of which he affirmed his belief in the historical accuracy of the Bible down to the minutiae of Eve's birth from Adam's rib. On July 21 the court found

Scopes guilty of teaching evolution in the school system, fining him $100. Five days after this technical but hollow triumph, Bryan collapsed and died in Dayton.

Mencken, of course, missed these dramatic events. Yet, in his Monday column in the Baltimore *Evening Sun*, he commented upon them as follows: "Has it been duly marked by historians that the late William Jennings Bryan's last secular act on this globe of sin was to catch flies? A curious detail, and not without its sardonic overtones. He was the most sedulous fly-catcher in American history, and in many ways the most successful. His quarry, of course, was not *Musca domestica*, but *Homo neandertalensis*." Bryan, he said, was not only the *reductio ad absurdum* of a major democratic leader, but the *reductio ad absurdum* of democracy itself.

With this incredibly savage "In Memoriam," Mencken stole the final glare of the spotlight from all the other principals. Had he carved an ear off Bryan's body, the readers of the Baltimore *Sun* could not have been more shocked, nor the editors of the *Sun* more conscience-stricken. On August 13 the Executive Director of the Baltimore Association of Commerce declared that because of Mencken's continuous assaults on Southern culture, the Southerners had organized a boycott against the city. This boycott was apparently nothing more than a phantasm conceived and announced by a local booster whom the Sage had often abused in the past. Yet it was discussed quite seriously in the Southern press. "We must assume," argued the Knoxville (Tenn.) *Journal*, that Mencken's "detestable vaporings would not be printed day after day in reputable newspapers unless they had the approval of the publishers . . . and of the community as a whole."

"If something doesn't check Mr. Henry Mencken," added the Cordele (Ga.) *Dispatch*, "the Southern people are naturally going to steer clear of Baltimore for business. And nobody in Baltimore could blame us." Not many papers shared the view of the Raleigh (N. C.) *News and Observer* that however much Mencken may hurt business, a little more of his "destructive criticism would certainly do North Carolina no harm."

*CHAPTER 13*

# Boston: the "Hatrack" Case

## [ 1 ]

EVEN BEFORE the Scopes trial, it was apparent that Mencken was overextending his line of communications. In September 1924, Joseph Patterson (no relation to Paul Patterson), then co-editor of the Chicago *Tribune,* had launched him as a syndicated weekly columnist. But few American newspapers (except the Baltimore *Sunpapers* and the New York *World*) could afford to print his column for any length of time, and it was passed from one organ to another like a hot potato. As to the *American Mercury,* with its more than sixty thousand subscribers, he had still not provided it with a smooth-working organization. While Angoff in New York took the greater share of the burden (and he was developing into one of the best managing editors in the country), the liaison between Baltimore and New York was defective. Mencken made no carbon copies of his letters. Absent-mindedly, he sometimes assigned two or more authors to the same article, and then left Angoff to make peace among them. He endeavored personally to review everything that went into the magazine. Yet in this state, he undertook the most difficult and hazardous operation of his career.

For eighteen years, the Reverend T. Frank Chase had

quietly dominated the intellectual life of Boston. Under a unique Massachusetts statute, the booksellers rather than the publishers were responsible for the decency of Boston's reading matter, but Mr. Chase, the secretary of the Watch and Ward Society, had taken this responsibility from them. Now as he sat at his desk, weighing the purity of a book or magazine, a committee of booksellers stood ready to circulate his findings, and the police to enforce them; and if he found a book unfit for circulation, no Boston newspaper would advertise it or notice it in its literary columns. Thus Mr. Chase had outlawed such modernist works as Ben Hecht's *Gargoyles,* Huxley's *Antic Hay,* Dell's *Janet March,* Anderson's *Many Marriages,* and Dos Passos's *Streets of Night.* Fourteen years before, when John Macy, then literary critic of the Boston *Herald,* had attacked him, the censor had (or so it was believed) quietly eased Macy out of his job, and now when Mencken asked various Boston newspapermen to repeat Macy's performance in the pages of the *Mercury,* they were not interested.

Undaunted, Mencken turned to A. L. S. Woods, a young reviewer for the Springfield (Mass.) *Union.* Working closely with him through several unsuccessful drafts, he obtained an article, "Keeping the Puritans Pure," which he published in September 1925. In the December issue he continued the attack with Angoff's "Boston Twilight," a study of the cultural poverty of Irish elements in the Hub city, with passing remarks about the censorship. In "The Methodists," April 1926, he had Angoff strike another blow at the Watch and Ward, this time under the pseudonym James Bernard. (Angoff had also written "The Baptists" for the February issue.) Mencken did not believe that any of these articles did justice to the subject but it soon became apparent that they had found their mark. After the December attack, Chase advised his friends that the *Mercury* was such a filthy magazine that sooner or later he would have to suppress it. After the April attack he found the pretext that he was looking for. It was "Hatrack," a study of a prostitute. At once he issued the order outlawing the issue. He had no reason to doubt that the wheels of his machine would roll as usual. But, since this was a very special case, he personally saw to it that Felix Caragianes, a news vendor in Harvard Square, was arrested for defying the ban; and on March 30 he issued press releases explaining that "Hatrack" was "immoral," "unfit to read," "full of filthy and degrading descriptions."

The next day, when a Baltimore *Sun* reporter phoned to ask for a statement, Mencken declared with rasping guffaws that could be heard throughout the office, "This report, if true, is very amusing. There is in Boston a lay Methodist preacher who has forsaken the pulpit in order to act as catchpoll of a gang of fanatics calling themselves the Watch and Ward Society," and so on. As to the censorship itself, he assured the reporter that it was a meaningless gesture. The stocks of the April issue had been almost completely sold prior to the ban. Besides, Boston was *Atlantic Monthly*, not *Mercury*, country. Unknowingly, however, he had been hurt far worse than he had realized, and when he put the phone down, the injustice of the thing suddenly fell full upon him. Months before, Mencken had selected "Hatrack" from Herbert Asbury's forthcoming book about his boyhood in Farmington, Missouri; of all its well-written chapters, this one had seemed the best. It ridiculed the evangelists who went through the town, railing against imaginary bawdy houses, while it spoke very compassionately about the town's one and only prostitute, called Hatrack because of her figure, who accommodated her customers in the cemetery. Had Chase argued that the study was un-Christian in its spirit, Mencken might have agreed with him; but of "filthy and degrading descriptions" there were none. Clearly, then, Chase's action was an arbitrary one, and the more Mencken thought about it, the more it annoyed him. "If Chase gets away with this minor assault," he declared, "he will be encouraged to plan worse ones, and what is more, other wowsers [censors] elsewhere will imitate him."

That afternoon the Knopfs, father and son, agreed to a showdown. The following morning, with Arthur Garfield Hays, one of the lawyers of the Scopes trial, as counsel, they drew up their plan of attack. Openly, Mencken would defy the bar by selling a copy of the outlawed magazine in the streets of Boston. He would be arrested, and the issue would then be taken to court. In all probability, Hays said, he would be found guilty of a violation of law; he would have to pay a heavy fine or serve a two-year prison sentence. But Mencken agreed to all these risks because on every count he was the most formidable contestant. As a citizen of Maryland in conflict with Massachusetts law, he could have recourse to the federal courts. By the daring of his defiance, he would attract widespread public attention, rallying a nationwide opposition to the Boston censorship.

Herbert Ehrmann, a young Harvard lawyer who served as Hays's Boston agent, added the final touches to the drama. He laid the opening scene on "Brimstone Corner" where the Park Street Church faces the Common and where (according to legend) the early Puritan divines had once spread brimstone to advertise the incandescence of their sermons. Also he arranged that when Mencken sold the outlawed *Mercury*, Chase would be the purchaser. The censor protested the indelicacy of the transaction. But Ehrmann warned him that unless he appeared at the time and place arranged, Mencken would commence a general sale of the *Mercury* on the street.

[ 2 ]

Early on Monday morning, April 5, Mencken appeared in the South Station with W. A. S. Douglas, a special correspondent for the Baltimore *Sun*, at his side. He was in good fighting trim, nervous but in high spirit. After registering at the Copley-Plaza Hotel, he went down to the city morgue and applied for a peddler's license—a necessary preliminary, but one very much to his taste. The clerk had no conception of what he was about. He advised Mencken that the permits were issued in various styles, one of which would authorize him to sell bones, grease, and refuse matter. Mencken remarked that since the classification of the *Mercury* was still a disputed point, he would prefer another permit, under which he could peddle anything except fish, fruit, or vegetables. He assured the clerk that he would not sell any fish.

At 1:30 P.M., a half hour before the assignation, three thousand persons had collected on Brimstone Corner under depressing New England skies. Men clambered up to the second-story ledge of the Park Street Church;

traffic cops abandoned their posts to keep the crowd from overrunning the street; and to judge by the newspapers, it would be a hot reception. The Boston *Post* had declared that "for sheer prurient vulgarity unrelieved by the slightest trace of art, the article complained of is quite the limit," and Mencken would be lucky to escape jail. The Boston *Herald* compared Mencken to Earl Carroll, the Broadway impresario, who trafficked in life-size photos of seminude chorus girls. Even the enlightened *Evening Transcript* was sarcastic about his mission. Had Mencken given Boston more notice, it said, an appropriate welcome would have been arranged for him with a parade of five hundred Babbitts surreptitiously chewing gum, oratory by the combined Rotary Clubs, a contingent of Lowells talking to Cabots, presentation of a garland of poison ivy by the Irish societies, a float carrying local Fundamentalists enveloped in a smoke screen of applesauce.

At 1:55 P.M., prompt as ever, Mencken marched upon Brimstone Corner. He wore a black topcoat and a gray fedora, and carried under his arm three copies of the outlawed *Mercury*. As he pushed his way through the crowd, he observed to his relief that his partisans, the Harvard boys, were in the ascendancy. Hays had preceded him, and the crowd was giving the lawyer its attention. "Don't let them deport him, Arthur," someone shouted. When Mencken took his stand beside Hays, he was beset with autograph seekers. One jokester threw a copy of the *Mercury* into the air to watch the scramble, and others threw half dollars at Mencken and Hays. "Where's Chase?" they chanted. Mencken took up the cry, "Yes, where's Chase?" A young man edged his way into the center. He said that he was Chase's assistant and would perform the ceremony in lieu of the censor. Mencken waved him aside. There was another interlude of waiting. Finally from the outskirts of the crowd came cries of "Here he is!"; "Is this a free country or not?"; "Why don't we fight the revolution?"—indicating that Chase, accompanied by a captain of the vice squad and a plain-clothes man, was making his approach.

The censor introduced himself—a brisk man with a trim mustache and a wide, bespectacled face. Mencken extended a copy of the *Mercury* to him; Chase, in turn, handed Mencken a silver half dollar. With exaggerated gestures and grimaces, the Sage put the piece in his mouth and bit it as if to test its soundness. "I order this man's arrest," Chase called out. At once the police moved in upon the editor from either side, the plain-clothes man seizing his left arm, the captain his right. With Mencken as the point of a wedge, the trio broke through the crowd and commenced their march of four blocks down to the police station in Pemberton Square. News photographers illuminated the route with their flash bulbs, while the crowd took up the rear. One camera caught Mencken, flanked closely by his police escort, holding an unlit cigar in his left hand and striding along with his flat profile turned aside somewhat grimly at a point of provocation in the distance.

Arrived at the police station, Mencken was booked on the charge of violating Chapter 272, Section 28, of the Public General Law of Massachusetts. At the same time, the vice-squad captain observed that Douglas, Mencken's Baltimore *Sun* colleague, was carrying a copy of the *Mercury*. "Look," he blurted, "he's got the filth in his hands!" Douglas was placed under arrest. He protested that he was only a newspaper reporter discharging his duties; but it took the combined remonstrance of the two principals, Mencken and Chase, to convince the captain that an injustice had been done. Later, when Ehrmann attempted to join the group, the captain again lost his temper. Mencken already had one lawyer, he said, and didn't need another. Meanwhile Mencken's comic spirit could not be damped. For the record, he gave his occupation as editor and clergyman, but he added that it would be best to leave out the clergyman half because it was a matter of no importance. Then he sat in a corner under guard, surrounded by some fifty reporters, conducting what they later described as "a class in journalism."

In the Central Municipal Court there were further altercations. The captain requested a week's delay in the trial, but Hays objected that such a delay would work hardship upon his client, and his objection was sustained. The trial was set for 10 A.M. the following morning; until then, Mencken was at liberty without bail.

Inevitably now, Mencken felt the tension mount within him; for the first time, he was fully conscious of his peril. From Ehrmann's office he wired one of the *Sunpaper* editors to make all necessary arrangements for his bail: the editor was to notify the Fidelity and Deposit Company of Maryland and the latter was to instruct its Boston agent to have the funds available.

Back at the hotel, he relaxed somewhat with a flood of sympathetic telegrams. From Sinclair Lewis, then in Kansas City: "We of the KC ministerial alliance hope that you insisted on T. Frank Chase disinfecting any money handed you"; from Maury Maverick in San Antonio, Texas: "I am with you. Run the jack-asses to the cemetery"; from the editors of the *Evening Sun:* "Straw vote taken hurriedly at two fifteen today show the Free State solidly behind you with the exception of Crabbe, Davis and Kelly [Baltimore reformers] stop Indignation meeting in Maryland Club stop Free State flag coming by special delivery." The Boston intelligentsia also assured him of their support with phone calls and dinner invitations. Yet it was not enough. In his skittishness, he was rankled by the silence of one or two Boston friends; and their defection loomed larger in his mind than the support of all the rest.

He was restless throughout a long dinner at Ehrmann's house because, he thought, the time would have been better spent rehashing legal points alone with Hays. At 10 P.M., he returned to the hotel for some social drinking with a couple of his confederates. One of them, a Knopf book agent and a native Bostonian, reported that the Irish politicians were militantly anti-Mencken not because of "Hatrack," but because of Angoff's "Boston Twilight," and that in the event of a jury trial they would pack the jury. The ringleader of the Boston booksellers, he added, was offering long odds that Mencken would be convicted. When Mencken retired at midnight, he was exhausted but, "in view of the news, sleep was somewhat delayed."

The next morning Mencken arrived in the courtroom promptly at 10 A.M. He was cheered by a delegation of Harvard and Radcliffe students. Also in the audience he observed many photographers and newspapermen, some of whom had come unofficially to enjoy the show. The representatives of the Fidelity and Deposit Company were present with bail money. But the most important of all his forces, his lawyers, Hays and Ehrmann, were nowhere in sight. They were detained with their petitions over in the federal court, his friends suggested. Whatever they were doing, it was harrowing to sit there without counsel, his case to be called at any moment. He relieved himself with an eruption of profanity until a young lawyer offered to fill in for the missing counsel. A former assistant district attorney, he advised Mencken to get the trial postponed to the following fall, when a less hostile set of officials would come into office. A few minutes later, however, Hays and Ehrmann arrived and Mencken was relieved of this bird of ill omen.

Mencken with his counsel, and Chase with his, stood in a little knot around the dais of the presiding judge, James P. Parmenter. Following the judge's example, they spoke so softly that the audience and reporters could hardly hear them, the judge apparently fearing that the evidence would be improper. Chase's counsel, John W. Rourke, opened for the prosecution. The burden of his argument was that Mencken had deliberately set out to "corrupt youth" with the indecent articles of the *American Mercury* and that "Hatrack" particularly would have the effect of demoralizing the young people of the country. The Massachusetts statute, he said, had been passed largely at the instance of Catholic citizens to erect barriers against such offensive matter as this. When Chase took the stand, he suggested that Mencken was nothing more than a publicity monger, emphasizing that the transaction at Brimstone Corner was Mencken's idea, not his.

For the defense, Mencken was the first witness, and he stood squarely upon the dignity of his magazine. It was, he insisted, an organ of quality to which such dignitaries as an Episcopal bishop and a United States Senator had contributed; its price was set at fifty cents in conformity with its tone, and its readers were, for the most part, highly educated men. Prodded by Hays, Mencken gradually turned his defense into a broad offensive in which his characteristically strong rhetoric delivered in strong masculine accents broke the calm of the courtroom. "I came to Boston to find out whether so-called reformers were or were not to dictate to the citizens of this country what they should read and what they should not read. These reformers can smell out what they term 'immorality' in any publication from the Bible down, if they are so minded. Now I should not want the prosperity of my magazine to depend on its being obscene. It appeals to intelligent and decent people and assumes that such matters are open to debate and discussion." He stood as erect as a slightly stoop-shouldered man could, his broad red face tilted up to the judge. He spoke without gestures and betrayed no sign of nervousness except that he continually knotted and unknotted his fingers.

Rourke tried to deflect Mencken's onslaught by asking him why he had not built his case around Caragianes and thus secured a test of the legality of the censorship without involving his own person. "I could have done so," the Sage replied, "but when the news-dealer is convicted on the Reverend Mr. Chase's testimony, he pays his fine and goes about his business. But then my magazine is ruled out of the city on an untried verdict as far as we are concerned." Mencken did not elaborate. He assumed that the Watch and Ward Society knew well enough that news dealers were easy victims, willing to plead guilty rather than fight an expensive legal battle. "That is my purpose in placing myself in the position I am now in," he concluded. "I intend to have my conduct governed by the properly constituted courts of my country, and not by professional reformers."

As others spoke on his behalf, Mencken followed the proceedings with intense concentration. He heard Asbury, the author of "Hatrack," swear that "Hatrack" was an honest portrait of an actual prostitute. He watched Hays, in his peroration, become transformed from an advocate into a mob orator, declaring that Mencken had been denied his fundamental rights as an American citizen. And when the opposing counsel shifted the attack from "Hatrack" to an obscure item in George Jean Nathan's "Clinical Notes" called "The New View of Sex," he was convinced that he had won the case. But whether the judge agreed with him, he could not tell. The latter rarely spoke, and then only on technicalities. His square face, with the drooping left eyelid and the down-turned corners of the mouth, was devoid of all emotion. Perhaps, while observing this man, Mencken thought of what he had told another judge in Baltimore just before his departure for Boston: that "every judge should be hit once a week with a bag of —— to keep him conscious of the fact that he is human."

"The issue is simple," the judge said finally. He had only to decide whether the "Hatrack" article was obscene under the terms of the law. He would read the article and give his verdict the following morning at 9:30.

That afternoon Mencken held so many press conferences that his hotel room looked like a Presidential campaign headquarters on election eve. In the evening he was entertained at dinner by the "literati" of the St.

Botolph Club, among whom were Ferris Greenslet of Houghton Mifflin and Edward Weeks, Jr., then associate editor of the *Atlantic Monthly*. But he could not get his mind off his terrible predicament. Repeatedly he questioned the Botolphians, as earlier he had questioned the reporters, about the character of Judge Parmenter. They knew only that the judge was a Unitarian. Wishfully Mencken generalized about the tolerance of Unitarians. But the fact was, they said, that many Unitarians were on the board of the Watch and Ward Society. As the evening wore on, all his confidence evaporated. When he returned to the hotel, he believed, as did everybody else, that he would be defeated.

The verdict was apparently so much a matter of course that few visitors attended the courtroom the following morning. Even some of the principals were missing. There was no sign of Chase. Hays had already returned to New York, and Mencken was accompanied only by Ehrmann and two others. The Sage listened to the judge's opening remarks: "I have read every article in the magazine given me yesterday and find them all intellectual and of a serious nature." With the thick features of his face grimly set, Mencken concentrated upon the flow of words from the judge's mouth. Any moment now he expected the argument to take a turn for the worse. But the turn did not come. "The one on 'Jazz' is technical," the judge continued. "I do not understand it wholly, but can see where those who love music can gather much meaning from it. So far as 'Clinical Notes' is concerned, I saw nothing there that seemed out of the way.

"I do not find anything in any other article that touches upon sex except 'Hatrack,' but there the subject is not made attractive—in fact, the contrary is the case. It is a rather frank expression, but at the same time an intellectual description of prostitution in a small town, and I found nothing in it that would arouse sexual impulses or lascivious thoughts as prohibited by the statute.

"The magazine is rather high priced and this makes it unlikely that it would get into the hands of youth, but if it did, the quality of its articles is such that they would not understand them and, accordingly, would suffer no harm."

It took Mencken a few minutes to grasp the fact that the complaint was dismissed and that he had won a signal triumph. When he did, the next two or three steps of his strategy were already crystallized in his mind. First, he directed Ehrmann to have the judge's opinion transcribed for the record. Then, at a press conference in Ehrmann's office, he let it be known that he was preparing libel suits against the Boston newspapers and damage suits against the Watch and Ward Society, especially against Chase, totaling several hundred thousand dollars. Pointedly he asked the reporters whether there was enough money in Boston to cover him.

At 12:30 he drove to the Harvard Union, a University dining hall. Two days before, the students had invited him to a reception. They did not know then, and they still did not know, that he would appear as a conqueror rather than as a martyr. They had converged upon the Harvard Union dining hall in mob proportions. Radcliffe girls, trying to crash the gates, were turned back by the yard cops. The hall that had accommodations for six hundred was filled with twelve hundred, standing in every conceivable space along the walls and in the balcony.

Mencken entered with Professors Felix Frankfurter and Zechariah Chafee and took his place at the head table. When Frankfurter announced the Sage's victory, the students cheered and stamped their feet. After dinner Frankfurter introduced the Sage. Mr. Mencken, he explained, was an individualist who wanted nothing more than the right "to drink his beer in silence" and who, in the present instance, "had done a dreadful and brave thing." "His was the courage to resist brutality." Chafee made a further introduction, and then Mencken rose.

He began his address with characteristic flippancy: "I did not intend to go to jail while I was here. The fate of my colleague Chapman shows too well the effect of jail life on a younger man than I." (Chapman was a Connecticut outlaw whose hanging was reported in the Boston papers side by side with Mencken's trial.) Then he explained that he had come to Boston "to force the censors to abandon back-alley assassinations" and to stand up in the courts of law. As an elder statesman of anti-Puritanism, he advised this rising generation likewise to prepare themselves for battle with the Puritans. Without mentioning his own part, he recalled the "Freelance" wars. "The censors were chased out of the Free State of Maryland years ago," he said. "They used to go around sniffing and smelling down there just as they are doing here, but they were knocked off just as you can knock them off. Such wowsers cannot exist in the Free State, and they've given up trying." At the end, Mencken abruptly turned, picked off his chair a black and yellow silk spangled flag, and handed it to Frankfurter, saying: "I want to give you something I know you will appreciate, thinking as you do. This is the flag of the Free State of Maryland of which

I have the honor of being a citizen." The Harvard cheer was then rendered, and repeated twice over in the space of two minutes. When the tumult had subsided, Frankfurter accepted the alien flag. "We thank you sincerely for the gift, and we appreciate its significance. It will be hung on the walls of this hall."

Outside the hall, the news cameramen made Mencken re-enact the flag scene. Most of his past battles had been fought in his private study; his triumphs had never before been a public ceremony. Now he stood before the cameras surrounded by bespectacled adulators, his face suffused with a sardonic grin as one cheek rolled up and the other rolled down with an explosion of creases around his wide blue eyes. He was obviously pleased, obviously benign towards the students on either side of him. He permitted a Harvard *Crimson* reporter to ride with him back to the Copley-Plaza. "Harvard men represent to me as sporting a crowd of undergraduates as I have ever seen," he remarked in the car. "Not a trace of the wowser about them. They came to greet me right or wrong. Now suppose this had been a hugger-mugger Methodist college!" He expressed admiration for the Harvard faculty as a cosmopolitan group of interesting, distinguished, and queer fellows. He praised several professors of English, and for a moment the reporter thought that Mencken was about to disavow his antiacademic past. Then the Sage explained that though Harvard was stimulating, it was altogether too stimulating for the creative artist. "Writing is the most lonely occupation in the world. A writer must be utterly cloistered to do his best work, the only work that matters. James Branch Cabell realizes this better than any other great contemporary author. Hergesheimer does too, of course."

Back at the hotel, Mencken was concluding the interview in his room, when a bellhop brought him a trophy of the battle. "Ah, my famous four-bit piece," Mencken explained to the student, holding up the coin with which the affair at Brimstone Corner had been negotiated. "I had my attorney demand its return. I shall cherish it for some time. Probably Mr. Knopf, my publisher, will have it framed against Borzoi batiks. It is what you might call my blood money." He searched in vain for his tooth marks on the face of the coin.

A few hours later, Mencken and a friend were on the New York express, celebrating their victory with a pint of whiskey and a steak dinner. In New York there were further celebrations at the Algonquin with the Knopfs and the Hayses; and that night, as the Sage later recounted, "I had the first really comfortable sleep for a week."

[ 3 ]

Had the Sage understood Chase's mysterious absence from the courtroom, he would not have slept so comfortably. The censor was no fool. Of all the principals in the affair, he alone had known the temper of Judge Parmenter's mind; and having divined what the verdict would be, he had not listened to it. Instead, he had taken the night boat to New York. There he appealed his case to a friend in the Post Office, who appealed it to the Post Office Department in Washington. On April 7 he succeeded in having the April issue of the *Mercury* officially barred from the United States mails.

Mencken received no direct notice of the action. He learned about it in a brief item in the New York *Record* while dining out in a Hoboken restaurant, but at once he grasped its meaning. Strictly speaking, the ban applied only to the April issue, and all the copies had long since passed through the mails. But suppose this ban should be followed by another against the May issue. The authorities could then declare that the *Mercury* was not a magazine in "continuous publication" and could withdraw its second-class mailing privileges. During World War I, Postmaster General Burleson had suppressed several radical magazines in just this way. With this dreadful possibility whirling in his head, he returned to Baltimore and took stock of the situation.

The "Hatrack" case had become a national sensation, not for any of its basic issues, but for the remarkable spectacle of Mencken in the toils of the law. "North, East, South, and West," all the interests that he had antagonized over the previous six years were joined in a chorus of derision. The press generally portrayed him as a salacious, publicity-seeking editor who deserved all the punishment that the courts or the Post Office could administer to him. Ministers of the Gospel denounced him as, at best, a superficial cynic "lost to the high ideals of life," at worst "a foul-minded satyr" with the morals of a streetwalker or a bootlegger. The Chamber of Commerce of Farmington, Missouri, the home of the original Hatrack, passed resolutions against him. The police officials of Ingham County, and Poughkeepsie, New York, banned the April *Mercury*, and elsewhere they threatened to follow suit.

Universally, librarians withdrew the magazine from their reading rooms, either because they deplored its obscenity or because it was so much in demand that it constituted a nuisance.

Within a month, the storm would spread to Canada, a Member of Parliament demanding that the *Mercury* be barred from the Dominion because its June issue contained a "treasonable" editorial about the decline of British culture. Nor would Mencken improve his foreign relations by his rejoinder: "I can only say that the *American Mercury* acknowledges no allegiance to King George V, and that it is interested in definitions of treason framed by Canadian politicians only as it is interested in other amusing imbecilities."

Standing with Mencken in this tumult was only a small group made up of college boys, Socialists, apostles of companionate marriage, miscellaneous freethinkers, and Sinclair Lewis, then in Kansas City. Lewis was at work on *Elmer Gantry,* with L. M. Birkhead, a freethinking clergyman recommended to him by Mencken, as his consultant. Yet he found time to prepare a scorching statement for the Kansas City press. "Yes, indeed," he wrote, "I am very glad to hear that Mr. Mencken—or Apollo as we usually call him at the Algonquin—is being properly dealt with by T. Frank Chase, the Postal Department, the smart set of Farmington, Missouri, and like authorities on art and good manners. This fellow Mencken has been going around insisting that all of us know what all of us know, and if such a doctrine were to be accepted, the Church and Calvin Coolidge would be ruined." A few weeks later, Lewis erupted under full steam. He stood up in the pulpit of a Kansas City church, declared his agnosticism, and defied God to strike him dead. By so doing, he succeeded in diverting some of the national indignation from the stout figure of the Sage of Baltimore to his own willing and slender frame.

In Washington, one other powerful voice was lifted in Mencken's behalf, that of Senator James A. Reed of Missouri. An isolationist, an anti-Wilsonian who had been denied a seat at the Democratic National Convention in 1920, a bitter antagonist of Prohibition, the Ku Klux Klan, and hundred-per-cent Americanism, and currently the chief thorn in the side of President Coolidge, he had long since been nominated as the *Mercury*'s candidate for President and he did not hesitate to reciprocate the favor now. He offered to plead Mencken's case against the Post Office without fee. His offer rejected (he declared, incidentally, that Mencken was the only man of his acquaintance who had ever refused his free counsel), he drew up a bill to strip the Post Office of its censorship powers. In the House of Representatives a Socialist Congressman gave the scheme a thorough airing. But nobody was interested. Other Congressmen regarded the Sage as the big, bad wolf forever beyond the protection of the laws; President Coolidge said that he never read the *Mercury* because he had heard that it was against him.

In the Scopes trial, the Sage had taken it for granted that in Tennessee, at least, he would be outnumbered by odds of hundreds of thousands to one: he had gone about his business heedless of the most violent protests. But this time his confidence was shaken. This time, he was confronted, not with a spontaneous mob reaction, but with what seemed to be nothing less than an organized conspiracy to drive him out of public life. From one end of the nation to the other, a trap was being set for him, and he could see no way of getting out of it. Plaintively, he looked at the forces arrayed against him. He could understand the hostility of the clergy, of the politicians, of the Comstocks; he could excuse the apathy of the literary people. What he could neither understand nor excuse was the attitude of the press. Why, he asked himself, did the other editors fail to realize that the "Hatrack" case was one in which all of them had a stake—that, in fact, he was now their standard bearer?

If Mencken's rationality had not been grossly distorted at this point, the answer to his question would have been perfectly obvious to him. In the first place, the classic champions of the press had not gone out of their way to belittle the achievements of their fellow editors, nor questioned the competence of their fellow reporters because they could not write an article of *Mercury* standards. In the second place, they had fought on issues in the main stream of American idealism (the greatest of them, Elijah Lovejoy, had been an Abolitionist), while in the "Hatrack" case only the most sophisticated newspapers, like the New York *World* and the New York *Times*, could understand why it was so important for Mencken to print an article about a prostitute. Finally, the champions of the press had all taken themselves quite seriously. And by biting the coin at Brimstone Corner, Mencken had simply confirmed the general impression that the "Hatrack" case was a publicity stunt in the regular Mencken vein.

In any case, he still believed that if only he could clear up the misunderstanding about his motives, many of his colleagues would come rallying to his banner. He wrote two appeals—the first a mimeographed sheet addressed to editors and publishers for their private information; the second a brochure addressed "To the Friends of the *American Mercury.*" In both of them he explained in unadorned, almost painfully simple prose, that the "Hatrack" case was a serious effort to destroy the Comstock tyranny in Boston and elsewhere. "We have made absolutely no effort to capitalize the publicity that has flowed out of the contest," he wrote. "We know that our friends will have no doubt of our bona fides."

The response to these appeals was not encouraging: only two papers, Carter Glass's Lynchburg (Va.) *News* and Arthur Vandenberg's Grand Rapids (Mich.) *Herald* were converted by them, the latter with many reservations. Meanwhile the *Mercury* office was flooded with orders for copies of the forbidden issue, and the circulation manager waited impatiently for permission to fill them. Any profit to be had therefrom, he argued, had already been offset by the loss in advertising revenues. Mencken, however, enforced the policy of bona fides as though his very survival depended on it.

A few days later he retreated behind even stronger defenses. Reviewing the proofs of the May issue, he noticed that it would contain an article entitled "Sex and the Co-Ed." The article was completely innocent, its conclusion being that the co-eds behaved themselves very well despite many legends to the contrary, and it was written by one of the most promising young *Mercury* authors, Bernard DeVoto, under the nom de plume "John August." Nevertheless, if only because of its subject, it would surely attract the Comstocks, and with a second and final ban by the Post Office hanging over his head, he could take no chances. Accordingly he instructed

Angoff to substitute "On Learning to Play the Cello," by Doris Stevens (then Mrs. Dudley Malone), for the sex article. This quick change involved the confiscation of thousands of printed or half-printed magazines and drained $8000 out of the *Mercury's* war chest, but it accomplished its purpose. On April 17 (only two days late) the May issue was delivered to its readers without dissent from the Post Office, Chase, or any other Comstock agency, and on April 18 Mencken breathed easily again.

[ 4 ]

By this time it was clear (to the outsider, at least) that most of Mencken's injuries had been self-inflicted as precautions against remote dangers and that in all other respects the case was progressing as well as could be expected. One week after the Parmenter decision, the Federal District Court of Boston had awarded him a second major victory over Chase's Watch and Ward Society. The Society was enjoined for two years from threatening news dealers, and at any time during that period it could be sued for damages up to $50,000. Almost at once, the Society's position had deteriorated. The Police Commissioner had declared that henceforth his own officials would review all the Society's rulings before enforcing them; many formerly active members of the Society had resigned, and in response to these pressures a new leadership had come to the fore. Through various intermediaries, they informed Mencken that Chase's action had never been authorized by them and that if only he would vacate the injunction, Chase would make a public apology.

In the personal feud between Mencken and Chase, clearly the latter had met his Nemesis. Since that fateful March 30 when he had first trod on the Sage's toes, his every action had miscarried. In three months of litigation, he could claim only one small success—the conviction of the news vendor Caragianes in the Cambridge courts; and as a result of his many failures, he had slipped from being the chief censor of the Watch and Ward Society to its whipping boy. Nominally he was still its Secretary, but even this could have afforded him little comfort, for if and when Mencken pressed home the damage suit, he would be expected to pay a large share of the bill. On October 25 he contracted pneumonia with pulmonary complications. In the course of this illness, according to the newspapers, he "suffered a shock which caused a relapse." He died on November 3.

The nature of this "shock" may have mystified the public, but it held no mystery for the Sage. Asked by his friends what had happened to the Reverend Mr. Chase, he said bluntly, "We killed him." Mencken wrote in retrospect: "His death did not greatly surprise me. Like all agnostics I am somewhat superstitious, and one of my superstitions is to the effect that men who set out to do me evil not infrequently die suddenly." This was, indeed, his spooky season: within little more than a year, three of his archenemies, William Jennings Bryan, Stuart P. Sherman, and now the Reverend T. Frank Chase, had been abruptly called away, all of them cursing his name at or near the end.

Still, Mencken was not satisfied. Chase's associates on the Watch and Ward executive committee, including the Harvard dignitaries, remained very much alive, and he was determined that, by one means or another, every one of them should be punished. Repeatedly he urged his lawyers to proceed with the damage suits. But after patient inquiry the lawyers informed him that this was not feasible, because the *Mercury* had suffered little damage in actual fact and none that would stand up in the courts. Reluctantly, Mencken agreed to a more moderate line: to force the Society to guarantee safe conduct for all Knopf publications in the Boston market in return for the lifting of the injunction. By this time, however, the Society had recovered much of its former assurance. The bait was attractive to its officers, but not attractive enough to induce them to make any serious sacrifices for it. In the ensuing stalemate, they gave Knopf all the protection that he had asked for, including safe-conduct for "Hatrack" in book form, but towards other publishers they were more intolerant than ever. In rapid succession they black-listed the works of Dreiser, Upton Sinclair, Jim Tully, Julia Peterkin, Lion Feuchtwanger, and Bertrand Russell.

Two decades later, when the moral climate had become less severe and the Boston censorship a national joke, Mencken would receive the vindication that was now denied him. Also, in the case of *Esquire* v. *Walker*, Thurman Arnold, once a Mencken protégé, but then a circuit court judge, would refer sympathetically to the indignities that his mentor had suffered from the Post Office, and would advise that agency to meddle no longer with the public morals and to stick to the "more prosaic function" of delivering the mails. But at this point Mencken knew only that he had plunged into the most dangerous venture of his career and spent $20,000 of the *Mercury*'s funds in order to destroy the Comstocks, and that, as a result, they were more strongly entrenched than ever. In April 1927 the Boston *Herald* asked him to comment on the latest victim of the censorship, Sinclair Lewis's *Elmer Gantry*. His reply was so bitter that it was not published. The *Herald*, the Watch and Ward Society, and the other Boston Comstocks, he declared, should complete their "long and heroic crusade" by suppressing Harvard University. "It is more dangerous to the moron *Kultur* than a dozen *Elmer Gantrys*."

*CHAPTER 14*

# Hollywood: the Dead-end Road

## [ 1 ]

DESPITE THE DISAPPOINTMENT of the Boston battlefield, Mencken had not only achieved his twenty-year ambition to set the nation on its ear, but had achieved it to a degree that Nietzsche, Shaw, and his other iconoclastic masters might have envied. Yet even this aspect of the case did not satisfy him. For when he looked at the portrait of himself that had been broadcast from one end of the nation to the other, he could hardly recognize it. The face was his, but the character was that of a bankrupt demagogue far different from the artist and man of ideas that he had always believed himself to be. And though it was obviously a caricature, drawn by "jealous and cowardly" editors, he could not at this point explain away its element of truth.

A few months after Brimstone Corner, his eyes were opened even wider at a dinner in a New York hotel with the screen star Rudolph Valentino. Valentino was also having celebrity troubles. The Chicago *Tribune* had accused him of starting a vogue of pink talcum powder among the male customers of Chicago hotels. In reply, Valentino in New York had challenged the editorial writer to a duel. But the writer had laughed him off and the press generally dismissed him as a publicity seeker. Somewhere he had read an article by the Sage of Baltimore; in his distress he had sought out this wise man to ask his counsel.

"You should have passed over the gibe of the Chicago journalist," Mencken advised Valentino. "Or better still—hit him back with one of your own. You should have kept away from reporters in New York. Now the mischief's done. There's nothing you can do about it. Let the farce die a natural death." But no advice could salve Valentino's wound, and stripping off his jacket as Mencken did, he poured out the whole story of his life and disappointments. As Mencken listened, all his preconceptions vanished. He discerned in his dinner companion not the vain, lecherous character that he had naturally attributed to Valentino (he had never actually seen him on the screen) but a gentleman "of relatively civilized feelings thrown into a situation of intolerable vulgarity." Moreover, between his own experience and that of Valentino, he found a strange and disturbing parallel. Fame had deceived them both. In neither case had it brought contentment; in both cases it had proved a disillusioning and somewhat degrading snare.

Meanwhile, Mencken prepared three more books for his shelf—*Americana* (a collection of items from the *American Mercury* department), *Prejudices: Fifth Series,* and *Notes on Democracy.* Yet even here he could not shake off his disgust and disillusionment. *Notes on Democracy* was to have been the definitive statement of his political creed; he had worked at it off and on for almost a decade. But now, after a few frantic weeks of mechanical writing, he sent it off to the printer fully aware that it was a "half-baked" book that would add nothing to his stature. After he had pieced together the other books in the same way, his friends became concerned about him. Lynn R. Meekins, the editor who had given him his first upward boost on the Baltimore *Herald,* told him: "It is about time you made a better distribution of the burden. Let a few skilled Georges relieve you of the things that are not essentially your own. You are too valuable to waste." Mencken became acutely conscious of the fact that he had had no vacation since his visit to the ex-Kaiser in 1922. On September 10 he wrote to Irita Van Doren, "I need 2 or 3 weeks of absolute idleness, or I shall blow up. I am a tough old man, but the last year has nearly finished me."

[ 2 ]

In this state of mind, Mencken naturally turned to Joseph Hergesheimer. Though most of his other literary friendships had lapsed, this one remained as secure as ever. Mencken admired Joe first as a stylist so gifted that even his grammatical errors were landmarks in literary history, and second as an aristocrat who was the very archetype of what the literary man should be. On certain aspects of the literary life, the two men differed. Joe was a gin drinker, not a beer drinker; he wore fabulously expensive silk pajamas; he adorned his elegant mansion in West Chester, Pennsylvania, with "suave beds" and early American appointments. But whenever Mencken attended one of the parties in the Dower House, he always dressed himself in an imaginary suit of velvet pants and an imaginary bagwig "like an eighteenth-century profiteer," and he always found relief for "what ailed him."

In June of this dismal year, Joe provided Henry with a particularly exhilarating week end, its chief attraction being Aileen Pringle, the most "civilized" of the silent screen stars. Joe "glorified" her as a "suave and fragrant woman," and Henry could find no fault except that when he discussed music with her, she insisted on doing all the talking. Henry drank a gallon of Bacardi rum (or, at least, Joe thought he did); for the first and possibly the last time, he danced to jazz music, with a derby on his head and with his bowleggedness very much in evidence. On the lawn he played croquet with Aileen, and when his game blew up, he threw the croquet balls at his partner. Meanwhile Hergesheimer ground away with his amateur movie camera, making a record of the scene so that later he could confront the sober Sage with the drunken. Henry needed no reminders of his dissipation. On his return to Hollins Street he wrote Joe: "I feel like the poor girl who went to San Jose with the sailor."

This party was such a success that all the principals agreed to have another one in Hollywood in the fall. Joe was expected there for some scenario work; Aileen, of course, would be on location; and Henry would at last get his "2 or 3 weeks, maybe more, of absolute idleness." On sober second thought, the Sage must have been surprised at the decision. Hollywood indeed! He had never sat through more than two or three films. He regarded the movie capital as a national fountainhead of intellectual and spiritual corruption, promoting "the mean admiration of mean things." Four years before, he had admonished Hergesheimer for selling his talent to the producers, and it would not then have occurred to him that he could find any more relaxation amid the scenes of Joe's moneygrubbing than in a nail factory. Yet under the warmth of Joe's friendship his prejudices had become tempered.

Whatever else Hollywood might be, one thing was certain: the town was no sanctuary from the press. Elsewhere his every movement raised a cloud of controversy, but in California the controversy began fully a month before his departure. On September 10, Upton Sinclair informed the Pasadena newspapers that he had invited the Sage while in southern California to stay at the Sinclair estate. Thereupon the head of the local Rotary declared that Mencken might speak to his followers. He explained that he knew very little about Mencken "except that he is a well-known writer," and "I am broad-minded enough to meet a famous writer on a friendly personal basis, whether he believes in the things I do or not." Quietly, other Rotarians convinced the leader that he was much too tolerant, and in a violent turnabout he withdrew the offer, saying, "If Mencken's attitudes and writings are such as they are reported to be, I don't think we care to countenance him." As to the rest of Pasadena, opinion was divided. The University Club barred the *American Mercury* from its reading rooms. The local boosters demanded that Mencken bring his furniture and move in with the rest of the literary colony.

But during his spiritual disillusionment Mencken had thought out, or felt out, a method of dealing with just such "a violent bath of publicity" as this. He was, after all, the master of anticlimax. It was his way, when he disliked something, not to shun it, but to embrace it with open arms and tickle it in the ribs. If the American press regarded him as a pornographer, an ogre, and a clown, he would turn the tables on them by giving them all the hokum they expected and more.

His schedule had been amended to include a swing from Richmond to New Orleans with Paul Patterson as a preliminary to his meeting with Hergesheimer in Hollywood. He would join Patterson in cementing relations between the *Sunpapers* and the liberal newspapers of the South. But on the eve of their tour the publisher was frankly uneasy about the outlook. If a remote settlement like Pasadena could be so violently stirred up by the prospect of a visit from the Sage, what would happen in the South, close at hand? Mencken did not share Patterson's qualms. On October 14 when the two men boarded the train in Baltimore, he was in a festive mood. While he expressed his regrets at leaving his home-brews, he said he would console himself by scattering hops and sauerkraut seeds from the car window on the bone-dry Southern soil.

In Richmond, Mencken made the opening bow of this devil's holiday. To the reporters who met him there, he was genial, infectious, and disarming. He called Richmond a perfect city. He explained that he had no other mission on this Southern tour than to meet people, have a good time, and call the attention of the Democratic electorate to the Presidential mettle of Virginia's favorite son, Governor Harry S. Byrd. His next stop was Chapel Hill, an oasis of civilization in the Southern desert. Here he talked with Professor Howard W. Odum in a hotel lobby while fifty college boys peered at him from behind the rubber trees. Yet again he had nothing but the most generous press statements about the citizenry of North Carolina. He proposed the nomination of North Carolina's favorite son, Governor Angus McLean. All of Patterson's skittishness evaporated when he observed that the local papers printed Mencken's benedictions on their front pages and discussed them editorially with great seriousness. Though some grumbled that Mencken's conversion was too late, the Winston-Salem *Journal*, among others, greeted it with cheers. "Mr. Mencken may be badly off on some things," it stated, "but he is sound as a dollar when he says that Governor McLean would make a good President of the United States. Maybe Mencken is not such a 'bad citizen' after all." From town to town and city to city, the two men moved so fast that they outdistanced the interstate communications. They were deep in Georgia before it was discovered that Mencken's enthusiasm for favorite sons applied to all states and that he was "parading through Dixie with his tongue in his cheek, having as big a time as a small boy who whacks hornets' nests with a switch."

Nevertheless, the Sage had created an unprecedented and indissoluble era of good feeling between himself and the South. Wherever he went, town dignitaries moved in to lionize him. So much hospitality was proffered the pair that they could have eaten every day and slept every night like a conquering army, living on the fat of the land. But it was Mencken's rule never to accept such hospitality. Instead, he beamed upon one and all—hard-fighting liberals and unregenerate Confederates. In Raleigh the two men called on the moralist Josephus Daniels; in his absence they "paid tribute to him by kissing his desk." In Columbus, Georgia, they visited Mr. and Mrs. Julian

Harris, the most thoroughgoing Menckenian editors in the South, bestowing upon Mrs. Harris the flag of the Maryland Free State as a reward for her very real struggles against bigotry. In New Orleans, Marshall Ballard, Sanford Jarrell, and others of the *Item-Tribune* throttled Mencken before he could urge the Presidential nomination upon their mayor, and they took him on the rounds of the French Quarter, where wines and absinthe cocktails flowed freely. The fire chiefs of Louisiana, Arkansas, Kansas, and Missouri, meeting in convention at his hotel, also regaled the Sage, and he graciously accepted their offer to make him an honorary member of their society. A photograph of Mencken with a cigar in his left hand and his mouth agape, wearing the chief's white hat and surrounded by delegates from the "Bible Belt," was printed in the rotogravure sections of many papers. Mencken's followers who saw it could not believe that this was the same man who had once taken so much delight in setting fire to his enemies' shirttails.

Amid all this fanfare, the Sage managed to bring cheer to the Atlanta novelist Frances Newman, whose unhappy life would be terminated by suicide two years hence. Sweeping through Atlanta, he took her with him to the nearby Stone Mountain, the Confederate memorial. She later annotated news photographs of this excursion for Cabell's benefit. "Observe," she wrote, "how pleased Mencken obviously is with Stone Mountain and how pleased I obviously am with Mencken." In a letter to Lamar Trotti, she wrote: "I wish you had been here to see the absurdity of Mencken with his hands in his pockets, gazing with the yokels at the Great Memorial to the Late Confederacy. And buying a half dollar for his little niece."

Mencken complained to Miss Newman because Cabell had been given a look at the page proofs of her forthcoming novel, *The Hard-Boiled Virgin,* whereas he had been neglected. She repaired the slight by lending him her only copy of the manuscript, though she needed it for proofreading. Somehow Mencken found time between Atlanta and El Paso to read this appalling memoir of sexual frustration and to observe how he himself was described there under a thin disguise as the one who had introduced the author to the great world of letters. Cabell had called *The Hard-Boiled Virgin* "the most profound book yet written by an American woman." Now Mencken sent the manuscript back from El Paso with the note: "I go with Cabell all the way and even beyond. You have done an original and first-rate job and I kiss your hand."

A few days later Mencken slipped into Hollywood alone and virtually unnoticed; Patterson had turned back at New Orleans, and Hergesheimer had not yet arrived. However, Mencken had lost nothing of his gift for press-agentry, and he used his brief respite to plan and stage-manage the most vulgar of all his extravaganzas—one that would shame even the professionals of the glamour capitol.

On November 3, an hour before Joe's arrival, he had the platform of the Southern Pacific Railway station surrounded with ten batteries of motion picture cameras (without films). He had a white open touring car properly chauffeured on the street, and a squadron of motorcycles mounted by actual police waiting to provide escort. All these props he had procured through the friendly offices of Walter Wanger. James R. Quirk, the editor of *Photoplay* magazine, Anita Loos and her husband John Emerson, and Aileen Pringle joined him to form the official welcoming committee. As the "City of Angels" thundered into the station, they all gathered around it, waving little American flags. When Joe finally stepped down from his Pullman car, he was given no time to stretch his legs or to grasp what it was all about. Mencken hugged him and kissed him on both cheeks. Aileen Pringle hung a garland of roses around his neck and presented him with a huge papier-mâché domino in memory of the games they had played together. Then the news photographers went to work. For one posed picture, Hergesheimer stood placidly in the center with his cheeks inflated and the brim of his hat pulled down over his tortoise-shell glasses, with Miss Loos holding on to his right arm and Miss Pringle standing off in the shadows on the left. Detached from the group, Mencken propped himself against the car step with his right arm, held his hat and an American flag in the other, and planted his right foot on the domino. To be sure, no matinee idol would ever have got himself into such a contorted position, but the Sage grinned self-consciously at the cameraman in the conviction that his show was a great success.

As the police escort cleared the way for them, this intellectual group rode conspicuously in their white car from the station to the Ambassador Hotel. At length Joe was installed in the lower floor of one of the hotel bungalows, "Siesta," Mencken having already pre-empted the upper. The Hollywood reporters were flabbergasted by the performance. They weren't sure who was fooling whom, but were inclined to believe that Mencken was the dupe. "They're making the old boy like it," one of them wrote. "This is the sort of thing he harpoons all the time and they're giving him a double dose."

For the next week or so, Mencken seemed more like himself again, exploring the "imbecilities of the Los Angeles area," sometimes with Hergesheimer, sometimes alone. In Pasadena, at a public luncheon arranged by Upton Sinclair, he bantered pleasantly with his old friend and chopping block; he suggested that Sinclair do his next muckraking novel on Duke University, "a great Fundamentalist college for yokels," and told him sententiously, "In a few more years the only place in America where you'll be able to make a Socialist speech without going to jail will be Maryland, and there are no Socialists there!" In Los Angeles, Mencken talked so loudly and so often about being baptized by Aimee Semple McPherson that soon Mrs. McPherson claimed him as one of her converts, though she admitted that the baptism didn't seem to take. Mencken had visited Mrs. McPherson's temple, but on that occasion his thoughts were, as he reported to Dr. Raymond Pearl, carnal, not spiritual. "I sat under Aimee yesterday. Her Sex Appeal is tremendous. But don't believe the liars who say that I am her new radio operator. I have troubles enough in Hollywood, what with the enervating climate and the general interest in literati."

In the evening, dressed in formal wear, he circulated around the movie colony. At Norma Talmadge's tea he was introduced to Jack Dempsey. He was also entertained by King Vidor, Walter Wanger, and other producers who told him about the problems of movie-making. They were all very intellectual, very serious. Mencken was impressed. "The movie dogs," he told Dr. Pearl, were very respectable craftsmen and "compared with the rest of the population, [they] actually seem like an ancient Italian noblesse." He was just beginning to feel at home in the movie colony when one night Jim Cruze, the producer of *The Covered Wagon,* gave him a party in the regular Hollywood vein. Jim Tully, the novelist, made all the arrangements.

The host greeted Mencken gruffly, "I'm Jim Cruze and I've never read a God-damned thing you ever wrote." To which Mencken replied, "Well, I never saw one of your God-damned pictures—that makes us both Elks." Later in the evening, Mencken found himself holding forth to an audience consisting of Hedda Hopper, Irene Rich, Aileen Pringle, and Betty Compson, who was, at the time, Mrs. Cruze. "When I was a youngster in Baltimore," Mencken said expansively, "the girls in the sporting houses called me professor." Betty Compson stopped him, saying, "I thought your face was familiar." At this, Cruze laughed so much that he spilled his drink. Tully, too, was highly amused, and he was amused again when he heard that Mencken's chauffeur was too drunk to drive home, and that Miss Pringle had taken over the wheel while Mencken and Hergesheimer held the chauffeur prisoner on the back seat. Still Tully was not satisfied. "The tragedy of it all," he confided to Nathan, "is there was so much out here for our friend to see, but he hung around with Hergesheimer, Quirk, and the intellectual ladies. Now he'll go home and be mad because he saw a chiropractic hospital out here, and I might have introduced him to damsels whose chins are still one."

On November 14, Mencken left Hollywood for San Francisco. Six years before, on a previous visit to the city, George Sterling, the poet, had provided him with one of the most memorable weeks of his life. Perhaps now he would recapture something of its *gemütlich* quality. Once more Sterling would take him on the rounds of the Bohemian quarters; once more he would find shelter from the inanities of the press. Indeed, with Hollywood behind him, Mencken believed that he had shaken off the curse of his notoriety once and for all; but in this, he was mistaken.

Weeks before, Sterling had accumulated a large stock of whiskey against Mencken's coming. Prematurely he had tested large quantities of it, and while Mencken was now speeding to the rendezvous, Sterling was down with a crippling attack of alcoholic neuritis. At the station in San Francisco the Sage was met, not by Sterling, but by Gobind Behari Lal, a science reporter for the San Francisco *Examiner,* who conveyed Sterling's regrets. Nor did Mencken find Sterling that evening, as he had hoped, at a dinner given by Charles Norris in his honor.

The next day, Mencken called on the poet at his room in the Bohemian Club to persuade him to come along on a round of studio parties. He knocked at the door, and hearing no response from within, concluded that the poet was asleep. On the upper floor he talked briefly with some of the club members who were playing cards. They assured him that Sterling had not left his room for several days. From the club, Mencken was taken by Lal to Russian Hill, to the studio of Idwal Jones, one of the *Mercury* authors. There he was treated to an extraordinary Hindu dish, a duck cooked in coconut milk and spiced with rare herbs. The Sage's face grew ruddier than ever as he swam in a hospitality that was very much to his taste. He exclaimed over the infinite loveliness of Jones's two-year-old daughter with her blonde hair in the shafts of the setting sun. He provided the company with what Lal described as a "gorgeous fireworks of humor." Nevertheless, he could not forget his friend's curious confinement; repeatedly he remarked to Lal, "I tremble for George."

The next day Mencken was inspecting the printing house of John Henry Nash, when an Associated Press man brought him the news that Sterling had been found dead in his room with a half-empty flagon of prussic acid at his side. It did not take the Sage long to reconstruct his own part in the tragedy. Sterling, obviously, had felt it a terrible humiliation that the Sage had come expressly to visit him and that, by his own indulgence, he had been unable to entertain him. The shame must have seemed unbearable as he lay in his room the night that Mencken called, and as the chatter and laughter of the company above came down through the ceiling. But this alone would not have finished him if he had not also been aware that at fifty-seven his body could no longer withstand his accustomed way of life. "It was almost an ideal finish," Mencken said to the reporters. "He had come to his time and he knew it. Like any other great poet, he must have thought long about suicide as the best means to end it all when the time should come. At the proper moment, George merely adhered to his theories. It was the best way out."

As the foremost literary genius of the town, the poet was entitled to far more impressive obsequies than the few words that Mencken spoke at a press interview. He would have a public funeral attended by numerous California dignitaries; Mencken, of course, would make a speech. But even before the autopsy had been completed,

Mencken shyly slipped out of the city. Soon his train was rolling through the salt flats of Utah, eastbound for Baltimore.

[ 3 ]

For almost two months Mencken had searched across the face of the nation for a new lease on life. And when he again assumed his labors in his Hollins Street office, he knew that he had failed to find it. First of all, no one had understood what he was about. Fame, like birth, death, and failure, was apparently much too serious a matter to be dealt with in vaudeville style; and the man who flouted it brought down on his head a notoriety twice compounded. While *Vanity Fair* thought that Mencken on tour had "never once compromised his position as commander-in-chief of militant public opinion in America," other observers were not so sure. When they were not utterly mystified by Mencken's antics, they decided that the publicity of the Brimstone Corner affair had gone to his head. In his "It Seems to Me" column, Heywood Broun conducted a lively discussion of the Mencken psyche, printing letters describing the Sage as "Napoleon retreating from Moscow" and as an idol who "gave himself the leg and landed in the middle of the photogravure section."

Discussing his own reactions with Nathan, Mencken wrote: "Your words in 'Clinical Notes' in the forthcoming *Mercury* on the motives behind the yearnings for rural peace are full of sagacity. I wish you would make a tour through the country as I did. You would come back as I have come back, thoroughly disillusioned and disheartened. I got an immense amount of notice but I believe that I could honestly say that ninety-nine percent of it was disgusting. It left me feeling lonely and miserable. . . . The rural retirement scheme is absolutely nonsensical and I can think of no satisfactory alternative. You, yourself, at least have something ahead in the way of a change. But I see no possibility of anything of the sort for me. I'd only be ten times more miserable."

Moreover, as he sat at his desk in Hollins Street, his disillusionment became more profound than ever. For seven years he had been trying to bring the "first-rate men" like himself into positions of power and influence, and thereby to inaugurate in America a new and more civilized era. Perhaps he had never been very clear about the fine points of his program; on many occasions, in fact, he had denied that he had any program at all. But when he looked at the total of his achievements, he could find nothing in it of honor or significance. His personal following was comprised in large part not of "first-rate men," but of shoddy craftsmen, college sophomores, and intellectual snobs. On the other hand, the third-rate men of the "booboisie" had remained, and clearly would remain, as firmly entrenched as ever. Even in the matter of stimulation of public debate he had apparently failed of his purpose. On all sides, by friends as well as enemies, he had been misquoted and misrepresented, and in retrospect his whole campaign was as vague as the last election contest between the Republican Calvin Coolidge and the Democrat John W. Davis.

No doubt while writing to Nathan, he thought of their "golden years" together on the *Smart Set*. He had been happy then. His daily life in New York had been a round of ribaldries, and at home he had produced his most enduring works, including the first edition of *The American Language*. Outwardly his position had not been very favorable: he was relatively unknown, and he could not reply very effectively to the patriots who harassed him. But if he had resisted his "irresistible impulse" to "crack their heads," if he had stuck to his old routine of "slow, steady striving," no doubt he would have been as happy now as he had been then. Perhaps he recalled that Nathan had warned him of this; perhaps he was still too proud to acknowledge his debt to the other. At any rate, he was determined that, by one means or another, he would resume the pattern of his former life.

Without fanfare he commenced work upon a project as far removed from the current scene as possible—a semi-artistic, semischolarly history of world religion. But here again he could muster none of his former enthusiasm. "I am constantly asking myself," he told Nathan, "if it is worth while to waste so much energy upon an enterprise whose rewards are so unsatisfactory." In another spasm of despondency he declared: "What could be more preposterous than keeping alive? Yet nearly all of us cling to life with desperate devotion, even when the length of it remaining is palpably slight, and filled with agony." Life, he concluded, was neither tragic nor comic, but simply a bore, and human progress (which he had once regarded as a glorious upward struggle towards the superman) seemed now simply a "progress to the death house—a gray emptiness." Still, he pursued the project. During the winter of 1926–1927 he made notes upon several religious encyclopedias and a hundred learned works. The following spring he typed out the first chapter of *Treatise on the Gods*. "The end is always a vanity," he explained dejectedly. "But the means remain. In them lies the secret of what is called contentment, that is, the capacity to postpone suicide for at least another day."

*CHAPTER 15*

# Retreat to Matrimony

[ 1 ]

IN THE SUMMER OF 1919, when Mencken was boasting of his bachelorhood and defying any woman to compromise it, Sara Haardt, his future bride, was upholding the woman's point of view as chairman of the Montgomery suffragettes. One day some fellow agitators, most of them Yankees, were arrested in her territory. Sara protested. Her brown eyes blazing with indignation, she dared the cops to lay hands on the women, belabored them hotly, and eventually routed them. Later the Mayor himself apologized to her for the incident and officially welcomed her friends to the city. There was nothing remarkable about this, for she was the daughter of a poor but locally well-connected family. Nevertheless, Sara failed to carry the state for woman's suffrage, and when the Nineteenth Amendment became part of the Constitution, she could take no credit for it.

In the fall she resumed her studies at Goucher College. She mingled with a class of wartime sophisticates who drank Coca-Colas and smoked cigarettes in defiance of the campus authority, edited the college literary magazine, and made Phi Beta Kappa—all the while paying her way as college postmistress. At her graduation she appeared to her classmates to be a "soulful high-brow." But below the surface her spirit was now in full revolt against "the cloying Southern air and everything in this cloying, sickish, decadent land!" Her plan was to live in Baltimore and continue her studies in English and psychology. For the moment, however, this plan was not feasible, and for the next two years she taught school in Montgomery. Meanwhile she was finding a niche for herself in Mencken's Southern Renaissance. She placed a series of sketches of Alabama types in the *Reviewer* in July 1922, and soon afterwards was discovered by the *Smart Set.*

It was upon her return to Goucher in 1923 that she was introduced to the Sage. The occasion was his annual Goucher lecture; the scene, the home of a faculty member. At twenty-four Sara was an exceptionally handsome woman. She was thin and tall (she and Mencken were exactly the same height, five feet eight inches), with large but shapely features, long brown hair, brown eyes, and a doll-like complexion. She laughed easily and carried herself with great poise. Indeed, she was then, and would remain henceforth, far more accomplished as a woman than as a writer. One of Mencken's friends later remarked that while Mencken had met many women authors, he had never before met one who was a thoroughgoing Southern lady. Mencken vigorously denied this, but it was unquestionably true that Sara made a very favorable impression on him.

After this meeting, Sara began to move in the aura of the Sage, with occasional correspondence and meetings. The next year, when Sara went to a tuberculosis sanatorium in the Maryland countryside, Mencken visited her and brought her gifts. He had always been dutiful in his attentions to the sick and after a tragedy in his own home, he was even more so. At Christmas time, 1925, his mother had died following a tonsillectomy at the Johns Hopkins Hospital. Some months previously she had suffered a stroke that had partially paralyzed her hand, and if death had not intervened, her remaining days would probably have been filled with agony. Almost two months later, Mencken still had not reconciled himself to it. "I begin to realize how inextricably my life was interwoven with my mother's," he confessed to Dreiser. "A hundred times a day I find myself planning to tell her something, or ask her for this or that. It is a curious thing: the human incapacity to imagine finality. The house seems strange, as if the people in it were deaf and dumb. But all my life, I begin to believe, resolves itself into doing without."

When Sara returned to Baltimore, she became inevitably a confidante and a full-fledged member of his circle. He helped launch her as a free-lance writer, either printing her articles in the *Mercury* or advising her which offers to accept and which to reject. He gave dinners in a private room of the Rennert Hotel for the Raymond Pearls, the Hamilton Owenses, the Paul de Kruifs, the Willie Woollcotts, and the Hergesheimers, in various combinations, at which Sara sat by his side. Hergesheimer was especially enthusiastic about this "tonic" person. He entrusted her with the research for his Civil War story *Swords and Roses*. Also, in 1927, she worked through some twenty-five volumes of Mencken's press notices, extracting the items for *Menckeniana: a Schimpflexicon.*

Of all the friends who saw Henry and Sara together, Dorothy Hergesheimer was perhaps the most penetrating.

She observed a certain mellow glow radiating from the rough heart of her friend, and in August 1927 she broached a match between the two. "The idea is charming!" Mencken wrote her. "Ah, that it could be executed! But I already have one foot in the cemetery, and spies hint that she is mashed by a rich Babbitt in Birmingham, Ala. One more book, and I am done." Meanwhile, his public pronouncements on the sex war indicated that he was ripe for capitulation on the most conventional terms. At one interview he said: "If any woman of the proper resolution had ever made up her mind to marry me, I'd have succumbed like the rest of the poor dogs and to the tune of pathetic hosannahs." Moreover, the Nietzschean who had once advocated ingenious devices by which first-rate men could multiply their kind, through liaisons with other men's wives, now condemned polygamy, free love, birth control, and allied things. "The younger generation with its theories of companionate marriage is full of gas," he wrote in 1928 in an attack on Judge Ben Lindsey. "A normal man does not marry a woman thinking of her as a possible enemy, as the companionate marriage experts seem to believe. He marries thinking of her as a perpetual friend. He is willing to show her his secrets and to give her his full confidence. He is, in fact, eager to do it. The whole source of his delight in her is his trust in her. His hope, if he is normal, is for a complete merging of their interests." The personal significance of these remarks did not become clear until two years later.

It undoubtedly took courage for Sara to marry a man who was at once twenty years older than she and one of the most articulate bachelors in the world. At forty-nine Mencken was no longer in the mood to mock the blessings of domesticity, but the stigmata of the free man were still upon him. Indeed, he had publicly confessed his chief failing. "Every woman who enjoys the honor of witnessing me," he said, "sees at once that I'd make an impossible husband. I am too vain for the office. My interest in myself is so inordinate that it is obvious that nothing remains for a possible wife and child." On the other hand, if his egotism demanded plenty of room in his work, clearly it also thrived on peace, affection, and stability at home. So when Sara weighed the Sage's qualifications against his disqualifications on the practical side of the question, she made up her mind that he was a good risk. "A bachelor is likely to be interesting because he has had a varied life," she remarked later. "Suppose he is set in his ways. That too has its advantages. It is pleasant to live with someone who knows what he wants. It is comparatively simple to manage things. It is fumbling indecision which clutters life up."

The ceremony would perhaps have been performed in 1928 or 1929 if Sara had not had two long sieges of illness, both of them requiring major operations, and if she had not taken time out for her first novel, *The Making of a Lady*. On July 28, 1930, Mencken informed Dorothy Hergesheimer that all the obstacles had been surmounted. "If any scandal-mongers call you up and try to make you believe that Sara and I are to be joined in connubial bonds on August 27th don't deny it, for it is a fact. The solemn announcement will issue from Confederate G.H.Q. at Montgomery in about a week. Your congratulations I take for granted, for you know Sara, and so you know what a lovely gal she is. If you write to her please say nothing about my heavy drinking, or about the trouble with the girl in Red Lion, Pa., in 1917. I still maintain that I was innocent of any unlawful or immoral purpose.

"Wedding presents are absolutely forbidden, on penalty of the bastinado. I shall continue my book-writing business as usual. Sara also proposes to engage in literary endeavor, but I suspect that cooking, washing, and ironing will take up a lot of her time. Her novel, by the way, has been taken by Doubleday, and will be published shortly. Thus in one year she gets launched as an author and marries the handsomest man east of Needles, Calif."

On July 31 Mencken confessed to Hergesheimer, "I begin to show the classic tremors but hope to recover at the altar." On August 2 the engagement was made public. Sara subscribed completely to her fiancé's doctrine that "being married with all your friends about you is as private and discriminating as eating in the window of a restaurant." And she joined him in planning a "very *pianissimo*" wedding. More concretely, Mencken feared the attentions of the "Hearst brethren, who threaten to be too polite. They are not above busting into the church and shooting off flashlights." Thus the public was informed that the ceremony would take place on September 3, while only a few intimates knew that the actual date was a week earlier. The reporters were suspicious when Mencken's name turned up on the books of the Marriage License Bureau prematurely on August 21. But in explanation they had only Sara's remark, "I guess he just wants to be sure to have the license."

Meanwhile Sara had decided to have the ceremony in Baltimore rather than in Montgomery. This decision precipitated another problem. As unbelievers, both of them would have preferred a civil marriage with no assistance from the clergy. Maryland, however, did not recognize such marriages. Mencken managed a compromise between the letter and the spirit of the law by summoning back from retirement the Reverend Dr. Herbert Parrish. The latter had but recently advocated a new and more civilized God for America in the *American Mercury;* hence he could be relied upon not to take the affair too seriously.

The Saturday before the wedding, Mencken attended a meeting of the Saturday Night Club as usual, receiving the felicitations of the members and a shower of gifts that he could appreciate—a gold purse, a diamond-studded belt, a Benedict medal, all from a notions shop. On Tuesday night, the eve of the wedding, Mencken wrote to Dr. Pearl: "I greet you from the brink of the precipice! Curiously enough, I seem to be holding up fairly well. Perhaps I'll wobble a bit tomorrow when I see the actual sheriff. I am taking him a couple of jugs this evening."

At 4 P.M. the next day, the little wedding party gathered in the Church of St. Stephen the Martyr. The church was a half-timbered affair in an unpretentious neighborhood. Mencken's brother Charles had come from Oil City, Pennsylvania, for the occasion, while the Haardt family was represented chiefly by Sara's mother from Montgomery and her sister from Cincinnati. There were no interlopers. The bridegroom arrived at 4:28, two minutes before zero hour, accompanied by his brother August, the best man. He wore a pin-stripe business suit, the bride a simple crepe ensemble in summer brown, with a felt cloche hat in deeper brown and a spray of orchids. They were married in a brief ceremony according to High Church Episcopal rites, after which they departed in a shower of rice.

It had been Mencken's plan to spend the honeymoon at Max Brödel's place in Ontario, where he knew there would be plenty of Canadian ale (if also summer sports that he could conveniently ignore). Sara was more attracted by the Old World atmosphere of eastern Canada and there they went. For two weeks they explored the St. Lawrence Valley, passing through Montreal and Quebec down to the Maritimes. At Halifax they stayed at a small hotel which Mencken found idyllic. "There is a brisk breeze from the sea," he wrote his friends, "and the good red sun shines down." He had feared that marriage would ruin his thirst, but later reported that he performed "honorably," not only upon the wines and beer that were on sale throughout the Dominion, but also on Scotch supplied by *American Mercury* "customers" en route. Yet even on his honeymoon, the Sage was not allowed to forget his mission in the world. The reporters met the couple in Montreal on the day following their marriage, and asked Mencken for his political views. "Ramsay MacDonald," he told them, "is a kind of Methodist evangelist." As to the Hoover Administration, then involved with a deepening depression, he remarked, "It's a comic government, but perhaps it's as good as any. When dreadful things happen, people laugh and take the situation lightly."

The intrusions of a curious public grew to major proportions on the couple's return to New York. While Henry was at the *Mercury* office, Sara was confronted in their Algonquin suite by a lady reporter, Hally Pomeroy. She apologized to the reporter for her green velvet negligee and the water-wave net on her hair, and made every effort to escape the inquisition of an interview. When the reporter asked her questions, she pleaded that she didn't know what to say. "I haven't the knack for clever sayings. Ask Henry. He knows how to do that."

Mencken arrived at length, complaining of the heat, searching loudly for the White Rock and ice, answering the telephone, yet at the same time beaming upon his wife, upon the reporter, and upon the world. Sara prodded him smilingly to explain to the reporter the code of politeness upon which their successful three weeks of marriage was based. "Politeness," he said after a couple of moments thought, "is the absence of the reformer complex, of any desire to improve other people. Leave them alone. They're doing the best they can, poor fishes, wishing they were in heaven and afraid to get there. But then, of course, it's easy for her. She's married to a perfect specimen of German manhood with good appetite, an educated thirst, and a generally serene and amiable attitude of mind." His eyes sparkled when Sara agreed with him. "Now she isn't quite perfect," Mencken went on, "but her defects are so small it would be pedantic to improve them. That, naturally, is as it should be." The couple looked at each other and laughed, Pomeroy reported, "as children and thoroughly happy people laugh." They laughed, too, when Pomeroy recalled that they had married a week ahead of time and thus foiled their well-wishers. Sara mentioned the wedding date, August 27.

"Aha, so you remember it, do you?" the bridegroom asked.

"Of course, Henry," she drawled in all seriousness.

When Sara slowly and gracefully went off to dress for dinner, Mencken stared after her with demonstrative pride.

"She doesn't know what to say to reporters," he explained. "She'll learn. She's seen so many of them lately, she's gun-shy."

[ 2 ]

As Mrs. H. L. Mencken, Sara was a principal of the most newsworthy marriage since that of the Charles A. Lindberghs a little more than a year before, and one, moreover, that was a landmark in the history of "modern" marriages. To the modernists it was, of course, disappointingly old-fashioned, but to the conservatives, by the same token, it marked the capitulation of one of their greatest tormentors. It was a tacit admission of error, like that of Henry IV at Canossa, or Galileo's at the Papal Court. Upon its first announcement, all of Mencken's friends, except a handful of the very closest, were surprised, if not stunned. When the news reached the *Sun* office, John Owens, editor of the morning paper, remarked, "Well, I'll be God-damned." The following day he recovered from his confusion. He assured *Sun* readers that the Sage would make "a good husband and a grand provider."

As the news spread out across the country, it provoked a great deal of smug speculation and rib-tickling at the Sage's expense. The Little Rock (Ark.) *Democrat* welcomed him to the "uncivilized majority." The Louisville (Ky.) *Times* accepted the news as evidence that behind the withering satirist was a milder Mencken, given to "mellow, lenient contemplation" rather than to angry rages. But many papers asked how the shades of Nietzsche and Schopenhauer would regard this apostasy. The Columbus (Ohio) *State Journal* surmised they would hang their heads in shame; the Fort Wayne *News-Sentinel* that they were chuckling together over it. "Babbitts" everywhere were delighted. The Cosmopolitan Club of Chicago congratulated Mencken on "his return to fundamentals" and invited him to explain his new code at one of its meetings. From the hand of his and Sara's good friend Grover C. Hall, he received a copy of a resolution of the Kiwanis Club of Montgomery, offering him honorary membership and a certified copy of the Confederate States' Constitution with the compliments and good wishes of the Cradle of the Confederacy "from which he is snatching his bride."

Meanwhile reporters demanded an explanation, and Mencken gave them their due, discussing the theory of his marriage probably as thoroughly as any newlywed husband has ever discussed wedlock, with full replies to long questionnaires. It was the reporters' especial delight to confront him with his former doctrine. At first he made light of the contradiction. "I was formerly not as wise as I am now," he said; or he argued around it on the supernatural plane of discourse: "The Holy Spirit informed and inspired me. Like all other infidels I am very superstitious and always follow hunches. This one seemed to be a superb one." But the existence of contradictions and the admission that he had changed any article of his creed were extremely unpleasant to him, and in the end he insisted that he had always believed in monogamy. "My point of view, in fact, never alters," he said. "I detest converts above all things. I can't ever recall changing my mind about anything of the slightest importance." Even Sara was hard put at times to explain to reporters how she could both subscribe to Mencken's written doctrines and believe in the possibility of a successful marriage with him. His writings, she said, must be viewed as generalizations: they did not apply in all cases. Most of the embarrassing quotations came from *In Defense of Women.* After Sara's death, Mencken would prevent another wave of public discussion by refusing to reissue the book, despite a continuing demand for it.

As a result of Mencken's apostasy, George Jean Nathan was left as the last great articulate bachelor in America; and when Henry deserted the mountain pass, he tried to get George to come down with him. Nathan was in Paris when he received a cable from his friend, announcing what had happened. It concluded: "How about a double-header? My pastor offers inside summer rates." The cable was something of a shock. George had met Sara and suspected the imminence of a marriage; yet on his departure for Europe he had been assured by Henry himself that "marriage has never been further from my mind." George cut short his vacation and returned to the States, declaring that his friend now needed advice more than ever. But apart from this single expression of concern, Nathan was in no mood to belabor Mencken for his fall. "Age changes and mellows earlier opinions," he remarked. "Consistency is unimportant. Mencken and I both used to believe in Santa Claus and the wisdom of the President of the United States, but the passing years have changed all that." Nathan's remarks prompted the reporters to speculate upon an impending alliance between Nathan and Lillian Gish. Mencken himself joined them. "If George Jean Nathan is not married on or before February 14, 1932," he declared, "I engage forthwith to shave my head, submit to public baptism by the Hardshell

Baptist rite and go on the water wagon for ten days." For the sake of the dramatic unities, George should have capitulated pronto, but he did not.

[ 3 ]

The newly married couple settled down in a third-floor apartment at 704 Cathedral Street in Baltimore. It was in a brownstone dwelling and looked out upon Mount Vernon Place, a fashionable square that was flanked by the palaces of Baltimore's historic clipper merchants and dominated by a statue of George Washington on his highest pedestal. Next door to the south was a Christian Science church, and next door to the north was the Alcazar, a center of various fraternal orders. If Mencken would be disturbed on Sunday mornings by the "moanings and roarings" of the Christian Scientists, the location had compensatory advantages, he said, in that it was close to "Schellhase's kaif and several other excellent saloons."

The apartment was a seven-room affair on two levels, with separate working and living quarters below for the two authors and spacious "public rooms" above. With the aid of Anne (Mrs. Edmund) Duffy, her best friend, Sara had virtually completed the furnishings in the month before the wedding. Her taste was unmistakably in evidence. The enormous high-ceilinged living room was lined with satin Victorian wallpaper, and the green hues of the curtains and of the broadloom carpet were blended and reflected in a large gold-leaf mirror. The room was filled with bric-a-brac—with old candlesticks on the tables, shellwork pictures on the walls, waxen flowers under bell jars on the marble mantelpiece, and rows of Sara's favorite china pin-boxes on every conceivable perch. In the drawing room there hung an ancient marriage certificate; engraved with cupids and garlands, it showed a Victorian bride in crinoline giving her hand to a bewhiskered groom in tight breeches.

Mencken had brought but few furnishings from Hollins Street. His baby grand piano was placed in the living room. An early abstractionist painting by Thomas Hart Benton, which he had bought fifteen years before from Willard Huntington Wright, was hung in the drawing room and the portrait of Kaiser William in his bedroom. A "couple of truck-loads" of liquor and brewing equipment were stored in the spare room. Mencken had also proposed to bring along his collection of cuckoo clocks and radiometers. Sara had an irrational prejudice against the clocks, but she countenanced the radiometers and placed them on shelves in the long hall. These radiometers were glass-enclosed vanes rotated by light. Commonly seen in the windows of optical shops, they delighted Mencken in his moments of relaxation. But his two most notable effects were a billboard installed inside the front door for the display of Americana—pictures of Elks in full regalia, and religious handbills—and an enormous poster of the Pabst Brewery plant showing myriads of chimneys belching smoke, framed and hung over a mahogany sideboard.

Living in bachelor lady quarters most of her adult life, Sara had little training for large-scale domestic management. On her first trip to the grocery store, she purchased, among other things, a huge stock of cream of tartar, one pint of which would have been sufficient for a lifetime.

Henry anticipated a cuisine on the strictest Alabama principles, "with gumbo in everything, including the coffee," and he asked only that she keep a plate of cold roast beef in the pantry for himself and other Yankees. Yet, aided by the advice of her friends, Sara learned very quickly and soon she was operating the household as elegantly as she had furnished it. She hired two colored servants, a cook and a maid. They served in full dress, with the silver shined, the finger bowls in order, and places set for four at all times, as though important guests were expected imminently.

Her precaution was well-advised. Her husband's friends included many of the most eminent and eccentric men in America. She had to cope with an unannounced midnight visit from Sinclair Lewis and his English publisher; with a persistent F. Scott Fitzgerald (whose wife Zelda had been her girlhood friend in Montgomery) inviting her out for wild drunken drives; with Governor Albert C. Ritchie arriving late at night for counsels of state; with an unmixable assortment of journalists, actresses, trial lawyers, professors, scientists, musicians, of all denominations and colors. Despite such difficulties, Sara could give dinner parties for fourteen and conduct herself with dignity as a hostess and with conviction as a conversationalist. In domesticating her husband, moreover, she carried on the tradition of Mencken's mother and sister before her. She modernized his wardrobe, replacing all his darned socks with new ones, and lectured him on how the necktie should match the shirt. Gently, too, she elevated his table manners. During her occasional absences from home, he expressed the fear that the maid would send her an unfavorable report on his backsliding.

The novelty of being the nominal head of such a household enchanted the Sage. As Sara expressed it, "Henry is a Victorian, although he won't admit it." On one occasion, she purchased a copy of *The Young Lady's Toilet*, published in 1841, and from it expounded the Victorian virtues to her husband. " 'Piety, contentment, moderation—' " "In drinking?" Henry interrupted. "In everything," Sara assured him. "Terrible!" he said, and he chuckled as she finished the recitation. " 'Innocence, good humor, mildness, truth, compassion and tears, fidelity, meekness and charity, circumspection.' Isn't it perfect?" Sara asked, half humorously. "These are the ideals by which I live." "Splendid! Wonderful!" Mencken boomed. "That book should be published again, now."

Henry joined Sara every afternoon between 4:30 and 6 in the "public rooms." He had frequently a little surprise for her—an odd piece of glass from an antique shop, or a jar of dill pickles. After the gifts, the two might sit at the piano and play "Chopsticks." Or Sara would tell Henry about books that she had enjoyed and that he had overlooked. Sara, for example, was a great admirer of Thomas Wolfe, yet Wolfe's naked lyricism rang hollow in the ears of her husband. At other times, they would discuss the family fortunes. Sara knew that she had not done herself justice in *The Making of a Lady*. It had received bad notices. Henry had attributed these to his enemies, who, he said, were not above striking at him through his wife. Yet he closely followed the planning and execution of her next novel, *The Plantation*. It was, he thought, such a promising work of art that it must not be allowed to miscarry.

At Christmas time the Mencken household was at its gayest. The apartment was then dominated by a large tree laden with gifts and ornaments, and issuing chimes as it rotated on its base. After the celebrations, Mencken would gather together his hundreds of Christmas cards and send them to the historical section of the New York Public Library to illustrate how a "typical" American family observed this holiday in the third decade of the twentieth century.

With these exceptions, Mencken observed his long-established routine without change. Sara believed that it was sound policy to steer clear of her husband at breakfast. "No one has anything to say at that time of day," she used to say. "I want my papers and mail, and Henry wants his." Henry came down to the breakfast table at eight for his orange juice, toast, and coffee and he was at his desk by the time Sara made her appearance. As always, he worked on through the forenoon and the early afternoon, stopping only for lunch at twelve and for the family hour before dinner. Though the fashionable neighbors in Cathedral Street dined at seven, this menage was so regulated that its master sat at dinner at six and an hour later entered into his last work stretch, which continued till nine or ten. On Saturday nights there was the club. Whether its functions were held at the Mencken apartment or at some other member's home, or at Schellhase's restaurant (after the repeal of Prohibition), Sara, like all the other members' wives, was virtually a grass widow at such times. But on Sunday afternoons, after a lavish meal at one, the family once more came into its own with a session of what Henry called "philosophical belching."

## [ 4 ]

From beginning to end, the happiness of Mencken's married life was shadowed by Sara's abnormal susceptibility to disease. Every time she recovered from some affliction, Mencken hoped that at last she had achieved a permanent cure, but he knew too much medicine to believe it. Six months after their marriage, in struggling with a winter affliction, she put on so much weight that Mencken observed, "She begins to look like a German soprano." "I tell her that obesity is far preferable to pleurisy," he wrote to Dr. Pearl. "In this I may be wrong, but such is my character that whenever I have said a thing I always stick to it. I carry this principle so far that I am still insisting that Hoover is a jackass." In the spring of 1931 he found his wife "vigorous and rosy" again.

The following Christmas, Sara had a siege of the flu for which her doctors recommended a change of air. In January 1932 the couple went off to Puerto Rico on a two and one-half weeks Caribbean cruise. Sara was improved by the very thought of this, her first sea voyage; and though she had forebodings that she would get sick at her first taste of the Atlantic swells, she took enough Coca-Colas, at Henry's suggestion, and enough apples, at the stewardess's, to develop her sea legs. Meanwhile Henry was barely serviceable as an escort. He had had the flu along with his wife and now suffered from the after-effects more noticeably than she did. Boarding the ship, he looked so run-down that the news photographers offered him a chair. This courtesy he refused proudly, but he suggested that they caption their pictures of him "This man is sick—not drunk." En route, between the hospitality of the North German Lloyd liner *Columbus* and the effects of the tropical climate, he made a remarkable recovery. Later Sara told their friends, "Henry was not only sober during the entire cruise, but he was also in good humor," for which endorsement Henry mumbled his gratitude.

Henry's good spirits, indeed, had embraced all his fellow passengers. He played shuffleboard with them. In the beer garden one evening, at the risk of serious aftereffects, he showed them what was left of his youthful accomplishments by putting down a liter of draught beer in one gulp. No man present could match this feat. Moreover, he serviced them clandestinely by editing the ship's newspaper, the *Caribbean Caravel.* The secret was, to be sure, shared by all hands; but in any case Mencken would have betrayed himself by a nonpolitical flight of fantasy that harked back to his Baltimore *Herald* editorials. In one issue, under the title "Confidential Information," he purported to reveal the blueprint of a new 1500-foot, super-luxurious liner soon to be launched by the North German Lloyd. The "Doppelschraubenpostexpressluxuskolossalriesendampfer," he wrote, was to have a half-mile cinder track, a stadium seating two thousand, and "a fourth-class for professors." The first-class accommodations would be, not cabins, but apartments; and of these, twenty would be penthouse apartments. "The ship's doctor will have twenty assistants and there will be a hospital equipped to extract fifty appendices and five hundred tonsils a day. There will be Catholic and Protestant churches on the top deck, and space for Communists, single taxers, birth controllers and other reformers will be provided on the boat decks, with free soap boxes. There will also be half a dozen speakeasies."

Sara's next prescription was a two months cruise to the Mediterranean in the late winter of 1934. This one was even more to Henry's taste. In two volumes, *Treatise on the Gods* and *Treatise on Right and Wrong*, he had but recently spread himself on the origins of Christian religion and ethics, and it is doubtful that any infidel before or since has ever looked forward with such anticipation to visiting the shrines of the Holy Land. "As you know," he told Boyd, "I have always had a peculiar veneration for Pontius Pilate, and it is my hope to visit his tomb and drop a tear. If the time offers, I shall also make a journey to the site of Gomorrah, my favorite town of antiquity." On February 10, Henry and Sara boarded the *Columbus* again and found among their shipmates three Catholic bishops, one of them a Mencken admirer who not only tolerated such talk but seemed to enjoy it. From the eastern Mediterranean, Henry reported strange portents to Dr. Pearl. "As we approach G.H.Q. the wonders of Yahweh increase in ingenuity. In Algiers (the home of statistics) I was flung clear out of a taxi on a hairpin bend and landed on my arse on the cobbles, but got only a small bruise. Today, at least 200 miles from the nearest land, we are in the midst of a violent sandstorm." When he arrived at last in the Holy Land, his attention was most palpably directed to the stucco houses of the Zionist settlers, but the sacred ruins piqued his imagination to a ribald climax. He returned to Baltimore laden with relics. "I have a valuable souvenir for you, and shall place it in your hands when we meet," he wrote Boyd. "It is a gallstone passed by Abraham back in the year 1700 B.C. It has been cherished as an heirloom in the Margolis family in Jerusalem, and was presented to me by the present head of the house, J. Lloyd Margolis."

Despite its many diversions, the cruise failed of its purpose. Sara had apparently enjoyed good health as she went the rounds of museums, ruins, and hotel restaurants with her husband. But now they discovered that they were both tired out, and that Henry had lost five pounds and Sara fifteen. Nor did Sara recover her strength in the April warmth. She developed a fever which the doctors could not diagnose—"probably something Mediterranean," they said. It proved to be not serious, and within a month it disappeared as mysteriously as it had come. That Sara's recuperative powers, however, were seriously on the decline soon became evident. In the fall she had another spell of pleurisy and was either hospitalized or bedridden at home throughout most of the ensuing winter. It was a harrowing period. Sara maintained her spirits by continuing to write magazine pieces and to block out the chapters of her novel. Henry also was optimistic: in the spring, he talked to her about a convalescent trip to the Pacific Northwest.

In the middle of May she was again in the hospital with an undiagnosed condition. When the nature of this last illness was revealed to him, Mencken knew that the end was at hand. For about a week, he stood the death watch. "Sara is in a hopeless state," he wrote to Dr. Pearl on the last day. "She has meningitis with t.b. bacilli in the spinal fluid. The headache has passed off, and she is comfortable. But the morphine is being pushed so hard that it is difficult to arouse her. All this, of course, was not unanticipated. But all the same it is dreadful to face the brutal reality."

Sara died at 6 P.M. on May 31. Disbeliever though he was, Mencken, as he later expressed it, found it intolerable to part from her without a word. The service was conducted at a funeral parlor with many friends in attendance, though none had been invited. Later her body was cremated, as she had requested, and her ashes buried in the Mencken family plot. Mencken was prompt to acknowledge the letters of condolence. "Her long struggle against illness was extraordinarily gallant," he told Boyd, "and I console myself with the thought that her last days were peaceful and painless." To others he revealed that he had always been "full of hopes" that she would finally recover, but "the long anxiety has left me a wreck." He was in the last stages of writing *The American Language* (Fourth Edition), and hoped to complete the work by August 1, but now he told Mrs. Clarence Darrow, "I feel so completely sunk that I am unable to do any sensible work." In the middle of June he abruptly pushed aside all his newspaper and magazine obligations and set sail for a few weeks respite in England. His brother August joined him.

Mencken bravely faced the few friends who saw him in London. He made no mention of the tragedy and spoke boldly of his work plans for the future. But they observed that he had to struggle to keep his mind on what he was saying and that his weary blue eyes bespoke a tremendous strain. Back in Baltimore in mid-July, he resumed his work in the Cathedral Street apartment, allowing himself only such delays as were necessitated by the miasmatic heat. He proposed to go on living there. "It is very comfortable and convenient," he told Dreiser, "and I suppose that I'll have to learn to endure the fact that my wife is no longer in it." It helped somewhat that in his absence Sara's dresses, jewelry, and china pin-boxes had been parceled out, as was her will, to her friends and relatives. And it helped, too, that his brother August would stay with him in the apartment until the end of the summer. But he had not counted on the long nights of the fall and winter. In March 1936 he reported to Hergesheimer that he would rejoin his brother at the old family house. "It turned out to be completely unendurable, living in this apartment. It was too full of reminders, and too dreadfully empty and lonely." Abandoning it, he took with him but a handful of pieces, among which were the dining-room set and the waxen flowers.

Sara's collection of books was willed to the Goucher College Library. It included, among its four hundred volumes, many autographed first editions presented to her by Robert Frost, Vachel Lindsay, Ogden Nash, Ellen Glasgow, Cabell, Lewis, Hergesheimer, and others; a complete set of her husband's works; and a shelfful of books on the South and on the Victorian era. Five months after Sara's death, Mencken made the formal presentation. While he talked briefly about the books, Hergesheimer, summoned especially for the purpose of sustaining him, sat close at hand. The president of the college officially accepted the gifts, and Dr. Ola Winslow, one of Sara's English professors, made an address on "The Meaning of Books to Mrs. Mencken and to Goucher." The two men of letters left the premises together, Henry remarking to Joe that Sara would have "larfed" to see these two freebooters in such unfamiliar surroundings. By the following spring, Mencken had compiled *Southern Album,* a book of Sara's short stories prefaced by a restrained memoir of his own. At the same time, he collected her literary scraps, including everything from published articles to rough outlines on the back of old letters, in six large volumes, had them handsomely bound in blue morocco leather, and deposited them in her Goucher collection.

To little Sara Anne Duffy, the daughter of Anne and Edmund Duffy, born soon after Sara's death and christened in her memory, Mencken discharged all the duties of a godfather and more. He brightened her gullible years with all manner of gewgaws—glass eyes, "No Trespassing" signs, and great packets of comic valentines. Even when she had begun to doubt the existence of Santa Claus, she still had to take into consideration an extraordinary whiskerless fat man who, on successive Christmases, sent her table silver for her hope chest.

# PART FOUR

# *The Reprobate*

*C H A P T E R   1 6*

# The Road Back

THE SAGE had not taken the depression very seriously. By the fall of 1930 he had noted the stock market crash, the idle factories, the estimates of six million unemployed and a thousand bank failures. He believed that a little business retrenchment was a good thing: it knocked people back to a more modest scale of living, based on thrift rather than on gambler's luck; he could himself live comfortably at half his old standard. The reports that men were starving seemed to him exaggerated, and the bread lines he regarded as nothing more than a hoax of the "charity racketeers."

When Angoff, his assistant in the *Mercury* office, informed the boss that the situation was fully as bad as reported, Mencken challenged him to find an actual case of destitution. Thereupon the junior editor led the senior down to Times Square, where the bread lines were longer even than the waiting line for Charlie Chaplin's *City Lights.* Mencken saw the shabby clothes and the pinched faces of the unemployed and of the children who stood with them. These people were undeniably destitute. The Sage fell silent while a surge of sympathy played across the ruddy masses of his face. Then the two men moved on down the street. "Well, after all," he said at length, "a good death rate would be salutary. The people who die aren't worth saving anyway. A few more slaves, a few less—what is the difference?"

Though these reflections were, of course, expanded and printed in the *Mercury*, nobody paid very much attention to them. The landmarks of Mencken's cosmos were fast disappearing. When the "boobs" were on the march, Mencken had performed a useful service by satirizing their "fear and hatred of their betters." But now that so many of them were destitute, his shafts went askew. Moreover, even by Mencken's standards, the boobs were no longer behaving like boobs. The postwar hysteria had subsided—and with it, all such issues as the disloyalty of the German-Americans during World War I, the red menace, the Ku Klux Klan, and Fundamentalism. With the ousting of the Republicans and the repeal of Prohibition two years hence, two more of his targets would "go down the chute." Even the Babbitts were becoming less vulnerable. A decade before, the editor of the *New Republic* declared, America had been compounded of 1 per cent Mencken and 99 per cent Babbitt; now it was 10 per cent Mencken and only 90 per cent Babbitt.

This was the critical year. Mencken had already been advised that unless he took a more constructive attitude towards the depression, he would pass into history along with the decade to which he had given his name. But how, indeed, could Mencken become more constructive? In his father's cigar factory, and later from Nietzsche, Herbert Spencer, and his other mentors, he had learned that no man has a right to live unless he can prove his worth in the open market, and that all efforts to improve the little man's plight are either futile or dangerous. In the course of his great crusade, this harsh capitalist dogma had become intermixed with many more compelling notions. At times he had ignored it entirely, allying himself with the reformers and against the capitalists. But now that the crusade was over, he was back willy-nilly at his starting point—and as cocksure about it as ever!

Some signs of disaffection in the Mencken camp had been observed as early as 1925. But after this critical year, they were legion. College boys taunted the Sage with the cry, "Why so hot, little man?" and dismissed him as "a blunderbuss firing noisy shots into dead corpses." Except for James T. Farrell and a few others, rising authors neither paid tribute to him nor asked for his patronage; instead, following Ernest Hemingway in *The Sun Also Rises,* they went out of their way to bedevil him. Gilbert Seldes, a critic, freely admitted that he had been wrong these many years, that the Mencken movement was devoid of idealism and as deadly as a cancer. Meanwhile, other movements and other Sages were coming into vogue. In 1929, when the Humanists, led by Irving Babbitt, came out of their retreats, they were received politely, if not enthusiastically. As the depression deepened, the Marxists were heard from; and such familiar *Mercury* names as Sherwood Anderson and Theodore Dreiser appeared occasionally on the front cover of the Communist *New Masses.* Significantly, when these people renounced their old chief, most of them employed the style and manner that he had taught them. And the two most successful magazines of the period still bore the marks of his influence—the flippant *Time* and the sophisticated *New Yorker;* yet this fact was little noted.

To all these indignities Mencken yielded with a remarkable passivity. He seemed to be more interested in his romance and impending marriage with Sara Haardt than in what was happening in the public forum. He attempted no restoration of his influence, and, adding a touch of masochism to the affair, denied that he had ever had any. "I have never tried to convert anyone to anything," he said testily to a reporter. "No man writing can avoid being pawed over by the imbecile type of person who is hunting for someone to follow—the natural subordinate, the Yes-man. Some of these vermin followed me. I have no more grievance in losing them than would a dog when the fleas which pestered him left him and fell on another dog. If the people who used to follow me are now following Irving Babbitt, my sympathies are with Babbitt: he's got the fleas."

On Thanksgiving Day, 1929, he confided to his brother August that after three years labor he had finished his masterpiece, *Treatise on the Gods,* "the first work of art on the anti-religious side after Huxley." It appeared in March 1930, and in a hostile atmosphere. During the late twenties, Jeans, Eddington, and Millikan had been busy reconciling science with religion, and as far as most critics were concerned, the gods were back on their perches, safely beyond the range of Mencken's skeptical pen. At the same time, the book astonished them. Despite its scholarly apparatus, it glowed at times with the inner light of a much earlier and much happier Mencken; also it was the most popular of his works so far, selling thirteen thousand copies in its first year. Thus, against heavy odds, the Sage had achieved a triumph of a sort. At the age of fifty, he had struck a new vein, both congenial and profitable. Henceforth, he would continue writing such treatises as this, even if no one read them and no one agreed with them.

With his other enterprises, however, he accepted the critics' verdict, and without complaint or demonstration of any kind retired from them. In 1927, when the initial sale of *Prejudices: Seventh Series* fell slightly below that of the *Sixth Series,* he abandoned the project, holding to a resolution that the *Prejudices* should never appear on a falling market. At the end of the year and for the same reason, he abandoned his weekly column for the Chicago *Tribune.* Most serious of all was the plight of the *American Mercury:* by 1930 it had slipped from its peak circulation of 90,000 to an unsteady 65,000 (official figures) and after Nathan's prearranged departure would soon slip to an unofficial 30,000. Again Mencken was ready to step down. But this time, his escape route was sealed behind him. Though the *Mercury* has proved as viable and impersonal as any other magazine, it was then regarded as a one-man show, and there was doubt that it had any better chance of survival under a new editor than under its co-founder.

This matter he discussed at length with the Knopfs. He agreed to stay with the magazine until it was restored to a "fairly firm footing," but admitted frankly that he had no heart for the job. After five years in the editor's chair, he complained, he had whipped the nation's "imbeciles" so thoroughly that they would no longer come out and fight. "Why not forget them?" suggested the Knopfs, echoing the general opinion, "and concentrate upon the more serious issues raised by the Hoover administration?" "Why not go back to the Nathan formula," suggested Angoff, whose burden was now heavier than ever, "and let us sink or swim as a cultural magazine?" But Mencken rarely took anybody's advice on editorial matters. And since his concern for "serious issues" was, as yet, not very great, he redoubled his attack on the retreating army of Prohibitionists and otherwise indulged his whims. In November 1931, as a kind of masterstroke of irrelevance, he featured "The Tragedy of the Sioux" by Chief Sitting Bull. At the end of 1933 he transferred his command to Henry Hazlitt, a conservative in economics and a modernist in letters. A year later the chapter was finally closed when Alfred Knopf sold the *Mercury* to Paul Palmer at the incredibly low price of $25,000.

Mencken's retirement coincided with the repeal of Prohibition. He celebrated the latter event with a half-hour radio show during which he nervously conducted the N. B. C. Symphony Orchestra and advised the nation on how to drink beer. Shortly afterwards, he expressed his relief at being rid of the *Mercury*. "This has been a job, a daily job. An editor's got to sit down at his desk once a day." Among his many irritations, he mentioned his fan mail of forty or fifty letters a day, and he added that he no longer bothered to read his press clippings. He was satisfied to remain in Baltimore as columnist and adviser to the *Sunpapers*. He had always regarded himself primarily as a newspaperman; all his other interests, he said, he had managed with his left hand.

In short order, all such rationalizations were exposed for what they were. History has yet to show a dictator, political or intellectual, who has ever been wholly reconciled to his downfall, or any man smitten with the messianic delusion who has ever entirely recovered from it. In Mencken, too, this madness was not dead, but asleep.

All he needed was some antagonist of sufficient size and offensiveness. And when such a man appeared at last, it would not matter to Mencken that he had grown prematurely old, that he had lost his magazine and his following, that his intellectual armor had become outmoded. He still enjoyed the prestige of his historical position, and even this he would expend in order once more to "stir up the animals" North, East, South, and West.

*C H A P T E R 1 7*

# *Putsch* on F.D.R.

## [ 1 ]

IN JUNE 1932, when the *Sunpapers* sent him out to cover the Democratic National Convention, Mencken had no idea that this fateful hour was at hand. His candidate was his friend, Albert C. Ritchie, Governor of the Maryland "Free State." Indeed throughout the preconvention campaign, he had served Ritchie as a kind of amateur Jim Farley. He had written Ritchie's speeches, dictated his platform, arranged his speaking tours, and attempted to sell him to Herbert Bayard Swope and other Democratic bigwigs. But Franklin D. Roosevelt won the nomination; and with Ritchie receiving few votes outside the Maryland delegation, Mencken could hardly suppress his disappointment. The great issue before the country, he said, was the repeal of Prohibition. On this count, the "civilized" Ritchie would have made a far stronger candidate than the "shallow and futile" Roosevelt. When he went to the polls in November, he cast his vote for the straight Democratic ticket, but with serious misgivings.

Following Roosevelt's vigorous action in the bank crisis, Mencken proposed that he be made king. On the face of it, this suggestion might have been taken as an overwhelming endorsement. But it was double-edged.

Mencken toyed with it for a couple of years, twisting the blade now one way, now another, as the mood dictated. In June 1933 he wrote Albert Jay Nock that there had been little response to his proposal. Roosevelt, he said, "is, to be sure, a fourth-rater. But even a fourth-rate king is better, it seems to me, than a fourth-rate President with his eyes on 1936." In the next letter, a few weeks later, he added: "The republic proceeds towards hell at a rapidly accelerating tempo. With the debt burden already crushing everyone, Roosevelt now proposes to relieve us by spending five or six billions more. I am advocating making him king in order that we may behead him in case he goes too far beyond the limits of the endurable. A President, it appears, cannot be beheaded, but kings have been subjected to the operation from ancient times."

A few months later the Gridiron Club, a select body of Washington correspondents, decided that Mencken would make an admirable devil's advocate when squared off, face to face, with Mr. Roosevelt. The season of anti-New Deal hysteria had hardly begun. With Hoover still observant and silent, the press cautiously critical, and the great industrialists forming their lines of battle around the Liberty League, Mencken looked to be not only a respectable journalist but the pioneer of a promising reaction. On the night of December 8, 1934, the club's four hundred guests gathered in the great banquet hall of the Willard Hotel. They included virtually all the effectual engineers, architects, and saboteurs of the American destiny. The government was represented by Mr. Roosevelt, eight Cabinet members, seven Senators, five Governors, a Supreme Court Justice, and General Douglas MacArthur, then chief of staff. Private enterprise was represented most conspicuously by Richard Whitney, president of the New York stock exchange. The captains of public opinion swarmed everywhere—Merlin Aylesworth of the National Broadcasting Company, chain publishers like Roy Howard and Paul Block, the publishers of the great New York dailies, and a host of others.

During the long dinner, skits were enacted by the club members and their wives; the New Deal was depicted as a train wreck blocking the tracks for the "Prosperity Limited." About 10:30 the Sage, in his boiled shirt, rose from his seat at the head table. "Mr. President, Mr. Wright [President of the Gridiron Club] and Fellow Subjects of the Reich," he began. For an ordinary after-dinner speaker, his address was hardly long enough for a warm-up. It consisted of a few speculations as to how long the New Deal would last. There was hope, he said, in that the New Dealers had left one article of the Bill of Rights still intact: as yet, no soldiers were quartered in any man's house without the consent of the owner. He cited the warnings of his pastor that it would be ten thousand years before the "smart fellows who ran the Republic were turned out." On the other hand, he took courage from the fact that those words "were uttered a little less than three years ago, in the forepart of the year 1932, and the camorra that the pastor referred to was not the Brain Trust, but the Anti-Saloon League."

When the President spoke in his turn, it was evident that he was not in the least disturbed by the gamut that he had run, and that, if nothing else, the club's cocktails were very much to his taste. Genially he referred to "my old friend, Henry Mencken." Then he plunged into his text. What followed was so unexpected that everyone was frozen in his chair. Instead of making a courteous retort, Roosevelt lashed about him like a mad Hessian, chopping down not only the Washington correspondents but their employers as well. The whole American press, he declared, was shot through with "stupidity, cowardice and Philistinism." "There are managing editors in the United States, and scores of them, who have never heard of Kant or Johannes Müller and never read the Constitution of the United States; there are city editors who do not know what a symphony is or a streptococcus, or the Statute of Frauds; there are reporters by the thousands who could not pass the entrance examination for Harvard and Tuskegee, or even Yale." As he continued the assault, it gradually dawned upon his audience that Roosevelt was not delivering another state paper, but simply quoting Mencken's "Journalism in America" out of *Prejudices: Sixth Series*. Nothing that the President could have said about Mencken as the bedfellow of the reactionary press lords could have been half so stunning as this: that is, as waving the bloody shirt of Mencken's almost forgotten war with the press at this time and place. Nearly eight hundred eyes peered through the smoky hall at Mencken's face, now coloring like an autumn leaf.

The Sage was embarrassed and irritated. He had not liked the easy familiarity with which Roosevelt referred to him as "my old friend." In his own speech, he had made what he regarded as some good-natured remarks about the regime in power—remarks which the White House secretaries had seen beforehand but which they had completely ignored in preparing the President's bombshell. "I'll get the son of a bitch," Mencken whispered to Governor Ritchie, who was seated next to him. "I'll dig the skeletons out of his closet. I'll throw his 1932 campaign pledge speech right back at him." Ritchie advised his friend to forget about it. But Mencken hastily jotted down a rebuttal to the effect: "I have written many things in the past that would embarrass me when brought up at a later date. But no matter how embarrassing they may be, I stick to them. While other people . . ." The Sage could not understand why Presidents of the United States should be privileged above satirists in face-to-face engagements. Yet when Roosevelt completed his remarks, all further argument was at an end. The President was wheeled out of the banquet hall, pausing gallantly on his course to shake Mencken's hand.

In 1935 it occurred to Mencken that the weak and charming Roosevelt of 1933 was nothing less than the long-heralded man on horseback. In the whole list of Presidents, he could think of none so offensive. For, while Roosevelt had gifts of rhetoric infinitely superior to those of "such clams as Coolidge," his principles were "fluid like the assets of a well-managed bank." If he thought that cannibalism would bring him votes, he would fatten up a missionary in the White House yard. Setting forth such observations in the March 1936 issue of the *American Mercury,* Mencken fired the opening gun of the Presidential campaign. He affirmed what the "smart politicoes" were saying: that the "jig is nearly up for the greatest President since Hoover." "If they [the anti-New Dealers] can beat him at all, which seems most unlikely," Mencken predicted, "they can beat him with a Chinaman, or even a Republican."

Mencken's volcano had been quiescent so long that he had almost forgotten what happened after a full-scale eruption. "The *Mercury* article," he told an old traveling companion, "was made up of stuff that had appeared in the *Evening Sun* here at least a dozen times. It made little, if any, impression in Baltimore, where the customers are used to strong meat. But it had hardly come out in the *Mercury* before I began to be bombarded with telegrams, some of them beautifully abusive, but most of them friendly." Even the conservative Democrats of the New York *Times,* soon to have their own inning against the New Deal, were disturbed by the vigor of Mencken's attack. In a leading editorial, they protested that Mencken "not only treats the Presidency with gross disrespect but reduces this kind of personal attack upon Mr. Roosevelt to the absurd." They recalled that in the past the Sage had cursed each and every President without doing much damage, but this time, they warned, he might be setting the pace for a very muddy Presidential campaign.

Mencken was not in the least disturbed by the warnings of the *Times* or of any other organ. After covering the conventions, he went out to Topeka, Kansas, to see Alfred M. Landon installed as the Republican challenger of the New Deal incumbent. It was a festive occasion for him. In his pocket he carried an "authentic" Maryland madstone for working miracles. On his new seersucker suit he wore the sunflower badge of a Landon partisan, as big and luminous as his eyes. Parading up and down the street, he asked a group of school children, "Who are you for—Roosevelt or Landon?" When they objected that they couldn't vote, he professed great incredulity. "Who says you can't vote? Why not?" he asked loudly. Informed that they were not yet twenty-one, he looked at them in mock amazement. "What? You mean you can't vote out here until you're twenty-one?" In the same spirit he retorted to bystanders who asked him what he thought about the beautiful women of the Bible Belt, "I haven't noticed them. I am from Baltimore where men and women agree, due to the humidity, to pay no attention to each other between May and October."

With these preliminaries, Mencken joined the Landon train. For thirty-two years he had been participating in political campaigns, but this was the first that brought the blood to his eye. He was conspicuous not in one capacity, but in three, each inconsistent with the others. As a reporter, he wrote honestly and in detail of Landon's failures as a stump speaker. As a strategist, he censured the candidate for having advocated "doles for lazy and half-witted farmers" and advised him to revert to the true conservative doctrine that "the only tolerable government is a really weak one." But in the third capacity, as a partisan, he tried by his rhetoric to do what his candidate was failing to do. His "Case for Dr. Landon" appeared in the *American Mercury* for October. Landon, he admitted, would not make a brilliant President, but he would balance the budget or bust. As for Landon's opponent, Mencken had long since reached his highest pitch of anti-Roosevelt invective, but the visiting British correspondents, sampling it for the first time, gasped for air. Mencken is assailing the President, one of them reported, "with a violence of vituperation unparalleled even in the hellfire and brimstone annals of American politics."

Until the very last day, Mencken maintained his hope and belief that Landon had "a good chance of winning the election." His earlier prophecy that if Roosevelt could be beaten at all, he could be beaten by "a Chinaman, or even a Republican," was put into more vulnerable form by the Scripps-Howard columnist Raymond Clapper, as "A Chinaman could beat Roosevelt," and in this form was endlessly requoted. Thus it came about that when forty-six of the forty-eight states went down the line for Roosevelt, Mencken the Sage and Prophet was almost as much a casualty of the landslide as Landon the Candidate. Commentators of both sides, but more particularly the liberal ones (then including Westbrook Pegler), had chortled loudly over the Sage rooting for a candidate who was a Republican, a Methodist, and an Elk. But they chortled even louder over the resounding collapse of the Chinaman prophecy. In December, Mencken again gazed into the future, telling the pro-New Deal Paul Y. Anderson of the St. Louis *Post-Dispatch* that he anticipated another big smashup. This time he was careful to disclaim infallibility. "I am saying these things to you," Mencken wrote, "solely because I have known you for a long time, and feel sorry for you. Please remember that, following the recent election, I formally resigned from the practice of prophecy. I have decided to devote the remainder of my life to translating Hebrew manuscripts. It's pleasant work, if you can get it, so if you hear of any one who has a Hebrew manuscript which he wants translated, don't forget to send him around."

Before Landon's train had quite reached its dismal destination, Mencken suggested that Landon interrupt the procession in the Free State and enjoy some of the famous dishes to be had there. Unfortunately the candidate had time only for a rear-platform appearance, but he promised that "win, lose or draw, I shall eat one of your meals when I again come through here." Landon was a Dutchman who gave weight even to his most casual words. On December 20 he turned up with Eugene Meyer, publisher of the Washington *Post*, and Ogden L. Mills, Hoover's Secretary of the Treasury, en route to the 1936 Gridiron Dinner. Mencken was fully equal to the occasion. In a private room at the Southern Hotel he had enough food and drink served up to hearten all the chieftains of the defeated party. The bill of fare included cocktails, choice Chesapeake Bay oysters, terrapin à la Maryland, Maryland beaten biscuits, sherry, chicken à la Maryland, cream sauce, grilled bacon, corn fritters, potato croquettes, Bordeaux wine, Maryland ham, Maryland hearts of lettuce, Maryland water ice, champagne. Half a dozen dignitaries of the *Sunpapers* assisted Mencken in the entertainment. When it was time for Landon to leave, the former candidate repeated over and over again that Mencken was the most gracious host to be found anywhere in the country.

[ 2 ]

As the full enormity of Mencken's transformation became apparent, his old followers turned upon him as an apostate. At Christmas time, 1933, two young men interrupted a meeting of the Saturday Night Club in the back room of Schellhase's restaurant. Their intentions were not clear. They were armed only with leaflets against war and Fascism, but when they were stopped at the door by the club's sergeant at arms, they clipped him on the ear. At once the whole club rallied to the defense. The youngsters wavered, and at the sight of Raymond Pearl's towering figure they fled. After a brief pursuit the fast-moving Sage collared them in the middle of the restaurant floor. Later he turned them over to the cops for a night in jail. He was not molested again, but henceforth wherever he moved among advanced intellectual circles, at the Knopf office in New York, or among the editorial writers of the *Sunpapers,* the shadow of his apostasy hung over him; at any moment, one of his old friends might remonstrate with him or argue the case of Communism or the New Deal.

What looked like apostasy to the intellectuals looked like conversion to sound principle to the local business magnets. In 1932 the last of the anti-Menckenites on the *Sunpapers'* board of directors retired; two years later, Mencken was elected to fill the empty seat. The other directors, mostly prosperous lawyers and bankers, under the chairmanship of Harry Black, received him with open arms. Soon afterwards one of them proposed him for membership in the exclusive Maryland Club. For a time the Sage kept his distance, being embarrassed once more by the ghosts of his disreputable past. He had often referred to the club as a refuge for Babbitts and Confederate sympathizers. Yet, ghosts or no ghosts, the Sage gravitated like anyone else into the circle which offered him the greatest hospitality. On the eve of his nomination, he nervously wagered his sponsor six dinners that he would be blackballed. But his precautions proved excessive, for he was elected without a single dissenting vote and with only a few snickers.

Admitted into the Baltimore business community as a full-fledged member, Mencken promptly took a leading role. On the constructive side, he devised a new constitution for Maryland. It was a curious document, so full of

Menckenian crotchets (it provided for the sterilization of criminals, for unrestricted divorce after the third year of marriage, for political disabilities for clergymen and lunatics) that it was never seriously considered. But its purport was safely reactionary: it would have made Maryland into a perpetual paradise for capitalism. Meanwhile, on the destructive side, he urged his boss, Patterson, to intensify the *Putsch* against Roosevelt. In the 1936 elections the *Sunpapers* had maintained a position of neutrality, but now, bit by bit, their editorials became almost as irresponsible and strident as Mencken's own columns. Still the Sage was not satisfied. When the editorship of the *Evening Sun* fell vacant, Patterson invited him to take over as interim editor and to show the staff what anti-New Deal journalism really looked like.

In February 1938 the Sage entered the editorial rooms with all the animation of an old dog digging into his bone hoard. He girded himself with a smoking jacket for protection against flying ink. He fondly exchanged first-name greetings with the veterans of the composing room. Then, setting to work at his desk, he swore so lustily and so profanely that the invisible walls of office decorum, lethargy, and precedent collapsed everywhere within earshot. Mencken had told Patterson that he had more ideas in a day than the average newspaperman had in a lifetime; but on this day he had a large reserve as well. He unloaded them on his staff like so many boulders, directing each man to assume responsibility for some social problem—Prohibition, highways, the City Council, the oyster war—and before the man could properly become expert in one subject, Mencken assigned him another.

The office was raw with excitement. The paper at last

was going somewhere, and nobody had any doubt as to its destination. Mencken did not have to lay down his editorial policy. He could take any editorial, whether it was written by the civic stalwart, Clark Hobbs, or the charmingly urbane Gerald W. Johnson, and by the editing of not more than ten words convert it into a characteristic Menckenian blast. Readers were startled to see the old *Evening Sun* editorial page burst its columns. Newspaper contemporaries were distressed by the "strangest items in American journalism in many years." For Mencken, without even forewarning his own staff, pulled two rabbits out of his hat. On March 4 he had Johnson write a seven-column editorial on the failures of the first five years of the New Deal (later he gave Johnson a chance to write a rebuttal under his own by-line). On another occasion he filled all but two columns with one million seventy-five tiny black dots, each dot representing one federal employee, as a graphic illustration of the dimensions of the governmental feed-trough. (The dots, however, were so faint that few readers got the point.) Upon Mencken's retirement from the chair in May, he went to the hospital with a disordered stomach. The staff was also badly shaken. And though none of them required medical attention, they could never forget this rough schooling.

[ 3 ]

During these years, it was generally believed that Mencken would gradually sink back into his origins as a Baltimore journalist and become simply another choleric old Tory of the Maryland Club. But the Sage was incapable of any such peaceful exit. For thirty years he had been successfully outraging his fellow countrymen. And if by now many of his heresies had become obsolete, or more or less conventional, he could always find more shocking ones to replace them.

Since the advent of Hitler in 1933, if not before, he had been quietly flirting with the newfangled doctrines of Nazism and Fascism. In absolute terms, he could not condone the suppression of liberties, or the arbitrary persecution of the Jews, or the "meretricious" chauvinism of the Nazi regime. On the other hand, compared with the New Deal, it had its points. It was a democracy that had turned against itself. It kept the masses quiet and well fed; it put the church in its place; and it seemed to protect property rights against reformers of all kinds. Nor did he dissent entirely from its racial theories, for he too had always arranged the races in a hierarchical order, putting the Germans above the Jews, but, unlike the Nazis, putting the Jews above the Americans. The more he reflected upon the Fascist experiment, the more he believed that Fascism, for better or for worse, had a promising future in the Western world, and that an "intelligent Fascism" operated by incorruptible naval officers might be just the thing for America. How he reconciled this notion with his plea for less government he never made clear. Nor, as a onetime Nietzsche scholar, did he show precisely how Hitler had fulfilled or perverted the Nietzschean dream.

No one understood just what he was driving at by his enthusiasm for crackpot demagogues like Huey Long and Father Coughlin, or by his friendship with Dr. Townsend and the Reverend Gerald L. K. Smith. His endorsement of the Townsend Plan was cryptic. "I'd like to see what would happen," he said. "I'd like to see a volcano erupt, too, and I've wondered what it would be like to see New York bombed from the air." In the spring of 1938 it was reported that Mencken was sailing for Hitler's Germany on the *Europa*. The inference was that he had become a Nazi. Yet his friends soon received from his hand Nazi postal cards glossed over with ironic inscriptions such as "Behold the Superman!" or "This proves that 'Der Führer' loves children," and later he confided to his correspondents that he had found all his German acquaintances, "save a few damn fools," covertly in opposition to the Nazi regime. He spent most of his time sight-seeing alone in a hired automobile, visiting the military cemetery at Tannenberg, the tomb of Eilhart Mencke in the Cathedral of Marienwerder, and the University of Leipzig to which he had given his collection of Ibseniana in 1922.

Returning to the United States, Mencken was no Nazi. But he sympathized with Hitler's program for European conquest, and this heresy marked him off from the bulk of his fellow Tories, "swimming and swooning in the British orbit." Thereafter, his descent was swift and inexorable. Within less than a year, indeed within less than six months after the Munich crisis, he had forfeited his brief respectability and found himself in the political wilderness with Colonel Robert McCormick of the Chicago *Tribune*, Father Coughlin, Colonel Charles A. Lindbergh and other notorious isolationists as his allies. His mind was full of the most gloomy forebodings. Soon Roosevelt would precipitate a showdown between Germany and the Anglo-Saxon powers. The United States would be converted into "a military despotism hard to distinguish from an Asiatic empire." Immediately upon the declaration of war, Schellhase's "kaif" would be closed by the police.

He reported the National Conventions of 1940 with the gloom of the prophet Jeremiah. "The odds against beating Mr. Roosevelt," he declared, "are something less than 10,000 to 1." He recommended that the New Dealers adopt as their campaign cry: "It is an act of lunacy, and not only an act of lunacy but also immoral and against God, to change barrels going over Niagara." Willkie, he thought, was to be pitied for even aspiring to the Presidency: it would be better if Roosevelt were made to bury "his own dead horse." Mencken had several private sessions with Willkie in Philadelphia, but the candidate impressed him as a "weak-sister," without enough common sense or honesty to declare himself on the side of the isolationists.

At the close of the Democratic Convention in Chicago, Mencken rose from his wooden bench in the press section, slammed on his straw hat, and with his cigar firmly clenched in his mouth went round shaking hands with his associates. "Goodby, old chap," he told one of them. "No, we won't see each other in 1944. This is the last political convention that will ever be held in this country." Upon Mencken's exit, a publicity man for the Democratic National Committee, standing near by, grinned at another correspondent and said, "That's Mencken. He's a card, isn't he?"

After the 1940 election, Mencken disappeared almost completely from the national scene. He no longer wrote for *Liberty* and the other mass-circulation magazines as he had in the early New Deal years. (Such free-lancing, he later explained, he had undertaken only to pay off the expenses of Sara's illness.) Nor did he appear any longer on the radio networks. Yet wherever he was heard in his more restricted sphere, he inspired not merely shock but a kind of bloodcurdling horror. In November he made a speech before the Women's National Press Club in Washington. It didn't make any difference to him who won the war, he told the ladies, for he could live happily under a totalitarian regime. Besides, the human race was "an inferior breed that deserved to be liquidated entirely." Meanwhile Mencken's position on the *Sun* was becoming increasingly difficult. He was bombarded from without by hostile letters, and he was isolated from within by the *Sun*'s editorials, which supported Roosevelt in all measures leading to war.

Mencken's New Year message to his friends was to the effect that 1941 would be the happiest year since the Black Death. A month later, he wrote what he believed to be his last signed article for the *Sun*. "I have quit my job in disgust," he wrote to a friend. "The paper is supporting Roosevelt in a large and even violent way. It seems to me that my continuance on the editorial page would be an affectation. I am on good terms with the brethren but I believe, and have so told them, that their editorial policy is insanity." When Mencken withdrew his column, he offered to resign also his position as editorial and news consultant. But Patterson would not hear of it. After a great to-do, Mencken finally washed his hands of all connections with the editorial department, but agreed to stay on as news consultant. Also, he insisted that since his job had been cut in half, he should receive but half his former salary.

Though he deserted the readers of the *Sunpapers* without a word of farewell, he had in effect already drafted his valedictory. It was a contribution to Clifton Fadiman's symposium *I Believe,* published in 1939. All his life, he there declared, he had strived to reveal the facts which alone could benefit the welfare of the race. Above all, he had fought to emancipate the intelligent and competent individual from all hindrances, including hindrance of government. "Today," he said, "no decent value in all the scale of human values is safe, and neither is any decent man." And yet "intelligence is at work all the while, though from time to time it has to go underground. Let us hope that it will emerge once more anon, and pull the reluctant race along another peg."

*CHAPTER 18*

# The Lance in the Closet

TWICE BEFORE—during World War I and after the Hollywood episode—Mencken had tentatively announced his withdrawal from the public stage. But following Pearl Harbor he buried himself in Hollins Street with such finality that it seemed doubtful that he would or could ever come out again. The tax collector could barely get out of him his annual federal income tax, for he took advantage of every allowance and deduction down to and including the purchase of a ball of twine. The Library of Congress no longer received his collection of documents, averaging annually nearly one hundred books and three hundred pamphlets; with the poet Archibald MacLeish as chief librarian, the Sage was convinced that that institution was no longer a library but a Communist-New Deal propaganda agency. When the Bundles for Britain organization appealed to him for aid, he sent their stamped return envelopes back to them sealed but empty.

How long Mencken could maintain this detached status in Hollins Street he did not know. He could, of course, count on his brother August as a wise, loyal, and self-effacing companion. During the evenings, while he worked in his front office, August, a practicing engineer, was in a back room, building magnificent inlaid chests and ship models or solving crime mysteries. At 9 P.M., August joined him in the "public rooms" and amused him with satires, at times even more bizarre than his own. In one instance, he proposed to Mencken that all the old people who were a burden to their children be gathered together and maintained on a government reservation. Again he proposed that the U. S. Army should be kept fit in peace time by a continuous war with Mexico. Meanwhile, Mencken's sister Gertrude made her weekly inspection tours of the household, and many of Mencken's friends contributed liquor, caviar, and other delicacies. Still, in March 1942, Mencken was talking as though he were completely on his own.

One evening he was interrupted in his retreat by a loud and ominous siren. It was the signal for Baltimore's first air-raid drill. Obediently he pulled down the blinds and dimmed his lights. But instead of creeping under his desk, as he had been instructed to do, he went downstairs, opened the door, and with August at his side stood defiantly on his white marble steps. Nobody could miss the two bachelors; they were the most conspicuous targets in the whole block. "Get back in the house, you damned fools," the warden cried out in the darkness. The Menckens did not reply; they withdrew into their home—but only for the moment. As soon as the warden had passed, they emerged again to invite another reprimand. By the time the all-clear signal was sounded, the Sage was hot and flushed from the encounter. But he was determined to carry on like this so long as grocery clerks and other "yaps" were empowered to ride herd over "decent" citizens in such a silly enterprise as this.

Oddly enough, no one complained except his two

colored servants; and upon further investigation, Mencken discovered that it was not his patriotism that they objected to, but his wage scale. It was a difficult situation: if the servants left, Mencken would have to sleep in a dirty bed and eat all his meals in a Greek lunchroom around the corner. But at the opportune moment, he upped their wages to $30 a week. And since they resumed their duties in complete silence (as Sara had trained them to do), he believed them to be perfectly satisfied. True, the maid did not always return the books and bric-a-brac to the satisfaction of his sister; but he explained to her that precision is not a Negro attribute but a German one. Nor in other respects did he make unreasonable demands upon them. On Thursday and Sunday evenings, he let them off. Then, having stocked up on pumpernickel bread and slices of cold ham, he and August entered the old-fashioned kitchen with its concrete floor and its steel cabinets and made picnic suppers for themselves.

In 1945 his domestic peace was again threatened—this time by his neighbor's dog. Where this dog came from, or what its pedigree was, he did not know. But its bark could be heard clearly through the thin walls that separated the two houses, not only in his "public rooms" downstairs, but also in his office and bedrooms upstairs. Mencken protested to the neighbor. But apparently the dog was too powerful even for its owner to handle. Months passed, and what had started as a mere nuisance now loomed up as the most serious of all Mencken's problems. He could neither think, write, sleep, nor entertain friends without awareness of that infernal animal. At last, when his efficiency had been so impaired that he could no longer meet his deadlines, he took the case to court.

Appearing before a friendly judge, Mencken declared that he had a "normal" knowledge of "normal" dogs (he might have added that he had kept his own dog Tessie for almost nineteen years, finally burying her with honors in his yard); by this standard his neighbor's dog was "markedly abnormal, unreasonable and extraordinary." The judge gave the neighbor fifteen days to reply, during which the dog was finally silenced. Along with the barking, Mencken had also heard the neighbor's baby crying. But this he had found soothing and relaxing, and he made no complaint about it.

While Mencken was holding his own in the vicinity of his Hollins Street home, the world at large heard little from him. Nor was this surprising. Shortly before his retirement from the public stage—in July 1939, to be precise—he had had a brief spell of dizziness accompanied by high blood pressure. For ten days thereafter he was kept in the hospital for a rest and check-up. "Just what fetched me," he told his friends, "I don't know." Nor did his doctor throw any light upon it. But as an amateur student of medicine he believed it to be a mild stroke; and the more he read about such things in the medical journals and the more he studied the medical history of his own family, the more certain he was of his diagnosis. At any moment, he believed, he would be seized by a massive cerebral hemorrhage which would finish him as painlessly, perhaps, as a hammer blow on the head.

At once he made all the necessary preparations. His literary papers were collected into several hundred volumes, bound in blue leather bindings (at roughly $50 a volume), and willed to various libraries. By special arrangement, his letters to his wife were stored in the Enoch

Pratt's fireproof vault and sealed for twenty-five years. His funeral was to be a very unpretentious affair. He was to be cremated without benefit of clergy and buried in Loudon Park Cemetery; the press was to pay no tribute to him. (Indeed, he had a note to this effect inserted in the obituary files of the Associated Press.) As an agnostic, he did not believe that there was anything more to death than a decomposition of the bodily alkaloids. Yet, again as an agnostic, he did not claim any certitude for this belief. Thus, among his other preparations, he also rehearsed his first day in Heaven. In his mind's eye, he stood before the judgment seat, surrounded by the Twelve Apostles, and with a simple but forthright apology declared, "Gentlemen, I was wrong."

Thereafter he readjusted his routine to his senility. Twice weekly he had his secretary, Mrs. Rosalind Lohrfinck, come into his office to take dictation for the outgoing mail; in the afternoons he took long naps. By writing only at short stretches, he cut his workday in half, from ten or twelve hours to six. He still subscribed for some seventy newspapers and magazines and received hundreds of books gratis from their authors, but he generally avoided books that would raise his blood pressure. Ignoring most of the new novels, he devoted himself to such large and substantial works as Carl Sandburg's *Abraham Lincoln: The War Years,* Van Wyck Brooks's *Flowering of New England,* Thackeray's *Letters* in four volumes, and Toynbee's *A Study of History* in the uncut edition. He enjoyed Will Durant's *Caesar and Christ* so much that he sent its author a fan letter.

He also made an effort to repair some of the gaps in his social circle. With so many of his friends dying off, and himself soon to be "an angel singing around the throne," it was patently absurd for him to hold grudges against those who remained. And when his friends, on their side, indicated the same disposition (particularly Nathan and Dreiser), they resumed their former intimacy. On visits to Hollins Street, he seated them in overstuffed chairs, offered them drinks and a complete assortment of stale cigarettes, and gave them the free run of his garden outside to relieve themselves. Then he took his place hard by a blazing fire and, with his brother sitting silently on his left hand, reminisced about their "golden age" together before World War I. Though many of Mencken's former circle availed themselves of this hospitality, it did not extend to all. He could not excuse any writer who had abused him too offensively, who had stopped writing, or who had, in one form or other, turned out to be a failure.

Fifteen years before, he had planned a magnum opus for his declining years. Originally this took the form of a treatise on man, a recapitulation in semi-scientific terms of all his earlier observations on sex, religion, ethics, politics, and other subjects. Since the death of Dr. Pearl, the chief proponent of the project, he no longer felt up to it, and he turned instead to the writing of his autobiography. Here again there were obstacles. His memory had never been very accurate, and age was not improving it. But as luck would have it, he had at hand, in his own home, a virtually complete archive of family history. Neither Mencken himself nor his mother before him had ever thrown away anything: his mother had stuffed the clothes closets with old household bills, including one paid to the doctor for Henry's birth and another for the purchase of the family's first piano, while Henry had stored in the cellar not only a complete file of his literary papers, but also such "documents" as the dinner menus, wine cards, and clothing catalogues of establishments that had long since gone bankrupt.

In the summer and fall of 1938, Mencken immersed himself in these treasures, reading, classifying, and re-arranging them. Depressed by the decline of his literary fortunes, he delayed the actual writing as long as possible. But as usual, when he finally sat down at the typewriter (in January 1939) he found it "easy going," writing three or four thousand words a day, and later six thousand, which was his all-time fastest pace. In the spring, he had half-completed a book covering his first twelve years. It made him "feel alive again"; yet its substance seemed so trivial and so personal that he could not believe very strongly in its success.

In March 1939, by prior agreement, he submitted a few chapters to the editors of the *New Yorker*. A week later they wired their acceptance. His stories of the Negro philosophers and German pedagogues of Victorian Baltimore, they told him, would add a new flavor to the magazine. They paid him at one of their highest rates, more than $300 a story, adding that if all the stories were of equal caliber they could use an unlimited number. Somewhat gingerly, they made four corrections—two on points of diction, and two suggestions for more plausible action. But Mencken neither demanded nor wanted special license. "All the suggestions seem to me to be sound," he told them. "I am firmly convinced that every author, however richly endowed by God, should be copy-read vigorously, and in my editorial days I never set up any of my own stuff without putting some poor fish to translating it into English."

In its final form, *Happy Days* was acclaimed both by critics and by readers alike. The New York *Times* called it the most diverting account of an American boyhood since *Huckleberry Finn.* On all sides, Mencken was urged to continue the series on the same scale and in the same vein. Yet again he was plagued with doubts. Compassion had never been one of his strong points, nor the more painful kinds of self-revelation; and the mood of paternal detachment with which he had viewed his childhood had vanished. "My teens," he explained to Dreiser, "were full of loud alarms, and it would sound idiotic to treat them as I deal with my first ten years. In my twenties I was gay again, and also in my thirties, but since the age of forty I have been full of a sense of human sorrow. This sense has frequently taken the virulence of an actual bellyache." However, by dwelling on all his more pleasant memories, and glossing over the others, he was able to resolve this dilemma. And between his memoirs and his scholarly works, including Supplements to *The American Language* and a *Dictionary of Quotations* ("better than Bartlett") that he had planned for twenty-five years, he could keep himself busy, he believed, at least for the duration of his life.

Thus, in his sixties, at the very moment when everybody, including himself, had given him up for dead, he had come alive again. Life, however, was by no means an unmixed blessing. Through his Hollins Street window he watched the terrible miscarriages of World War II—half the human race starving, "Asiatic barbarians" firmly entrenched in Western Europe for the first time since

1683, "labor racketeers" stronger than ever, a President of the United States worse than Roosevelt and too much even for a democracy to bear. It made him restless. At times he was tempted to speak out and tell the world "I told you so"; but at other times he reflected that, after all, nobody was interested in the "truth" any more. "If I were 40 again," he told reporters, "how I would love to have a go at the quacks now on tap. But the Heavenly Father does not permit. Besides for twenty years I had a platform of my own, and that is enough for any man."

On several occasions Patterson urged him to resume his *Sunpaper* column. But here, too, he observed his oath of silence; and if he showed his hand at all, it was through quiet backstage maneuvers rather than through the printed word. As a news consultant, he worked to improve the quality and originality of reporting, and to make editors observe the code of ethics that he had framed in 1902: namely, that no newspaper employee should accept any favor, however slight, from theaters, circuses, or political parties. As a member of the board of directors, he was called in for many delicate negotiations between the *Sunpapers* and the outside world—with the labor unions, the Catholic Church, and the paper-rationing authorities of the federal government. In the first instance, his fellow directors gave him credit for having singlehandedly broken the Newspaper Guild's campaign against them. Also it was at his suggestion that the space devoted to the *Sun*'s patriotic editorials was sharply curtailed.

A few months after V–J Day, an incident occurred that vindicated Mencken's constraint. Ezra Pound, the poet, was brought back to Washington under charge of having broadcast Axis propaganda over the Italian radio and, pending his trial, became a mental patient at St. Elizabeths Hospital. As soon as he could, Mencken went over to see him. The meeting took place in a padded dining room; the poet was even more distraught than Mencken had expected. Indeed, if Mencken's name had not been announced to him beforehand, it is doubtful that he would have recognized the visitor. Yet Mencken found it a very enlightening experience. Though he had had only an occasional correspondence with Pound, and in general disapproved of his poetry, they had once been joined in common hostility to the Puritan tradition in letters. More recently, they had been joined again in the intellectual precincts of Fascism; and but for the grace of God, he too might have ended in some such hideous predicament.

*Courtesy, Alfred A. Knopf*

At Six

*Courtesy, Alfred A. Knopf*

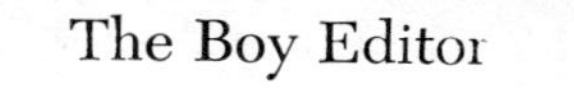

The Boy Editor

*Photos by A. Aubrey Bodine*

1524 Hollins Street

ABOVE: Sitting Room BELOW: His Office

*Photo by Brown Brothers*

Co-Editors of the *Smart Set*, 1920

*Acme Photo*

Brimstone Corner, April 5, 1926

*Acme Photo*

Under Arrest, Same Day

*Baltimore Sun Photo*

Posing for Nicol Schattenstein, 1927

*Baltimore Sun Photo*

Testing 3.2 Beer, April 7, 1933 with Hamilton Owens, at Extreme Right

*Photo by A. Aubrey Bodine*

With Sara in the Cathedral Street Apartment

*Wide World Photo*

At Work, Progressive Party Convention, 1948

AT LEFT: Norman Thomas

*Photo by Carl Van Vechten*

The Ageless Mencken

# Notes

IN WRITING the above portrait, I have made every effort to keep it within the bounds of truth. I have consulted literally thousands of sources. I have had Mr. Mencken himself read the text and authenticate it insofar as his memory would permit. In the few cases where the facts remained in doubt, I have drawn my own conclusions, and have so indicated below. Yet I claim no infallibility. Other students of the subject will doubtlessly arrive at different conclusions with equal or greater justice.

For the public aspects of his career, I have used the Mencken press clippings, collected in some eighty-odd volumes (350 pages each) and located in the Enoch Pratt Free Library of Baltimore; for the private aspects, I have drawn upon the Mencken letters of the Princeton University Library collection and the Dreiser letters in the University of Pennsylvania Library. Three book-length studies of the subject are now extant—two works of criticism, Ernest Boyd, *H. L. Mencken* (New York, Robert H. McBride, 1925) and Benjamin De Casseres, *Mencken and Shaw* (New York, Silas Newton, 1930), and one biography, Isaac Goldberg, *The Man Mencken* (New York, Simon and Schuster, 1925). Of these, I have found the latter the most useful for my purposes, being full of odd facts (and some fancies) about the man gathered from him in his prime. For the atmosphere of the twenties, I recommend Frederic Lewis Allen, *Only Yesterday* (New York, Harper & Brothers, 1931) and Lloyd Morris, *Postscript to Yesterday* (New York, Random House, 1947). A complete bibliography of Menckeniana has yet to appear, but for the earlier period, Carroll Frey's little book (Philadelphia, Centaur Book Shop, 1924) will be found useful.

In lieu of footnotes, the more detailed acknowledgments are made by chapter, section and paragraph. Thus, the symbols 2.1 under Chapter 3 refer back to the first paragraph of section two of the chapter in question. When brief quotations appear in the text unassigned, they are always to be attributed to Mencken, either to his published works or to his letters.

### CHAPTER 1

This chapter represents a blending of several actual episodes that occurred during the years 1911–1913. The streetcar incident, for example, was described in Mencken's "Freelance" column in early May, 1911. For other accounts of the young Mencken, cf. Louis Untermeyer, *From Another World* (New York, Harcourt, 1939); Ernest Boyd, *Portraits: Real and Imaginary* (London, Jonathan Cape, Ltd., 1924); Channing Pollock, *The Adventures of a Happy Man* (New York, Thomas Y. Crowell, 1939).

## CHAPTER 2

1.2 Johann Burkhard Mencken, *The Charlatanry of the Learned,* edited by H. L. Mencken (New York, Alfred A. Knopf, 1937).
1.4 Goldberg, *The Man Mencken,* Chapter II.
1.5 Ibid., Chapter III.
2.3 Mencken, "Larval Stage of a Bookworm," in *Happy Days.*
2.6 Romantic poetry quoted in Goldberg, op. cit., Chapter VI.
2.7 Mencken, "The Educational Process," in *Heathen Days.*
2.12 Mencken, "Allegro Con Brio," in *Newspaper Days.*
2.14 Mencken interview in New York *Herald,* May 21, 1906.

## CHAPTER 3

1.4 Mencken, "The Scent of the Theatre," in *Newspaper Days.*
1.9 Mencken, *The Philosophy of Friedrich Nietzsche,* pp. 319 ff.
1.10 Ibid., p. 58.
2.1 Harrison Hale Schaff to Isaac Goldberg, August, 1925, in Goldberg, op. cit., p. 371.
2.4 *The Philosophy of Friedrich Nietzsche,* p. 267.
3.3 Mencken, "The American: His Language," in the *Smart Set,* August, 1913.
3.6 Mencken, *The American Language,* Preface to First Edition, date-lined Baltimore, January 1, 1919.

## CHAPTER 4

1.2 For the prevailing literary values during this period, cf. Fred Lewis Pattee, *A History of American Literature Since 1870* (New York, The Century Company, 1915).
1.3 Percival Pollard, *Their Day in Court* (Washington, Neale Publishing Company, 1909), p. 408.
1.4 Theodore Dreiser to Isaac Goldberg, August 24, 1925, in Goldberg, op. cit., p. 379.
1.10 For Mencken's popularized medicine, cf. Leonard Keene Hirshberg, *What You Ought to Know about Your Baby* (New

York, Butterick Publishing Company, 1910). Hirshberg supplied the facts and Mencken wrote the text.

1.11 Mencken, "Fifteen Years," in the *Smart Set,* December, 1923.

1.12 Mencken, "The Leading American Novelist," in the *Smart Set,* December, 1923.

2.3 From Mencken's review of Pollard's *Their Day in Court* in the *Smart Set,* February, 1910.

2.4 Mencken, "Ambrose Bierce," in *Prejudices: Sixth Series.*

2.8 Burton Rascoe, " 'Smart Set' History," in *The Smart Set Anthology,* edited by Rascoe and Groff Conklin (New York, Reynal and Hitchcock, 1934).

2.9 Isaac Goldberg, *The Theatre of George Jean Nathan* (New York, Simon and Schuster, 1926).

## CHAPTER 5

1.1 For a more sympathetic treatment of W. H. Wright's editorship, cf. Rascoe, op. cit.

2.2 Goldberg, *The Man Mencken,* pp. 187 ff.

2.8 In *Pistols for Two* (see below 3.5) Nathan credited his partner with having discovered more authors than any other editor. Like most of *Pistols,* this tribute must be taken with a grain of salt. It now appears that Somerset Maugham, James Joyce, F. Scott Fitzgerald, and others were brought in largely by Nathan's efforts.

2.13 Mencken, "Puritanism as a Literary Force," in *A Book of Prefaces,* p. 277.

3.5 The Mencken-Nathan legend was fostered in Owen Hatteras's *Pistols for Two* pamphlet (New York, Alfred A. Knopf, 1917) and in a series of "Conversations" in the *Smart Set* beginning 1920; it is discussed at length in *The Intimate Notebooks of George Jean Nathan* (New York, Alfred A. Knopf, 1930), pp. 94–121.

## CHAPTER 6

1.1 Nathan's championship of Eugene O'Neill was in many ways comparable to Mencken's of Dreiser. By printing "The Moon of the Caribbees" and two other one-acters in the *Smart Set* (1916–1918), he gave the playwright his first appreciative audience. As a critic Nathan probably did more for O'Neill's reputation than any contemporary. "Were it not for Nathan," wrote Vladimir Kozlenko in *The Quintessence of Nathanism* (New York, Vrest Orton, 1930), "I question whether we would have had Eugene O'Neill as he is today."

2.1 Robert H. Elias, *Theodore Dreiser* (New York, Alfred A. Knopf, 1949), Chapter IX.
2.5 Press statement quoted in Ibid., p. 175.
2.6 For Dreiser's rebellion, cf. Mencken, "Theodore Dreiser," Section Five, in *A Book of Prefaces.*
3.10 Mencken's reaction to *The "Genius"* case was expressed in "Puritanism as a Literary Force," op. cit., pp. 269 ff.; Dreiser's in "Life, Art and America," in *The Seven Arts,* February, 1917.
3.11 Quoted in Elias, op. cit., p. 175.

## CHAPTER 7

1.1 Mencken, "Winter Voyage," in *Heathen Days.*
1.2 Mencken, "Ludendorff," in *Atlantic Monthly,* June, 1917.
1.6 Mencken, "Gore in the Caribbees," in *Heathen Days.*
2.6 Mencken, "On Being an American," in *Prejudices: Third Series,* p. 46; also, "Advice to Young Men," in the same volume.
3.3 Mencken, "Hymn to the Truth," in *Prejudices: Sixth Series.*
4.2 Madeleine Boyd, *Life Makes Advances* (New York, Reynier, 1936), pp. 414 ff.
4.3 Rascoe, op. cit.
4.5 Quotation from *The Intimate Notebooks of George Jean Nathan,* op. cit., p. 42.

## CHAPTER 8

1.6 Quotation from a one-day revival of the "Freelance" column, in the Baltimore *Evening Sun,* April 18, 1921.
1.8 Mencken, preface to *In Defense of Women,* typescript, dated 1937, in Pratt Library collection.
1.12 Mencken, preface to *Heliogabalus,* typescript, undated, in Pratt Library collection. Years later, each of the playwrights claimed the invention of the twelve-girl bed as his own—Mencken in the typescript (undated, but about 1937) and Nathan in a galley correction (November 1949). I take this as another evidence of their very close collaboration during the period in question.
1.13 Since then, *Heliogabalus* has continued to attract theatrical bigwigs behind the scenes—William Gillette in the later twenties and John Barrymore in 1936. But playgoers have seen nothing of it, except such of its devices as have been pirated in other men's shows.

3.3 Cf. Geoffrey Hellman's profile of Alfred A. Knopf, *The New Yorker,* November 27, 1948, and subsequent issues; also, Mencken in *Alfred A. Knopf, Quarter Century* (New York, Alfred A. Knopf, 1940).

## CHAPTER 9

1.3 The first full-length critical studies of the subject were Burton Rascoe's "Fanfare" in the Chicago Sunday *Tribune,* November, 1917, and Vincent O'Sullivan's "La Littérature Américaine" in *Mercure de France,* January 16, 1919. Both were reprinted in a Knopf brochure in 1920 under the title *H. L. Mencken* but more generally referred to as "Fanfare." Sherwood Anderson's quotation is taken from his *Memoirs* (New York, Harcourt, Brace, 1942), p. 251.

1.4 Anderson, *ibid.,* p. 293, recalls that Mencken's reaction to the manuscript of *Winesburg, Ohio* was no more enlightened than that of other readers and that, years later, he wrongly proclaimed himself one of Anderson's discoverers. The facts seem to be as follows: Anderson came to Mencken with Dreiser's strong recommendation. Mencken (and Nathan) would not print the stories, mainly, I suppose, for fear of censorship. But when the book appeared in 1919, he was highly enthusiastic. The best of Anderson, he wrote in February 1922, "belongs to the very first literature of the country today."

1.5 Ludwig Lewisohn, *Expression in America* (New York, Harper & Brothers, 1932), p. 439.

1.6 Edmund Wilson, Jr., "H. L. Mencken," in the *New Republic,* June 1, 1921.

2.1 Lewisohn, op. cit., pp. 415–451, for a full and inspired account of this battle.

2.2 Mencken, "Five Men at Random," in *Prejudices: Third Series,* p. 178.

2.3 Stuart Sherman to Ellery Sedgwick, quoted in Jacob Zeitlin and Homer Woodbridge, *Life and Letters of Stuart Sherman* (New York, Farrar and Rinehart, 1929). Volume II, p. 480.

2.5 Mencken, op. cit., p. 177; Sherman to Henry Seidel Canby, quoted in Zeitlin and Woodbridge, op. cit., Volume II, p. 533.

2.7 Carl Van Doren, *Three Worlds* (New York, Harper & Brothers, 1936). As to what was said on this occasion, I have chosen Mencken's version in preference to Van Doren's.

2.10 Stuart Sherman, "Mr. H. L. Mencken and the Jeune Fille," in *Americans* (New York, Charles Scribner's Sons, 1922). Cf. *Jurgen and the Censor,* edited by Barrett H. Clark and others (New York, Privately Printed for the Emergency Committee, 1920).

3.2 Irene and Allen Cleaton, *Books and Battles of the Twenties* (Boston, Houghton Mifflin Company, 1937), Chapter One.

3.4 For Mencken's participation in the revolt of the Young Intellectuals, cf. The Critics' Questionnaire, in *Vanity Fair*, April, 1922; also, *Civilization in the United States*, edited by Harold Stearns (New York, Harcourt, Brace, 1922). For the English reaction, cf. C. E. Bechhofer, *The Literary Renaissance in America* (London, William Heinemann, Ltd., 1923).

3.5 Fred Lewis Pattee, *Sidelights on American Literature* (New York, The Century Company, 1922), pp. 56–97.

3.8 Burton Rascoe, "Notes for an Epitaph," in New York *Evening Post* "Literary Review," March 4, 1922.

## CHAPTER 10

1.5 Mencken, "A Boon to Bores," in the Baltimore *Evening Sun*, January 1, 1921.

2.2 Burton Rascoe, "The Literary Spotlight: H. L. Mencken," in *The Bookman*, February, 1922.

3.2 Mencken in Frank Case, *Tales of a Wayward Inn* (New York, Frederick A. Stokes, 1938). For further details of his private life in New York, cf. Rascoe, *A Bookman's Daybook* (New York, H. Liveright, 1929).

3.4 Mencken stanchly maintains that he never attended either of the two clubs. But Nathan, whose memory is more reliable, recalls many sessions with him in the Fifty-eighth Street Club, though none in the France-Angleterre.

4.1 Hergesheimer to Mencken, December 21, 1921; Lewis to Mencken, January 21, 1922; Fitzgerald to Mencken, May 4, 1925. All these letters are located in the Enoch Pratt Library collection, pasted appropriately in the correspondents' books.

4.4 Mencken, "Chiefly American," in the *Smart Set*, December, 1920. Huneker to Mencken, October 6, 1920, quoted in *Letters of James Gibbons Huneker*, edited by Josephine Huneker (New York, H. Liveright, 1936).

4.5 Huneker to Mencken, December 27, 1920, quoted in Ibid.

4.8 Quotation from Mencken, "On Living in Baltimore," in *Prejudices: Fifth Series*, p. 242.

## CHAPTER 11

1.1 Nathan, op. cit., p. 110.

1.2 Mencken, "Footnote on Criticism," in *Prejudices: Third Series.*

For Nathan's historic role as a drama critic, cf. *The Theatre of George Jean Nathan,* op. cit., and *The Quintessence of Nathanism,* op. cit. He "sounded his tocsin" for Ibsen, Strindberg, Andreyev, Schnitzler, Hauptmann and Tchekov (not to mention Eugene O'Neill) and so spelled the doom of the prewar "pap-fountains."

1.3 Frederic Lewis Allen, *Only Yesterday,* Chapter Three.

1.6 Gerald W. Johnson and others, *The Sunpapers of Baltimore* (New York, Alfred A. Knopf, 1937), Chapter XIX.

1.11 Frank R. Kent, who was then managing editor under Adams, cannot recall this *Putsch.* The only offer of resignation, he says, came from John W. Owens, and this was before the national conventions, not after. I have followed Mencken's version as given to me in conversation, 1947.

2.2 Goldberg, op. cit., pp. 200–202, 217–224.

2.4 Mencken, "Fifteen Years," in the *Smart Set,* December, 1923.

3.1 Ernest Boyd, *Portraits: Real and Imaginary,* Chapters I and IV.

3.4 Quoted in Goldberg, *The Theatre of George Jean Nathan,* p. 68.

3.7 George Jean Nathan insists that Dreiser's break with Mencken had absolutely no connection with his. As I see it, the two incidents had their origin in the same remote cause—namely, Mencken's transformation into a political pundit.

3.9 For the cream of *Mercury* articles, 1924–1944, cf. *The American Mercury Reader,* edited by Lawrence E. Spivak and Charles Angoff (Philadelphia, The Blakiston Company, 1944).

## CHAPTER 12

1.8 Emily Clark, *Innocence Abroad* (New York, Alfred A. Knopf, 1931), pp. 109–126.

1.12 Cf. Virginius Dabney, *Liberalism in the South* (Chapel Hill, University of North Carolina Press, 1932).

1.13 Mencken, "The Husbandman," in *Prejudices: Fourth Series,* p. 58.

2.5 Mencken, "Inquisition," in *Heathen Days,* pp. 231–234; also, "The Hills of Zion," in *Prejudices: Fifth Series.*

2.12 The general store episode is based on the account in the New York *World,* July 17, 1925; Mencken did not take it seriously either then or later.

2.15 Mencken, "In Memoriam: W.J.B.," in *Prejudices: Fifth Series,* p. 64.

## CHAPTER 13

Virtually all the material in this chapter is taken from Mencken's unpublished six-volume monograph on the "Hatrack" case (1937) in the Pratt Library collection—the subjective material from his own narrative and the supporting evidence from the documents attached. For the lawyers' point of view, cf. Arthur Garfield Hays, *Let Freedom Ring* (New York, Liveright Publishing Corporation, 1937), pp. 157–194.

## CHAPTER 14

1.1 Mencken, "Journalism in America," in *Prejudices: Sixth Series.*
1.2 Mencken, "Appendix from Moronia," in *Prejudices: Sixth Series,* third section.
1.4 Mencken, preface to "Notes on Democracy," typescript, dated 1937 (Pratt Library collection).
2.9 Frances Newman, *Letters,* edited by Hansell Baugh (New York, H. Liveright, 1929).
2.14 Mencken, "Appendix from Moronia," op. cit., first and second sections.
2.15 Jim Tully, *A Dozen and One* (Hollywood, Murray and Gee, Inc., 1943); Tully to Nathan, quoted in *The Intimate Notebooks of George Jean Nathan,* op. cit., p. 76.
3.2 Quoted in Ibid., pp. 98–99.
3.3 Mencken, "The Human Mind," in *Prejudices: Sixth Series,* third section.
3.5 Ibid., second section.

## CHAPTER 15

1.1 Mencken's preface to Sara Haardt, *A Southern Album* (Garden City, N. Y., Doubleday, Doran, 1936); for further biographical details, cf. Sara Haardt's novel, *The Making of a Lady* (New York, Doubleday, Doran, 1931).
4.3 Quoted in *The Intimate Notebooks of George Jean Nathan,* p. 121.
4.4 Mencken, "Vanishing Act" and "Pilgrimage," in *Heathen Days.*

## CHAPTER 16

1.1 Charles Angoff, "Mencken Twilight," in *North American Review,* December, 1938; also, Mencken, "The State of the Nation," in Baltimore *Evening Sun,* January, 1932.

1.5 For the Humanist revival, cf. Gorham Munson in *Saturday Review of Literature,* August 9, 1930; *Humanism and America,* A Symposium, edited by Norman Foerster (New York, Farrar and Rinehart, 1930). For the Marxist or quasi-Marxist critique, cf. V. F. Calverton, *The Liberation of American Literature* (New York, Charles Scribner's, 1932); Louis Kronenberger's essay, "Mencken," in *After the Genteel Tradition,* edited by Malcolm Cowley (New York, W. W. Norton, 1937); Michael Gold, *The Hollow Men* (New York, International Publishers, 1941).

1.7 Rev. John E. Graham, *The Way of the Sceptic* (New York, The Dial Press, 1931), is the Catholic reply to "Treatise on the Gods."

1.9 One event of this period is noteworthy: In December 1931, Mencken's remarks about a lynching on the Eastern Shore of Maryland caused the natives to boycott the *Sunpapers* and to cancel $150,000 worth of contracts with Baltimore business houses.

## CHAPTER 17

1.1 Mencken, *The Making of a President.*

1.2 Quoted in Albert Jay Nock, *A Journal of These Days* (New York, W. Morrow and Company, 1934), p. 190.

1.7 Other anti-New Deal blasts were written for *Liberty* magazine during 1934–1935, *e.g.,* "Capitalism Won't Die," August, 1935; his case against the proletarian school of letters was summed up in "Illuminators of the Abyss," in *Saturday Review of Literature,* October 6, 1934.

2.3 Mencken's constitution for Maryland was printed in the Baltimore *Sun,* April 12, 1937.

2.4 R. P. Harriss, "Life with Mencken," in *Gardens, Houses and People* (Baltimore), May, 1949.

3.2 Mencken, *Treatise on Right and Wrong,* pp. 284–294.

3.9 Quotation from Mencken's credo in *I Believe,* edited by Clifton Fadiman (New York, Simon and Schuster, 1939).

## CHAPTER 18

1.2 Among his literary activities, August Mencken has edited a collection of reports on hangings, *By the Neck* (New York, Hastings House, 1942).

1.14 His suppressed political views later found expression in an interview with Roger Butterfield. Cf. "Mr. Mencken Sounds Off," in *Life,* August 5, 1946.

# Chronology of His Books

*Ventures into Verse*. Baltimore, Marshall, Beek and Gordon, 1903.

*George Bernard Shaw: His Plays*. Boston, John W. Luce & Co., 1905.

*The Philosophy of Friedrich Nietzsche*. Boston, John W. Luce & Co., 1908.

editor, *The Players' Ibsen: Little Eyolf* and *A Doll's House*. Boston, John W. Luce & Co., 1909.

editor, *The Gist of Nietzsche*. Boston, John W. Luce & Co., 1910.

*What You Ought to Know about Your Baby* (with Leonard K. Hirshberg), New York, The Butterick Publishing Co., 1910.

*Men versus The Man* (in collaboration). A Correspondence Between Robert R. LaMonte, Socialist and H. L. Mencken, Individualist. New York, Henry Holt and Co., 1910.

*The Artist*. A Drama Without Words. Boston, John W. Luce & Co., 1912.

editor, *Blanchette and the Escape* by Brieux. Boston, John W. Luce & Co., 1913.

*Europe After 8:15* (with G. J. Nathan and W. H. Wright). New York, John Lane Company, 1914.

*A Little Book in C Major*. New York, John Lane Company, 1916.

*A Book of Burlesques*. New York, John Lane Company, 1916.

*A Book of Prefaces*. New York, Alfred A. Knopf, 1917.

*Pistols for Two* (with G. J. Nathan and under pseudonym, Owen Hatteras). New York, Alfred A. Knopf, 1917.

*Damn! A Book of Calumny*. New York, Philip Goodman Co., 1918.

*In Defense of Women*. New York, Philip Goodman Co., 1918.

*The American Language*, A Preliminary Inquiry into the Development of English in the United States. New York, Alfred A. Knopf, 1919.

editor, *The Free Lance Books: Ventures in Common Sense* by E. W. Howe and four other volumes. New York, Alfred A. Knopf, 1919–1921.

*Prejudices: First Series*. New York, Alfred A. Knopf, 1919.

*Heliogabalus* (with G. J. Nathan). A Buffoonery in Three Acts. New York, Alfred A. Knopf, 1920.

*The American Credo* (with G. J. Nathan). A Contribution Toward the Interpretation of the National Mind. New York, Alfred A. Knopf, 1920.

*Prejudices: Second Series.* New York, Alfred A. Knopf, 1920.

*The American Language,* Revised Edition. New York, Alfred A. Knopf, 1921.

*Prejudices: Third Series.* New York, Alfred A. Knopf, 1922.

*The American Language,* Third Edition, again revised, New York, Alfred A. Knopf, 1923.

*Prejudices: Fourth Series.* New York, Alfred A. Knopf, 1924.

editor, *Americana: 1925.* New York, Alfred A. Knopf, 1925.

*Notes on Democracy.* New York, Alfred A. Knopf, 1926.

*Prejudices: Fifth Series.* New York, Alfred A. Knopf, 1926.

*James Branch Cabell.* Booklet. New York, Robert M. McBride & Co., 1927.

*Prejudices: Sixth Series.* New York, Alfred A. Knopf, 1927.

editor, *Selected Prejudices.* New York, Alfred A. Knopf, 1927.

editor, *Essays* by James Huneker. New York, C. Scribner's Sons, 1929.

*Treatise on the Gods.* New York, Alfred A. Knopf, 1930.

editor, *The American Democrat* by James Fenimore Cooper. New York, Alfred A. Knopf, 1931.

*Making a President.* A footnote to the saga of democracy. New York, Alfred A. Knopf, 1932.

*Treatise on Right and Wrong.* New York, Alfred A. Knopf, 1934.

*The American Language,* Fourth Edition, corrected, enlarged and rewritten. New York, Alfred A. Knopf, 1934.

editor, *A Southern Album* by Sara Haardt. Garden City, N. Y., Doubleday, Doran and Co., 1936.

*The Sunpapers of Baltimore* (with Gerald W. Johnson, Frank R. Kent, and Hamilton Owens). New York, Alfred A. Knopf, 1937.

editor, *The Charlatanry of the Learned* by Johann Burkhard Mencken. New York, Alfred A. Knopf, 1937.

*Happy Days: 1880–1892.* New York, Alfred A. Knopf, 1940.

*Newspaper Days: 1899–1906.* New York, Alfred A. Knopf, 1941.

editor, *A New Dictionary of Quotations on Historical Principles from Ancient and Modern Sources.* New York, Alfred A. Knopf, 1942.

*Heathen Days:* 1890–1936. New York, Alfred A. Knopf, 1943.

*Supplement I, The American Language*. New York, Alfred A. Knopf, 1945.

*Christmas Story*. New York, Alfred A. Knopf, 1946.

*Supplement II, The American Language*. New York, Alfred A. Knopf, 1948.

editor, *A Mencken Chrestomathy*. A selection from his out-of-print writings. New York, Alfred A. Knopf, 1949.

# *Index*

# Index

: DUE

| | |
|---|---|
| FE 3 '86 | |
| | |
| | |
| | |
| | |
| | |
| | |
| | |
| | |
| | |
| | |
| | |
| | |
| | |
| | |
| | |
| | |
| | |
| | PRINTED IN U.S.A. |